YOU MIGHT
FEEL A LITTLE
PRESSURE

Finding Wonder After Miscarriage

A memoir by
Mary Adkins

 THIRD RAIL PRESS

You Might Feel a Little Pressure: Finding Wonder After
Miscarriage

Published by:
THIRD RAIL PRESS LLC
P.O. Box 20285
Albuquerque, NM 87154
www.thirdrailpress.org

Paperback ISBN: 979-8-9912123-2-8
Ebook ISBN: 979-8-9912123-3-5

Printed in the United States of America

Praise for YOU MIGHT FEEL A LITTLE PRESSURE

"In this frank account of pregnancy loss and infertility, Mary Adkins gives us an intimate view into more than just reproduction. Weaving together threads on body image, achievement, and life purpose, *You Might Feel a Little Pressure* becomes a portrait of what it's like to be a woman in today's society. It is at once personal and universal, shocking and comforting—Adkins will not only hold up a mirror to your own life but hold your hand through it."

Jessica Zucker, PhD, psychologist, & author of
I Had a Miscarriage and *Normalize It*

"Mary Adkins pulls a stunning kind of hat trick with this memoir. One of the most hopeful and life-affirming stories about loss I have ever read, I inhaled every page as though it were oxygen. I will never forget the way reading it made me feel: expansive, unafraid, surprisingly whole and human. What a gift."

Simone Gorrindo, author of *The Wives*

"Mary Adkins has done the impossible: written an unflinching memoir about loss that shimmers with life. *You Might Feel a Little Pressure* is about three gut-wrenching miscarriages, yes, but it's also about the blink-and-you'll-miss-it beauty and hilarity of raising a toddler, the maddening hijinks that come with having a body, the deep satisfactions of marriage, the inside jokes with friends, who are only a text away, no matter what. This book has arrived to remind us that life, whatever else it may be, is this: a miracle."

Greg Marshall, author of *Leg*

"Mary Adkins takes you on a journey of love, hope, grief, and acceptance. It's heartbreaking, tender, and beautiful. *You Might Feel a Little Pressure* is like the friend you want to call in your darkest hour, reminding you that you are not alone, reminding you that others have gone before you and that there is a path forward. This book is for every woman who has loved and lost and loved again."

Meadow DeVor, bestselling author of
The Worthy Project

For the mothers of ghosts

PROLOGUE

JULY 2021

MY PREGNANCY APP TOLD ME he was the size of a blueberry when the life in him snuffed out, and so that's what I keep thinking about: blueberries. The big, bulbous ones pumped with chemicals, the tiny, wild ones I bake into muffins. Which was he, and will I get to find out?

I'm lying stiffly on my side of the bed on top of an old towel I've long meant to throw away. We've had it for way too many years. It used to be yellow, but now it's dingy and fraying, an embarrassment.

It's almost ten at night, and the cramping has been going on for a few hours, but still, no blood. I'm waiting for the blood to come like the doctor told me it will, but it feels more like I've just finished watching something impossibly sad like *Beaches* and just need to shake it off, let it pass, wake up anew. After I bleed, I can go back to being me, and this will be a movie I warn friends about: "Have your tissues handy!"

All day, I've played down the big-dealness of this. I've apologized for crying, joked about how now I can drink again, focused on the practicalities: the medicine, the towels, the pads. What's happening to me, I learned from the print-out the doctor gave me, is technically called "Medical Management of Missed Miscarriage." The miscarriage took place in my body while no one was looking, and only once we caught it on an ultrasound did we realize we have to manage it.

Management is something I can get my head around; miscarriage is not. Here are the ways I plan to manage:

First, I won't get blood on the furniture. I inserted the four tiny—so much tinier than I would have guessed—white, round pills into my vagina as soon as we arrived home from the appointment, around five o'clock. I was surprised they stayed up there, but clearly there was plenty I didn't understand about my own body, since until this afternoon, I thought I was still pregnant. The pills were supposed to make me start cramping within four hours, but I put a pad on immediately, just in case.

Second, I won't get blood on the bed. I am lying on a towel now.

Third, I won't let Finn, who just turned three, see any blood. My husband, Lucas, has laid down with Finn in his room for the night in case he wakes up with the urge to visit us in our room, which he often does. So, I'm on my own.

Fourth, I will get this over with as quickly as possible so I can move on with my life. The doctor gave me extra pills in case I "don't bleed enough" (whatever that means), so I'll just take them if I think there's more that needs to come out, based on my scientific assessment of what constitutes an appropriate amount at just over eight weeks. I am a novelist who weaseled my way out of high school chemistry, so surely my assessment will be accurate.

And finally, I will study the fetus, which means I have to be awake when it comes out. I haven't told Lucas this, because I don't tell him things I think he'll try to talk me out of when I really want to do them. I will find the fetus, and I will look it in the eye. I don't know why—I just have to in order to know that it was real, that he was real.

I sit up. I've already decided not to sleep, lest I miss my chance, but the pain is acute enough that there's no point trying to rest.

I climb out of bed and amble to the bathroom, where I pull down my underwear and take a seat on the toilet. I'll just wait here.

Has our HVAC system always been this loud?

At thirty-nine, I pride myself on my unflappability, the term a boss once used to describe me just before offering me a promotion. I can probably count on one hand the number of times I've raised my voice at another person—not because I'm never roused to anger, but because anger doesn't get you better outcomes. Calmness might. That, or I just want to be seen as stable, steady. Steady people get respect. And promotions.

Years into our relationship, Lucas once wondered aloud, "Have I ever seen you cry? *Do* you cry?" When he said it, I felt as if I'd been deeply complimented, as if being stoic was a virtue, shoving down feelings an achievement.

Slumped on the toilet with my sweats at my ankles, after keeping up my guard all day, I flap.

"I don't understand," I say aloud to the empty room.

I say it again—louder this time, a plea: "I don't understand!"

My body begins to rock forward and back. I press my arms into my cramping belly.

Why is this happening to me? *Why?*

It wasn't even a baby yet, I've told myself all day. *Barely eight weeks. Not even measuring that much.*

When a rush of clumps finally splashes out of me around midnight, I turn around and plunge my hand into the toilet.

For years, as a teenager and into my early twenties, I did the same thing with my food, fingering clumps of it to assess just how much of a meal I managed to purge. *Magic*, I thought the first time I succeeded at fourteen, having learned the technique from a *Lifetime* movie about a bulimic gymnast. Purging seemed like a genius solution to my inability to starve myself, and I didn't have to tolerate the depressing feeling of fullness, evidence of my poor willpower crowding my belly. I could make it disappear. Poof!

Now, nearly twenty years since my last purge, I crouch, once again with one hand in the toilet water, cupping the tissue in search of my blueberry with eye sockets.

I lift it over the sink and rinse it off to get a better look, but I can't make out anything resembling the archetypal image of a fetus, that signature bean with its alien head and shriveled body.

Find the bean, where is the bean…

Could it be too early? No, even on ultrasounds, they looked that way by now. I've already had one kid; I remember.

When a trickle of liquid begins to tickle my leg—I'm still pantsless and standing at the sink—I finally flush my maybe-fetus, the "products of conception" in medical terms, and resume my station on the toilet.

I stay seated until the bleeding subsides then pass out in bed sometime in the wee hours. The next morning, I brush my teeth and, meeting my gaze in the mirror, make a decision. No more flapping.

"How was the night?" Lucas asks, entering the bathroom.

"I think it's mostly over," I say, as if we both—or either of us—know what "it" means.

"Was it painful?" he asks.

"Not too bad," I say, leaving it at that. I need to make Finn some breakfast and pack his lunch for daycare. "Just contractions for a few hours."

Back when I was dating, my coping mechanism for breakups was to skip over the hard part of being lonely and jump right into the next relationship. I'd post a dating profile (the perfect balance of funny and sincere!) mere hours into singledom.

I'm moving on! I'd think, wiping away my tears as I frantically scrolled in search of my next boyfriend, well aware that what I was doing was anything but healthy.

Now, I have decided that I will simply get pregnant again, as soon as possible. This sucks, sure, but it will be a blip in my story, not the outcome of it. Of that, I'm sure.

I'll get pregnant again, so I won't have to wonder what my night managing a missed miscarriage meant. I won't have to wonder why the idea of loving a fetus makes me so uncomfortable, and I won't have to feel this sadness I don't know what to do with.

I will just fix it.

Magic.

PART I

DAY

1

HOLES

I DIDN'T QUITE REALIZE how much I still low-grade hated my body until I got pregnant with my son and the hate fell away.

When I peed on a cardboard stick in our tiny Queens bathroom in 2017 and watched, thrilled, as a second hot-pink line bloomed, I had, in my mind, fully recovered from my purging days. I didn't diet. I ate pastries and would never in a million years buy a Skinny Girl-brand margarita.

But in the days after that positive test, pregnancy woke me up. The shame that had become such a part of me that I no longer recognized it receded like a tide. Somehow, knowing my body was creating a miracle allowed me to see myself as one.

Even as my pants (skinny jeans still being in style) stopped zipping, and flaming zits surfaced all over my jaw, and a visible baby bump was still months away, I looked in the mirror and saw a different woman than had been there five weeks, then six weeks, then twelve weeks earlier. No—the woman was the same. My eyes were different.

As my pregnant belly ballooned, so did my appreciation for a body that, previously, had never *quite* been good enough. My phone holds dozens of photos charting its growth in mirrored profile shots I took only for me, and what I noticed in them is my face. I look so…at *peace*. I have a *Mona Lisa* vibe going.

Then I scroll, scroll back, pre-pregnancy, and the mirror shots are still prevalent, but these are for a different purpose. These aren't tracking growth but assessing how much reduction is warranted, how much smaller I need to get in order to look right, be right. In these, my forehead is scrunched into an eleven. I'm critical. I'm far from anything da Vinci painted. I'm looking to change her, alter her, shrink her up.

When did it begin, the mission to shrink?

When I mine for an answer to that question, what I uncover is a memory of when it *wasn't* there.

I was seven, hiding behind a Rhododendron plant in our side yard while my neighbor counted, feet away in our garage. When she reached fifty and ran off in the direction my sister had gone, I was left alone, huddled behind the bush, waiting.

Buried in those glossy emerald leaves, my skin tingled, and my tongue suddenly tasted metallic.

What am I? I thought.

I wasn't a robot. I wasn't a cartoon. I wasn't a dog or a squirrel or a leaf. I was a person—but what *was* a person? *Why* was a person?

It suddenly seemed so completely outrageous, so utterly bizarre, to exist at all as a human: to be able to talk, to conceive of a God—and my family was big on God—to feel sad, to sing and play.

I had no answer or even a guess. But the question I felt to my bones: *Why are we here?*

When I heard the other children approaching, I leapt up and sprinted to "base," and by the time I had a moment to myself again, the tingles had passed.

I wanted them back. I loved how it had felt to ponder the reason for humanity. It had felt...real.

At that time, I could recite the sixty-six books of the Bible at record speed (literally—I'd won Bible Drill at church) and belt I AM A C-H-R-I-S-T-I-A-N louder than anyone. This felt different, a deep and important mystery that I, Mary Patricia Adkins, age seven, had stumbled upon.

I knew that a grown-up would probably have an answer for me, but grown-ups always seemed so certain about things, and I'd already intuited that this was anything but certain.

Besides, I was newly dubious of grown-ups, having determined that the Bible, which all the grown-ups I knew revered, was hypocritical. You weren't supposed to kill, but you could if someone was bad enough, due to "an eye for an eye"? That didn't add up. Nor did Cain and Abel's families populating the entire earth when they were brothers—uh, wasn't that incest (a word I had just learned)? When I'd pointed this out in Sunday school, the teacher had phoned my mom, upset that I'd introduced the class to the concept. My mom, who found it funny, welcomed my scrutiny, at least in the privacy of our home. But this one felt too big to share, even with her.

I kept the experience behind the bush a secret, and I worked to summon it back.

I tried returning to the same bush, assuming the same position, and closing my eyes. I tried playing hide-and-seek with the same kids in case that was what had triggered it. But no matter what I did, the feeling was gone. And in its wake grew a hole.

If the feeling of the deep mystery had been warm and safe, the hole it left behind was the opposite. That hole was an emptiness that made me feel like a freak because other people didn't seem to have it. Others, kids and grown-ups alike, seemed perfectly confident in their right to be walking around the planet, just assuming that they belonged.

Not me. My wondrous secret had become a dark secret: Inside my skin and bones, there was no answer to the question *Why am I here?* There was only space.

The only thing that came close to filling it was affirmation—affirmation was a distraction that worked, at least temporarily, to ease the existential pain. I could forget, for a moment, the emptiness. And so I began to seek it out above all else: I'd get A's. I'd become popular. I'd find a boyfriend once I was as old as my babysitters, and he'd look at least a little bit like Zach Morris in *Saved by the Bell*.

By eight, I lay in bed at night plotting how to become a person the world would admire—maybe a senator or, even better, Miss America. She was beloved: People listened when she spoke *and* thought she was beautiful. But my mom shut down that idea.

"Nope, no pageants," she said. "Too expensive."

But I didn't need her permission to shape myself into a person I thought people could love, one who wasn't void on the inside. So that's what I did. I studied how the cool girls dressed and acted, and when my mom took my sister and me on our annual shopping trip to Atlanta for new-school-year clothes, I begged her to buy me outfits that looked like what those cool girls wore. (I'll never forget my elation in sixth grade at spotting a Dillard's look-alike for Kate Griffin's crocheted J. Crew vest.)

I was twelve when I watched the *Lifetime* movie about the bulimic gymnast and realized that, to be admired, I needed to be skinny—bony, preferably—a far cry from my pudgy, half-child, half-teenager body. So I would have to not eat. When that proved too hard because I was hungry, I taught myself to throw up.

By high school, I was years deep into crafting a Mary people could admire, like, perhaps even love: a member of student government, the captain of the dance team, an honors student who volunteered for a literacy program after school and won piano competitions. I started a nonprofit *in twelfth grade*. The Mary I'd spent a decade building showed up to college scholarship interviews and performed her way into several full-ride offers, garnering praise from teachers and parents' friends and church members and so-and-so's uncle, praise that was supposed to feel like I was being filled up but instead felt like pouring water through an open tube. There was no bottom. No praise was strong enough. No scholarship large enough.

When I wasn't performing Mary, I was rebelling against her, smoking Marlboro Lights out the driver's window of my Volvo sedan between school and church youth group, refilling the vodka bottle in our basement freezer with water, and skipping class with my unmotivated, rich boyfriend to sit by his pool and pretend to drink Bud Light, which I found gross, while his yellow-haired mom watched from the kitchen window. But this wasn't me, either.

Whether I was performing a Mary persona or revolting against it, all of it amounted to the same thing: a dance around a center of nothingness. If I got too close, I might fall in, so I stayed back, keeping my footwork safely in the Mary-as-rebel or Mary-as-good-girl zones.

Except for every now and then, when I slipped up. When I chose, for my senior quote in the high school yearbook, lines from Samuel Beckett—"I could not have gone on through the awful wretched mess of life without having left a stain upon the silence"—my parents expressed concern.

"Are you okay?" my mom asked. The quote seemed…dark. And what silence was I staining?

My mom was right. That quote was more real Mary—hollow and unexplainable—than curated Mary. I swapped it out for an innocuous Ani DiFranco lyric: "When I look down, I just miss all the good stuff/When I look up, I just trip over things." Balanced, wise-sounding but still cool: curated.

I would go on to curate Mary until my thirty-ninth year—I would curate her so reflexively, so instinctually, that, like with any habit, it became automatic. Eventually, even I believed curated Mary was Mary. I'd made her; I'd made a Me. What had begun as an intentional act of curation became so ingrained that I no longer knew the difference between me and my own persona. I didn't, in other words, see myself as deceptive.

I was a novelist—my dream job since I was a girl—who'd published two novels and was about to publish a third. I'd graduated from law school with honors. I'd run marathons and gotten married and had a kid and opened an IRA. I braked for squirrels and held the door and voted for the people who didn't hate immigrants. I owned, with my husband and a heavily invested bank, a townhome.

This was doing life right, right? I was, on paper, doing pretty damn well, or so I thought.

Even as I believed myself to be the Mary I'd carved out of the opportunities life had served up, the hole had grown and grown, branching into tributaries as real as my own blood vessels. I was porous. No part of me felt solid.

I never spoke to anyone about it. Not friends, not therapists (whom I viewed as people I'd enlisted to help me get better at what I was already doing, curating a self, because wasn't that what self-improvement *was*?), not my husband. Asking, "Do you also feel a gaping emptiness inside that nothing fills, and why do you think that is?" wasn't a great conversation starter.

But in the pages of my private notebooks over the decades, I would occasionally scribble the words, "Fill the holes, fill all the tiny holes" without knowing what they meant. The phrase would pass through my head and onto the page: *Fill the holes, fill all the tiny holes.*

And then I got pregnant with my son Finn, and I had a purpose, and all I wanted was to hold onto it after he was born, keep it close to me, cradle it like a second child I was more than willing to nurture, no matter what it took. Good God, it was so precious—I'd have awoken at 3 a.m. to feed it and sacrificed hair-washing if that meant I could retain this feeling about myself, this view of *me* as a miracle, too.

Around two months postpartum, barely having gotten the clear from my OB to have sex again and having only had it once or twice, I found an old pregnancy test—a cheapie—from a stash I'd long since tucked away. I had no reason to take it. I wasn't late for my period. I didn't even know if I'd resumed normal cycles. Nor did I want to be pregnant—we had an *eight-week-old*—and I was still dealing with the aftereffects of giving birth. Recently, I'd tried to jog and taken five steps before peeing a bladderful all over the sidewalk.

But in a new-mom stupor, wishing for a way to feel differently about myself and my body, I thought, *But what if I was?*

I sat on the toilet staring at the negative pregnancy test, desperate for a second line to appear, willing it with my eyes.

A flash of clarity.

Uh, Mary, you wish to be pregnant again at a terrible time to be pregnant again because that's the only way you've ever found to be nice to your body. Is this maybe…a problem?

Gulp.

I did not see myself as a casualty of a tragic cultural phenomenon, the institutionalized body shaming of women ingrained in us from birth. I saw myself as a failure, a person with a private struggle for which I alone was responsible. Why couldn't I just like and care for myself? What was my *deal*?

I resolved to do a better job of caring for my body. And I tried. I bought a device to exercise my Kegels, and I used it a whole four times. I subscribed to a meal kit service so I could cook nutritious dinners. I left Finn with my mom or Lucas and trotted down the street for $40, half-hour massages to ease my throbbing hips and lower back, now perpetually sore from childbirth or nursing. But no matter what I did, the magic was gone. When I looked in the mirror, I saw a flabby, tired me who could really afford to get her (aching) butt on the rower.

I didn't talk about it to people, because the world is full of interesting things to talk about, and my run-of-the-mill, tropey body shame was not one of them. It felt stupid and embarrassing and unworthy of conversation. It felt impossible to escape, a tax on womanhood—what woman *actually* liked her body? It seemed as rare as finding someone who couldn't use more money in their bank account.

So I waited. One day, I would get to be pregnant again. We both wanted a second child. It just seemed a matter of time. And the next time, farfetched as I knew this was, perhaps I could find a way to hold on to the feeling of being a miracle, too.

2

THE HALO

"HOLY SHIT! WHAT IS THAT?" Everyone at the resort was squinting up at the sky, hands cupped over our shades. Around the sun, a circular rainbow had formed. It was too bright to look at for long but impossible to resist trying.

"Aliens are coming!" someone hollered as everyone yanked out their cell phones. I settled back into my lounge chair, rattled, and started to google "circle rainbow around the sun," but between my phone's glare and its alarming heat, gave up and shoved it back into my bag.

It was May 2021—just over three years since I'd sat on the toilet wishing I was pregnant again so I'd like myself. Since then, the world had fallen into a pandemic and was finally tiptoeing out of it. Women had borne babies by laboring in masks without their partners present. Newborns at risk of COVID had been quarantined. It hadn't been a good time to try for a second kid; that had seemed so obvious, we didn't even discuss it.

But things were looking up: People were traveling again, for instance. Here we were in Mexico, our first trip as a couple since having Finn. Vaccines were a thing.

It was time.

I was thirty-nine and not worried about my age. In my mind, forty was when my fertility window began its creaky, crawling closure. I'd known friends to have babies into their late thirties and early forties, and with Finn, we'd gotten pregnant the first month we tried.

Plus, it was good timing for another reason. Lucas was finally at the end of a six-year-long career pivot from the performing arts to the sciences.

When we'd first started dating in 2013, he'd been a professional singer. On one of our first dates, I'd found myself sitting in his New York apartment meeting his two best friends for the first time—all three of them performers, two of them currently in Broadway shows—and when they pulled out a guitar to launch a singalong, Lucas said, "Mary, sing 'Part of Your World' for us."

I'd frozen, terrified. He was my new boyfriend, with whom I'd secretly shared that I'd sung the song from *The Little Mermaid* in my third-grade talent show. I was the only non-professional singer in the room, but I didn't want to seem like a poor sport.

His friend Wes pulled up the chords on a laptop and started to play.

"Look at this stuff," I sang quietly. "Isn't it neat?"

Lucas was beaming at me. I sounded ridiculous, like a child.

"Wouldn't you think my collection complete?"

"*Commit!*" Lucas yelled suddenly in his deep baritone voice, staring into my eyes like this was my shot, my moment to shine. He could not have seemed more earnest, more passionate about my performance on his couch in my green tank top and cutoffs. "*Commit!*"

What else could I do?

"*Wouldn't you think I'm the girl, the girl who has everything?*"

I belted that song like I was Jodi Benson, the voice of Ariel in the 1993 movie, and his friends were kind enough not to let out a single, audible snicker.

But being a performer had burned him out, and, approaching forty, he saw it only getting harder in the years ahead: tougher to get roles, to pay bills, to sustain the hustle. A performing actor is only as good as his next gig.

When I pointed out after we'd been dating a few months that he read medical journals *for fun*, the possibility of a career change came up. Sure, he was thirty-five. But so what?

The morning after our wedding, we'd sat side by side in the airport while he did his first Chemistry 101 assignment and I snacked on lemon bars from our reception the night before. My mom had packed them for me in a Styrofoam container. Over the next four years, he endured calculus placement exams and four-hour chemistry labs with eighteen-year-old lab partners who called him "Dad."

In the meantime, he became one—we had Finn just as he was wrapping up Physics II and Organic Chemistry.

And right after Finn turned one, Lucas applied to his dream graduate program in genetics.

He wasn't home when I saw the admissions email come in on his desktop monitor, which we kept in the living room. Finn was playing on the floor at my feet. It took all my willpower not to click on it, but I waited for his phone call: He'd been accepted.

I rushed to my closet, where I'd hidden everything I bought to celebrate, in case it went exactly as we hoped—balloons and streamers in the university's colors. I blew up as many as I could until I grew too dizzy and found a country music station to blast from my phone when he came in. A month later, we packed up and moved to Nashville.

His two-year grad program had coincided almost perfectly with the pandemic.

Now, finally, he was done. Two weeks before we left for

Mexico, he'd walked in cap, gown, and mask—all with matching insignia—across an outdoor stage on a vast, green lawn, where Finn and I cheered from our folding chairs, stationed a generous six feet from our fellow spectators. And in just a couple more weeks, he'd start his new job making his first annual salary as an adult, a job as a clinician and researcher that would give us health insurance, which had been the most constant stressor in our lives to date.

Under his sun hat, margarita in hand, he seemed the most relaxed he'd been in the eight years I'd known him.

Around us, people were still ogling the circular rainbow. I set down the novel I was reading. Sun blindness be damned; I needed to know what this thing was.

"Halos around the sun," I read on my phone, "are caused by the thin cirrus clouds that often precede a storm."

A storm? But the sky was all blue, only blue.

Lucas turned to me, grinning, and mouthed, "Is that Steve?"

The night before, sitting on an outdoor patio, listening to live music over cocktails, he'd suddenly said, "Don't turn around, but I'm 99% sure Steve Bannon is sitting behind you."

I'd turned, of course, ignoring Lucas's groan.

He was right—with his splotchy jowls and hooded eyes, the man *really* looked like Steve Bannon.

There is a game Lucas and I play in public sometimes. We'll find a person in the room who resembles a celebrity or someone we both know, then we say, "I didn't know Kathleen was here," or "I didn't know Martha Stewart was here." The other person has to figure out which stranger is Kathleen or Martha Stewart.

But Lucas wasn't playing that game.

"It's him," he'd said decisively.

I'd "gone to the bathroom" and instead, hovered behind a tree, peering at maybe-Bannon's table.

"Not him," I'd said, returning to ours. "Different hairline."

"Are you sure?"

"My long-distance vision is better," I'd said. But non-Steve was indeed an incredible doppelgänger, and we were having fun. We were *playing*. When had we last played?

Lucas had once told me, completely earnestly, "I remember the first time I ever laughed out loud. I was fourteen."

It had sounded like a bit. I'd cracked up.

"No, it's true!" he'd insisted.

"It's obviously not," I'd said. "You laughed before you were a *teenager*."

He'd shrugged, conceded that he probably had, and I'd made fun of him for it ever since.

But that week in Mexico felt, indeed, like the first time we'd laughed in years, or ever.

I'd gone off birth control to track my cycle. We weren't timing sex, but we weren't using protection, either—if it happened, it happened. And it was vacation; we were having a lot of sex. At some point, I opened my fertility tracking app with curiosity to find that I ovulated on May 19th—the day of the halo.

Months from now, when I'd look back on photos from the trip, I'd find a ten-second video Lucas took of me. In it, I'm cross-legged by the pool in my swimsuit, holding my forthcoming novel, *Palm Beach*, to face the camera. I grin widely and do a stupid little shimmy then crack up, because it's ridiculous that we're trying to make a promotional gif, something I've only ever seen other people do.

When I stumble on this video, I will replay it ten, fifteen times thinking, *she is someone else.* That shimmying woman will seem as distinct from my person as Steve Bannon's doppelgänger at our resort. Because by the day I find it, I will have miscarried and will know that the girl in the video only appears to be carefree. In truth, she is so afraid. She is in perpetual flight, terrified that if she stops flapping, she'll fall and never stop falling.

And fall she will. In her uterus, the egg and sperm have already formed a zygote, and the cells are rapidly multiplying. She's already pregnant, but this pregnancy will not end in a child, nor will the one after that, or the one after that.

The rain didn't come until three days after the halo, as we were scrambling with our suitcases to meet our airport transport, scurrying from palm tree to palm tree, getting soaked through the shields of our fingers.

3

GLOWING

TWO WEEKS AFTER MEXICO, at 7:30 a.m. on an already-hot Sunday morning, I stood in an empty Walmart bathroom in Mustang, Oklahoma, holding a three-pack of pregnancy tests I'd just scanned through the self-checkout.

It was the last day of our visit to Lucas's family for Memorial Day weekend. We'd rented a car more reliable than our own and driven ten hours with Finn across three states. Underslept and hungover, we would head back to Tennessee in the next couple of hours.

After our Mexico vacation, I'd not even unpacked, apart from swapping out my dirty clothes. But there was one thing: After realizing I'd ovulated on vacation, I tossed in an expired pregnancy test from the back corner of my bathroom cabinet, one left over from having Finn that had somehow survived almost four years and a move.

I calculated that the earliest I could possibly test positive—ten days after ovulating—fell on the day we'd leave Oklahoma to head back home.

That morning, Finn shook me awake at 5 a.m., well before any other human in the house had risen. In my twelve-year-old nephew's bathroom next to his NASA poster, I peed on the expired stick, and, to my surprise, made out a line just faint enough to wonder if my eyes were playing tricks. Was it possible? How lucky would that make us? We hadn't even been "trying" yet, not like we had with Finn. With Finn, we'd called my ovulation week "fuck fest 2000," a callback to the nineties Y2K obsession. Sperm-friendly lube had been involved that we (I) expedited via Amazon.

It's expired, but I think there's something?? I texted my sister.

Invent a reason to go to Target! Say you need tampons! she wrote back.

As soon as Lucas had stumbled into my in-laws' living room, groggy and in search of coffee, I announced, keys in hand, that I was venturing out for "road snacks." The line was so pale that it was still very possible I was imagining it. I didn't want to tell him unless I was sure. Before he could ask questions, I was pulling our rental sedan out of the driveway in the sweats I'd slept in.

Now, in the eerie and oppressive blue light of a desolate Walmart, I tore open the three-pack, then peed on the first two tests in quick succession. Instantly, each bloomed a second pink line. No three-minute wait required.

In the movie version of this story, the frame freezes here, and we zoom in on the matching sets of double lines until they blur and we're inside the dream—the family of four I'd default envisioned since girlhood. It was going to come true! It was happening!

But more immediately, there was the matter of my body.

Oh, the body. *That* necessary evil. I toted her out for a jog because I felt better when I exercised, clad her in colorful clothing, craved the sun, and delighted in any bright dress that could double as a festive tablecloth. But trying to like (or, God help me, "love") my body, as the Dove campaigns of the aughts encouraged, was akin to speaking French fluently: After an entire childhood's worth of education, it wasn't going to happen. She, my body, and I had far too rocky a history to launch a love story. My reflection in a mirror was like someone I was a little embarrassed by but knew I shouldn't be. I understood intellectually that she deserved love, but really, I just wanted her to be different. Enter guilt on top of the embarrassment.

I hadn't purged in years, but the truce I'd made with my body was more Cold War than peace. What I *could* manage was pretending I didn't even have a body; I simply lived in the world of my mind as much as possible.

Except for one brief, beautiful period of reprieve.

Pregnant with Finn, I had been a woman with one foot in this life and one outside of it. I was channeling creation itself, holding hands with the mysterious beyond. Straddling two worlds, this one and whatever is beyond it, like those tourist attractions where you can stand with one sneaker in one Carolina and one in the other. My God, it had felt like a magic trick: I actually liked my body. My thighs had just been my thighs, my underarms just my underarms.

It was finally finding the right eyeglasses prescription. It was hearing for the first time. It was acquiring a new sense. *This* was the drug I'd always wanted; this wasn't even body neutrality. The voice in my head, an asshole I'd muzzled for almost fifteen years, had retired and been replaced by the president of my fan club.

"Look at what our body is doing today!" she sang. "It's amazing!"

Miracle, indeed.

And listen, there's a reason I've never tried hard drugs, and it isn't D.A.R.E. (well, it might be). When I discover a magical potion for living, I have a hard time walking away.

I'd hoped that the miraculous, drugged feeling would survive Finn's birth, but the my-body-is-a-wonder attitude dissipated as soon as he was born.

In the hours after his birth, Finn hadn't been getting enough milk from my breasts, so a lactation consultant had shown up in my hospital room to help us navigate nursing.

"He's not quite latching right…" she said, pinching my nipple over and over and stroking it against his tiny lips while he alternated between whimpers and screams.

He'd latch, then stop. Latch, then stop.

She used one finger to pry open his mouth and peered inside. "Oh," she said soberly. "That's it." A tongue tie, she explained. A bad one. He wouldn't be able to nurse unless we got it clipped.

"Where do we do that?" I asked, assuming it was like a circumcision, offered on site. But no. The hospital would clip your genitals, but not your tongue.

"There's no one who does it in Manhattan. You'll have to go out to Long Island." Long Island? How? We didn't have a car. What kind of procedure wasn't performed in Manhattan, and why was she whispering?

Over the coming days, after going home, my quest to nurse grew relentless, frantic. I hired two more lactation consultants, who came to our apartment in Queens and performed various versions of the same nipple-pinching. "Like a pancake," everyone said over and over, squeezing me between their thumb and forefinger.

The day we rented a car and drove out to Long Island for the tongue-tie surgery, Finn was three weeks old. As the doctor clipped the thin strip of skin that attached his tongue to his gums, he wailed, and I'd turned to the wall unable to bear it, sobbing along with him.

But two days later, he still wasn't getting enough milk.

The last lactation consultant had told me she suspected he had a tight neck and recommended a chiropractor in Queens who performed craniosacral massage on newborns. I booked his first available appointment—7 p.m. on a Tuesday night.

"We're taking him to a chiropractor?" Lucas said, wide-eyed. He and my mom exchanged glances like, *do we let her do this, or do we stop it?* But that Tuesday, Lucas and I stood across from Dr. Vela, the chiropractor, as I explained Finn would only nurse on my left, not my right.

"Can I see him?" he asked. I handed Finn over.

"All I ask is—please don't do anything to crack his bones," Lucas said like he'd rehearsed the line.

"Oh, I won't," said Dr. Vela. Finn, who had been crying, grew quiet in Dr. Vela's hands. It appeared that Dr. Vela was simply holding Finn, nothing more, for several seconds. Finn remained calm until he was handed back to me. "Try now."

I let the right strap of my dress fall off my shoulder and lifted Finn's face to my chest. He latched and began to nurse. No struggle, no resistance, no fight.

What was this witchcraft?

I was overjoyed.

"You did it!" I said, gushing. "Thank you!"

"And how are you doing?" Dr. Vela asked.

"Me?" I asked. He nodded.

"Oh, um, great? This is amazing. I can't believe it," I said, staring at Finn nursing happily for the first time in the three weeks since he'd been born. I could feed him now. I could give him what he needed.

"No, I mean you," Dr. Vela asked. "How are *you* doing? Are you okay?" He and Lucas were both looking at me.

"Yeah," I said, thrown. "I'm fine." What did this have to do with me?

In the days that followed, I would sit on the couch feeling overwhelming affection and gratitude for this miraculous person lying in my lap while swallowing disgust at the rolls of flesh stacked beneath my swollen breasts. Typical newborn parents, Lucas and

I operated on four-hour stretches of sleep, subsisting on takeout Thai and cheap wine, frayed and bleary and raw with how much we loved this tiny person and how terrified we were that we'd make some stupid, grievous mistake—let him roll off the sofa, fail to feed him enough. Every decision felt dire, every morning a fog, and my body, the site of his crash landing on the planet. I couldn't even look at it.

Then, twenty-seven days after Finn's birthday came my own.

My mom stayed with him so Lucas could take me shopping for a new dress. It was either his idea or hers—I just know this was announced to me and that I saw they wanted me to feel beautiful in my three-week postpartum skin, and though I felt anything but, I was willing to try.

Lucas and I took the subway from our Queens neighborhood into Manhattan. I had no idea what size I might wear now. My belly below the waist was still baggy and inflamed.

Was it wishful thinking, or just delusion, that I walked into the first store and pulled garments in my old size?

I emerged from the dressing room, fully dressed in my own clothes, to meet Lucas's expectant face.

"Nothing fit right," I said, as if it were the clothes' fault.

At store after store, we did this dance. Even once I started pulling larger sizes, I could barely peek at my image in the three-way glass, much less step out to show him.

Finally, at Express, I tried on a long, hot-pink wrap dress that featured my enormous, milk-full chest in a way that seemed to distract from my loose middle and allowed myself to step out of the fitting room.

"It looks fantastic!" said Lucas sweetly. I agreed that it looked fine.

Shopping bag in hand, we headed to happy hour at one of our favorite restaurants, Rosa Mexicana, where I rushed to the bathroom to address my throbbing breasts. Having not yet left home for this long since they'd become Finn's nutritional source, I'd not known this would happen, so we'd swung by a CVS when I'd realized I wasn't going to make it through our date. I bought a hand pump for twenty bucks. As I stood there squeezing it and hoping no one was waiting outside the door, I cradled anticipatory shame over the queso I was about to eat.

But it's my birthday! I countered the voice in my head. *And I just had a baby!*

So? Some moms come home from the hospital looking just like they did before they ever got pregnant.

And so on. The glowing goddess with a cheer squad taking up residence in her head was a phantom, a good dream I wanted back.

All of which is to say that in that Walmart bathroom, the universe was offering me what I was most hungry for—more, I dare say, than a child itself: I got to be *her* again.

I gathered the ripped packaging and, still clutching the two tests, hurried through the aisles in search of a cute way to announce the news to Lucas.

I spotted a toddler t-shirt that read "Amazing Big Brother." It was hideous, a black and lime-green basketball decal with bubble letters. It was also $3.99—perfect. I figured as we were packing, I'd hold it up and say something to Lucas like, "Where'd this come from?"

I texted my pregnant friend Emily.

So I'm alone in a Walmart in Oklahoma, and I may not be able to lend you my bassinet.

Within seconds, she was calling.

"We're pregnant together!" we screamed as I walked across the lot to my car. (A secret of womanhood: A friend often knows before the partner.)

I was planning to see Emily in a few months for a girls' trip. We discussed how we'd take pregnant lady photos with our bumps. When we hung up, we were exuberant, giddy with joy.

A year from now, both no longer pregnant, both without babies, we would be having very different conversations—about life, about fertility, about what it means to let go of a dream. But in that moment, we were overjoyed to be expecting together.

Driving back to the house, I turned on the radio in search of a song I could celebrate to. When I landed on one I vaguely recognized from my high school days, I turned it up and rolled down the windows. Though I couldn't recall the title, I somehow remembered the words.

"That's all a part of me!" I belted. "Because that's who I am!"

The flat Oklahoma skyline, now a deep orange, felt like a promise. I drove down wide streets with no cars but my own, letting the wind rush through my fingers as my hair snapped across my face, half-blinding me.

A thank you ballooned from the bottom of my gut. Thank you. *Thank you.*

Back at the house, I found Lucas in our nephew's room, which we'd taken over for our stay. He was flustered and irritated, trying to pack as Finn "helped" by unfolding clothes Lucas had already placed in a suitcase.

Lucas eyed the Walmart bag with the t-shirt in it, not road snacks.

"Let's go ahead and hit the road as soon as we're packed," he said.

It was now or never then for my little stunt. I pulled the shirt out of the bag.

"Here, dress Finn in this," I said, holding up the shirt. I watched as his face played out confusion, more confusion, then terror.

"Oh my God," he said. He looked like he might throw up,

but also, this was his schtick: looking like he might throw up when I announced a pregnancy. He'd done the same thing with Finn.

"You're pregnant?"

I nodded, beaming.

"Dammit," he said. I looked at him like, *come on, man.*

"I'll bring the enthusiasm," I said.

He'd shared a twin bed with Finn for most of the night, and Finn was now screaming that he'd gotten poop on his hands. And we had a ten-hour drive ahead of us. He walked over to hug me. "Sorry," he said. "No, I'm excited. I am." He pulled away. "Wait," he said, panicked, "you don't actually want to dress him in that right now, do you?"

"God, no!" We both laughed. How absurd that would be, to share the news with his entire family, currently eating egg biscuits on the other side of the wall. That would be reckless; I was barely pregnant. Anything could still happen.

Technically.

Because I didn't actually believe that anything would. Declining to announce our happy development felt more like a social norm I was agreeing to observe for the sake of appearances than a choice based on any real possibility of loss.

Even as a woman of "advanced maternal age," I felt confident we'd have our baby.

Later that evening, six hours into our drive, we stopped for the night at a Holiday Inn west of Memphis. I drew Finn a bath and climbed in with him. I never bathed with Finn. I was always too focused on getting through the bedtime routine as quickly as possible: washing hair, rinsing hair, drying off, getting him in pajamas to brush teeth (which we called making his "eees and ahhs"). But this night, I felt in less of a rush.

Finn and I shaped animals out of bubbles: a rhino, a blowfish, a T-rex. From the other room where Lucas sat, I could hear the TV playing softly. Already, my body was softening into a friend, one I hadn't seen in a while.

I'm pregnant, I thought, and thought it again. *I'm pregnant.* It was a warmth, an embrace. It was a cloud of light that hovered around me. I was seven again, breathless in the bushes, with a precious secret.

4

SAVED

BACK IN NASHVILLE, home from our trip to Oklahoma and five weeks pregnant, I stood in the front yard with Finn jumping in the baby pool and squealing every time I splashed him, and behold…my head was quiet.

Normally, I hosted a chatterbox on my shoulder. Nothing as exciting as an angel or devil, more a nagging HR manager who couldn't help offering up a performance review on every. Single. Action. Or inaction, for that matter. *Nice work on X! Let's try to do more of Y next time, though, 'kay?*

From *remember, you haven't emailed that person back yet* to *yikes, check out the period in that text, she's probably mad!*, this 24/7 feedback hotline was so persistent, so *annoying*, that by the pandemic, I decided to try a new tactic: giving it a platform.

See me in 2020 making a poster to hang on my bedroom wall. At the top are all the tasks I hope to accomplish every day: Meditate, Do Yoga, Cook, Write, Experience Joy. On the left side of the poster board are dates. I get to check every box I complete. I'd granted my HR overlord a full-on chart in my house.

No wonder I got weird (I mean, who wasn't during that time, if they were healthy enough to be?). Soon, I was drinking mushroom tea instead of coffee and had joined an online women's self-help forum where people posted thousands of words every day as if sitting in front of our screens for hours and hours, typing out our fears to strangers, counted as facing them.

I'm not unusual in possessing this meddlesome roommate as an internal mouthpiece. I just happen to have one that likes to focus on the past, scrutinize what's already happened, rehash and make predictions based on my errors. Mine is a two-hour podcast recap of a one-hour TV show—that's the level of depth of her critiquing.

One way I tried to muzzle her was to dwell more in the future than in the present or past. The future, that beautiful thing, hadn't happened yet, so the talking head had nothing to critique. I could flee into dreaming about what lay ahead, into fantasies and plans that were quieter without all the chatter.

Perhaps this was one reason pregnancy was so effective at shutting her up. It was the ultimate future-dwelling state. Who, me? Oh, I'm just over here preparing for later, for my new life kicking off in about eight and a half months. This is the warm-up, the pre-game, the red carpet—all the fanfare and none of the pressure. There are no losers yet, only possible winners. You look stunning. You look gorgeous. How are you feeling? How are you feeling? How are *you* feeling? It's all sequins, white teeth, hope.

But dare I say, I think it ran even deeper.

I had long since walked away from religious life. If you pinned me down and asked me what I believed, I would say something about how I was pretty sure life was bigger than we understood, that it probably went on in some form, that love survived death, and that whatever happened after death cosmos-wise had very little to do with what gender we have sex with.

But another belief I felt in my bones, even if I wouldn't have articulated it this way, was that as hard as I'd worked to prove otherwise over the years, my existence wasn't justified. Mary Adkins: secretly expendable.

I'd gone to law school and been a lawyer for five minutes (seven months). I'd left that job when I was miserable and tutored the LSAT to pay my bills and managed to write several publishable novels around my tutoring schedule. It wasn't that I wasn't proud of what I'd done. I was. I'd kicked my crappy job to the curb and pursued what I really wanted to do, which was write, a choice that fortunately had worked out.

But none of it was ever enough. *Fill the holes, fill all the tiny holes.*

Pregnancy was categorically different. Is it possible to disappear a void? Because that's what it felt like. That it disappeared a void I'd spent a lifetime working around.

At eight, I asked my minister dad, sitting next to him in the passenger seat of our car parked in front of the First Baptist Church, "What if I don't believe in God?"

Between children's choir, Wednesday night church supper, mission group meetings, Sunday School, Bible Drill Club, regular Sunday morning church, plus weekday afternoons when we went with dad to work, I spent almost as much time at the church as I did at home. This wasn't an appropriate question for me, frequent pulpit soloist and "PK" (preacher's kid) with a personalized Bible embossed with my name, to be asking.

My dad, who epitomized the *un-* in unflappable long before I was ever called as much, calmly said something like, "God would know and would love you anyway."

Huh.

I climbed out of the car feeling watched...and still doubtful.

It wasn't that I didn't believe in God. I just didn't feel like I believed in anything. *Belief* didn't sound like something you could decide on, like what to eat for breakfast. It sounded like something you either had or you didn't, like the chicken pox or a decent singing voice.

I didn't *not* believe in God any more than I did—I just hadn't a clue how I was supposed to control that. The messaging around me, however, was very clear: We belonged to a community where there wasn't room for being anything other than a confident Baptist with Jesus in my heart, so I learned to fit in quickly, singing the songs, reciting the prayers, and memorizing the books of the Bible (have I mentioned I can still list all sixty-six from start to finish?).

One Wednesday night in the fall of my freshman year, I was at Wednesday night supper, a weekly buffet in the fellowship hall. I'd spent the summer trying not to eat very much, having gleaned that high school popularity required a few things: being skinny, having a car, and having access to beer. I didn't have a car or booze access, but I did have kid pudge to lose.

The gleaming silver tub of steaming, oily yeast rolls was impossible to resist, and I ate two or maybe three. And then, full of shame, I thought, *Maybe I can take it back.*

And then I remembered the *Lifetime* movie.

I think she even died in the film, or at least was hospitalized. I didn't care. It gave me the idea.

I made my way to a remote bathroom far from the dining hall, near where the church choir ascended to the rafters each Sunday, and I fell to my knees before the toilet.

I shoved my pointer finger down my throat.

Nothing happened.

I tried two fingers and let out a small gag.

I stood, now twice a failure: once for having eaten and twice for failing to puke.

But over the coming weeks, I improved. It wouldn't take many more tries to find my trigger, buried in the soft folds of my throat. And once I did, I was done for. Within a period of days, purging went from something I'd seen on TV to a temptation at every meal. A demon took up residence in my brain, where it would squat and torment me for the next ten years.

Then I turned sixteen. My youth group traveled to Houston for an event called the Baptist World Youth Conference—a gathering of five thousand teenage Baptists from around the world.

I'd never been in a room with five thousand people. We entered the stadium from the back. The room was dark except for the stage, a football field away, where a spotlight illuminated the band—a woman at a mic, a guy on a keyboard, and another at a drum set. They were the size of my pinky nail. It was echo-y and breezy, like the Sam's where we stocked up on frozen vegetables. In the dark, I followed the cluster of First Baptist kids, my peers, up one of the dozens of aisles radiating from the main floor. We climbed and climbed a staircase that kept going and going. Alongside us, people who didn't dress like me or anyone I knew—many in their national colors—sang. Some of them held their hands in the air, but it didn't look like it did when the annoying kids back home held their hands in the air at Young Life, the high school Christian club (which I joined to fit in). It looked more sincere. It didn't make me avert my eyes out of secondhand embarrassment.

We found our assigned section, where, instead of singing, I surveyed the room, in awe of the sheer number of human beings and our diversity. It was like a miniature Earth.

Over the next three days, I listened to the stories of people from countries in which believing in Jesus was criminal, stories of persecution and persistence, stories that left me quiet and confused. Praying had never been anything but required for me. It was the *opposite* of risky; it was risky *not* to love Jesus, never mind not believe in him. If none of my family believed—if my government had outlawed it—would I? It wasn't a hard question. The answer was no, I wouldn't. I wasn't even sure I did as it was.

The reverence that some people I was meeting held for the institution and idea of church, the fervor and devotion evident in their eyes as they talked about homegrown churches they'd sculpted from nothing because they cared about forming a place in which they could gather—it flipped me upside down. I walked around speechless, bewildered by how much these people cared about God, a character whom I had spent sixteen years mostly pretending to believe in.

My parents weren't the kind of Christians who used words like *saved*. They weren't fearmongering. I wasn't even sure if they believed in hell. If they did, it was probably more like time-out—temporary and instructive.

But more than one person at that event had asked me, "Are you saved?" in the kind of tone you use when you exclaim, "You have to see this sunset! It's fantastic!" People spoke of being "saved" like it was amazing, not just relief at being off the hook, where the hook was eternal misery. These people acted about God the way I imagined I would act if Jonathan Taylor Thomas had called me up in response to the lengthy fan letter I'd mailed him: euphoric.

At the final service, in Baptist revival fashion, the preacher invited anyone who wanted to commit or recommit "their lives to Christ" to join him on the stage.

Grace Pate went. Alan Smith went.

And suddenly I was going. I climbed down a million steps, walked to the front of the stadium, and knelt.

Then I was weeping. I was weeping because the people around me had found something I hadn't, and I wanted it so badly, what they had.

I cried because I had hated my body so, so much, plunging my hand down my throat again and again because I didn't believe I would be lovable otherwise.

I cried because, more than anything, I just wanted to belong to something meaningful, the way all these people did.

I was not crying because I suddenly believed Jesus could save me. I was crying because oh, how I wanted to.

At the airport, awaiting our flight home from Houston, a few of us went to a Mexican restaurant where a basket of chips was placed in the middle of the table.

For the previous two years—an eighth of my life, the majority of my adolescence—I had regarded restaurant baskets of tortilla chips as my greatest enemy. At Corona's, the restaurant where my family and I would have lunch most Sundays after church, I would steel myself with warnings (*You must have willpower!*), mantras (*You can do this!*), and compromises (*You can have exactly ten chips!*), but these had worked precisely zero times. I would binge on the chips, shoveling them into my mouth until the bottomless basket's bottom appeared for an instant before being refilled. Then I'd shovel again. As soon as the opportunity presented itself, I purged.

But on this day, I just took a chip without panic. I dipped it into the salsa, tipped it back, and brought it to my mouth. I took another chip. Did it again.

It struck me that I was not tempted to binge.

I ate a few more chips. And then I stopped—not because I was lecturing myself but because I didn't want any more.

Who *was* I? What alien had overtaken my body?

I left that restaurant without having binged and without feeling like I needed to purge. I'd just...eaten. Like a regular, non-bulimic person. I simply felt full.

For a month or two, the feeling lingered: a feeling of having a core that I didn't need to stuff full of something else, some substitute, but eventually it passed, and I was back to old habits.

A year or two later, I was at another church camp when someone asked one of the worship leaders what it felt like to "know Christ" (this is the way Christians talk).

"Like how you feel after a really good meal," she said.

I know exactly what she means, I'd thought.

I wasn't "a believer"—I wouldn't call what happened to me Jesus. But *something* had happened when I'd knelt in that stadium. It was a relinquishing, a surrender, like when I stopped fighting what I actually felt and believed, I could just be.

The closest I'd ever gotten to feeling that again had been while pregnant with Finn. And now that I was pregnant once more, it was back.

From the earliest days after that positive test, I could sense something in me where nothing had been before. I wasn't the one wondering, *How do I believe in Jesus, like those people do? How do I make myself believe so I can have that kind of joy?*

It was blooming inside me.

Whether this was the cause or effect of my kinder attitude toward my body is a chicken or egg. Was it that my outside stopped looking wrong to me because I had an inner sense of purpose, or did the fact that the HR overlord had shut up give me the space to recognize how miraculous pregnancy is?

I don't know. I just know that the shift was invisible and subtle and everything—a ragged hangnail finally cut, a monster zit after it heals, the red and weeping kind that I somehow *still* get in my forties. A splinter, gone. Tinnitus, subsided. Something miniscule that, once resolved, makes you want to cry from relief.

My friend's dad has had the hiccups for ten years. Ten *years*.

The hiccups, a splinter's sting, the ringing in my ears—they all stopped.

The wind blew as I stood ankle-deep in the cold water of the baby pool. I wore my favorite dress, a bright-orange tent with cream flowers on it, and my sun hat. I held onto my hat in the breeze and watched Finn march to the edge of the lawn, then turn around and stand at attention, waiting for my command.

"Ready... Set... Go!" I yelled.

He sprinted toward me in his oversized swim shorts and dinosaur swim shirt, a hand-me-down from his older cousins, giggling so hard as he ran that he almost toppled himself over before splashing into the pool and soaking me—the goal.

"No!" I yelled on cue.

He squealed and splashed around on his stomach, then stood and started jumping.

"Jump, mama! Jump!"

I jumped.

Over the coming weeks, ordinary life took on a new gloss, a shimmer. We went to the mall to get new eyeglasses for Lucas, and Finn tried on pairs alongside him, preening in the mirror like an adult. He wrote his name for the first time on our front patio with sidewalk chalk. He found ways to catch my eye and abruptly widen his to make me laugh.

One morning, wet from the pool, Finn shivered for the first time. Delighted, he exclaimed, "I just *shibbered*!" He'd learned the word before living the sensation and paired the two. I witnessed the spark happen, a candle catching a flame.

A baby meant all these moments of wonder would repeat, that I would get to do them again: the sidewalk chalk, the widening eyes, the shibbers.

Pregnancy was a filter on daily existence that brightened it while also rendering it inconsequential—it was difficult to care all that much about any petty grievance (a traffic jam, a hefty water bill, a rude stranger) because something, *someone,* miraculous was coming.

And not just anyone, but someone who, like Finn (and only Finn), could bust through my bullshit, slice it right open. When he laughed or asked to cuddle, the most urgent email became unimportant, even ignorable. By nature of being my son, it seemed, he had an unwavering power to reprioritize my to-do list simply by existing.

My friend Kate tells the story of how, one day, her six-year-old had an accident, soiling his clothes. When he was too embarrassed to leave the bathroom covered in poop, she didn't hesitate to give him her own shirt and walk home through the streets of Brooklyn in her bra.

That kind of love.

I had it with Finn, and I was going to get it with someone else too? It felt almost too good to be true. (Almost.)

Then there was the ice cream.

Upon the publication of my latest novel, a friend had sent a batch of gourmet ice cream, and after I had taken a bite and been floored by how utterly sensational it was, I'd discovered that it was French pot ice cream, made with heavy cream and eggs. When I wasn't pregnant, I spent many an evening trying to talk myself out of even a small dish of it.

But pregnant, I would happily fetch the carton I'd bought myself and spoon out a ramekin's worth each evening to enjoy, either alone or with Lucas on our front porch rocker. Like eating tortilla chips after my unexplainable spiritual experience as a teen, it felt magical. Suddenly, I had a blank permission slip for being a person.

It was like a mad lib, and the fill-in wasn't "noun" or "verb" but "something you normally want to do but don't allow yourself to for whatever reason." Fill-ins: Nap. Go to bed early. Say "no" as a complete sentence like the feminist memes demand. Eat as much ice cream as you want.

Meanwhile, the present became fleeting and thus precious: Our family of three would not be a family of three for much longer, and I found myself thinking, *relish it, Mary. These are the days before things change.*

And Finn had fallen in love with the morning ghost moon.

"Let's go find the moon!" he'd declare as soon as we came downstairs in the morning, yanking the front door open in his footie pajamas, his hair bushy from slumber. Since his sleeping hours fell just between sunset and sunrise, finding the moon amounted to scanning the pink sky for a pale remnant.

One morning, he sat on my lap in our front porch rocker and, as we looked for the moon, the sky flooded with what appeared to be tiny birds. What was happening? A migration?

But they weren't birds.

"Bats!" I said. Thousands of them washed over us, from the trees across the street to somewhere beyond our house.

"Bats!" Finn yelled, matching my glee. "Onetwothreefourfive—" He counted as quickly as he could, skipping fifteen, like he always did, and forgetting the thirties. But there were far too many, hundreds squealing across a peach backdrop.

It became our morning routine, to wait on the porch at dawn for the bats. They'd trickle out, then rush as the sky turned tangerine.

I couldn't believe it, that the whole time we'd lived in this house, we'd gone about our business making coffee and eating cereal, unaware that the bats were communing just outside our door.

The bats, the moon, the baby blooming in me—stitches in a shimmering tapestry whose brilliance blinded me to my regular preoccupations: weight, productivity, whether I was doing life "right."

This time, perhaps even after the baby came, I could hold on to the feeling of being a part of that tapestry, of being bigger than the calories in a cup of ice cream, bigger than the books I'd written with their mediocre sales.

Pregnant, I had a reason to be here. With Finn, that feeling had departed my body when he had. But this time, if I could just capture it somehow, then even after the baby came, I could stop searching and just live.

5

_____

FADING

WHEN DID THE FEELING begin to fade?

Or was it always fading?

When I look back at photos from those first few summer weeks I was pregnant, I feel it in them, lingering: making pizza from scratch with Finn. Visiting the zoo, where he ate a hot dog and saved his bun to feed the ducks. Trips to the YMCA swimming pool, where, clad in his bulky lobster puddle jumper, he devoured half a cantaloupe by himself.

Like cresting the peak of a hill, I find it difficult to pinpoint precisely where the decline began.

The day we'd driven home from Oklahoma, the same morning I first tested positive, I'd booked my initial ultrasound appointment on my phone from the passenger seat.

Under our new health plan's "maternity bundle" through Lucas's job, having a baby would be free (free!) as long as we delivered at the university hospital. The online scheduler had required me to provide the date of my last period before it would offer up appointment options. When I input my actual last period date, I wasn't shown any slots until late July, but when I fudged it and moved it back a week, I was given slots in June.

I chose a date in June.

Was I already sensing that something was wrong? I was lying to lock in an earlier initial ultrasound. In my mind, it was mere reassurance that I wanted. I'd read somewhere that once a heartbeat is detected—as early as six weeks—one's chances of carrying to term were over 90%. I wanted to know that this baby's future wasn't going to be taken from me—nor that this feeling would be.

I knew that not everyone felt the way I did about being pregnant. Multiple friends had described the first trimester as terrible—and not even just the physical symptoms. For an aerialist I knew, who performed physical feats in minimal clothing for a living, pregnancy had been terrifying and existential: How would her body's changes affect her professional identity?

Not me. No aerialist, I.

I relished my swollen, tender boobs, the extreme fatigue a small price to pay for the deep sense of belonging I felt with a baby on board. I wasn't nauseous, which worried me a little since I'd heard that nausea signaled a healthy pregnancy, but I hadn't been nauseous with Finn, either.

Another friend, though, shared my experience of pregnancy as a welcome shift in perspective that transcended body image. Pregnant, Kate and I both found that we asked for (or took) what we needed: a seat on the subway, an afternoon nap, a hand carrying groceries. We said "no" more often and felt less guilty about it. We coined a term for this newfound self-regard: *pregnancy swagger*.

We both wanted to figure out a way to bring pregnancy swagger into our lives all the time, even when we weren't pregnant. She was done having kids, so when I'd gotten my positive test, we'd decided to make it a project. We'd email back and forth during my pregnancy and talk about how pregnancy swagger felt different from regular life. She'd share memories of her two past pregnancies, and I'd share my current state of mind in real time. Maybe, we thought, we could capture whatever made being pregnant so magical—and find a way to make it last.

Our pregnancy swagger emails were daily and long. We wrote about how hard it was to like our bodies when we weren't pregnant, how cruel and hateful we could be toward them. We wrote about how easy, on the contrary, it was to be kind to ourselves while pregnant. When she wrote this—*For me, I think some of the joy of pregnancy was the knowledge that every minute of the day I was doing something valuable, worthy of the space I was taking up on earth*—I knew I could have written that exact sentence.

Leading up to the first ultrasound, I was increasingly anxious. I would still daydream—*Where will we put the nursery? We could turn part of the playroom into a nursery, maybe build a wall. Should we replace the rug?*—but I also found myself constantly checking the odds-of-miscarrying calculator I'd discovered online, inputting my age, height, weight, and number of prior live births. Sometimes, I'd redo the demographics, altering one thing—tweaking my live birth history or age—to watch the likelihood of my *not* miscarrying climb a smidge: 88.2%, 88.6%, 89.3%.

I longed almost desperately to show, to have a visible bump. It was said that women show sooner in pregnancies after their first, and I couldn't wait. On Instagram, I searched #twelveweekbump and #twelveweekbumpsecondkid for an idea of how I might already look pregnant by the end of summer, and I wished I could skip forward in time to get there.

At 6 weeks 3 days, I took a profile selfie in a full-length mirror and texted it to my mom and sister with this caption: *Is it possible I'm already showing?*

It wasn't. But if I stared long enough...

I bought a coming-home outfit online. It was a set of cotton knits and a tiny, tan sweater with matching booties I'd found through an Instagram ad, the world of targeted marketing having quickly picked up on my pregnancy. (Side note: It's a lot slower to pick up on a miscarriage. I'd get the same maternity-wear ads for months, and, after that, ads for diapers and formula, the algorithm built to track only the most optimistic version of a gestational calendar.)

The morning of our checkup, I knew I was precisely seven weeks pregnant; my cycle had been regular, and I'd tracked it.

Waking up, I had an uneasy feeling. I tried to shoo it away. This was supposed to feel like Christmas morning: I'd been counting down the days. Instead, a mild sense of foreboding scratched at my back.

Of course it did. I was a thirty-nine-year-old mom on her way to a first ultrasound. I'd be delusional not to be nervous.

When Lucas and I parked and entered the facility, I was shocked by its size. A shopping center that had been converted into a massive medical complex, it still had nineties mall vibes and lighting. As we approached a bank of escalators, my stomach sank.

My OB back in New York, the doctor who'd delivered Finn, worked from a small office in a charming brick building overlooking Central Park, a cozy warmth matched by her demeanor and bedside manner. When I'd been diagnosed with gestational diabetes at twenty weeks, she had called to tell me personally that it wasn't my fault. As she'd sewn me up after delivering Finn, while the nurses wiped him down and crowned him with a knit beanie (my favorite thing about humans is that when we arrive on the planet, the first thing we're given is a hat), she'd quoted Khalil Gibran: "Your children are not your children...and though they are with you, yet they belong not to you."

Before I'd even held my son for the first time, I'd committed the line to memory. He was on loan to me, and I would do my best to care for this precious, borrowed soul.

It was hard to imagine any doctor in this dimly lit omni-plex showing such warmth.

Mary, you haven't even met the doctor yet, I told myself.

I took a breath and a seat next to Lucas in a sea of plastic chairs. As the minutes ticked by, I grew more and more uncomfortable. The chair was too hard. The air was chilly in that recirculated airplane way that makes you feel like you're not getting quite enough oxygen.

Ten years earlier, on my first day of work as a lawyer at a job that I'd blindly worked my butt off to get, I'd stood in my new office on a high floor of a skyscraper, peered out at the Manhattan skyline, and thought, *oh no, I've just landed in someone else's life.*

It was the best way I could describe it to people.

"I don't hate it," I'd say, even though I did hate it a little bit. "It's just like I'm in a play, and it's a play I don't even like."

It had taken me seven months to wriggle my way out of that job, and the whole time, I felt like an actor who couldn't get my lines right.

Sitting in that plastic chair, my feeling was similar. This was not where we were going to have this baby. This was someone else's doctor's office.

Finally, we were called back and led to a room where, I noticed right away, there was no ultrasound machine.

Wasn't the entire point of this visit to perform an ultrasound, confirm a baby was in there?

"Have a seat," the nurse said, motioning to a set of chairs. Lucas and I sat as she launched into a series of questions that felt more like an interrogation than a pregnancy intake.

Did I do drugs? (No specific drugs. Just "drugs.")

Did I know anyone who did drugs?

Was I around people who did drugs?

Drugs? I wasn't even using my regular *sunscreen.*

"You have me down for a pregnancy appointment, right?" I finally interrupted, genuinely concerned that she was mistaken about the purpose of my visit.

"Yes," she said before proceeding to the next question.

When she left us alone to wait for the doctor, Lucas turned to me and said, "Do you think we'll get better treatment if I put on my badge?" He pulled out his lanyard with ID showing that he was on staff at the institution and looped it around his neck as a nurse practitioner came in and introduced herself.

"Congratulations," she said. She was smiling and friendly, and I hated her. We aren't old college pals, woman! Look at my cervix! Find my baby and give it an A-plus!

I'm changing doctors, I thought. *I don't care what it costs.*

"Thank you," I said. "Um, are we going to do an ultrasound today?"

"We'll have to schedule that for you separately at one of our ultrasound locations," she said. "You can book that on your way out."

I swallowed. No. No, no, no, no. I had to see the baby.

"Can I book it for today?" I asked, trying to keep my voice from trembling.

"They may be full, but they hopefully can get you in over the next few days."

The next few days?

My scathing Google review was writing itself when she said, "Listen, we do have an old ultrasound machine here. I'm not an ultrasound technician, but if you want, I can at least confirm there's a baby in there."

I let out my breath.

"Yes," I said. "Thank you."

She disappeared as I climbed onto the table and spread a blue paper blanket over my thighs, managing to eke out a smile at

Lucas.

She is going to make sure there's a live baby in there. That was all I needed.

I lay back and closed my eyes. After a couple of minutes, she returned, rolling a dusty contraption on a cart. She pressed a button, and it whirred like a jet firing up.

"We don't have a transvaginal wand here, so we'll do our best with this abdominal one."

Oh, right, the wands. I'd forgotten since my last pregnancy how it worked. Very early in the first trimester, the baby is so small that it's only detectable by a wand inserted into the vagina. After that, it's big enough that equipment outside the belly can pick it up. At seven weeks by my calculation, I was almost certainly too early in my pregnancy for a belly ultrasound.

They didn't have a single transvaginal wand anywhere in this massive medical stadium? Was it 1959?

"Maybe you're farther along than you think," she said. I was pretty sure I wasn't, but I'd take what I could get.

Changing doctors, I thought again. She switched off the light so we could better see the screen, wiped gel over the machine's nub, and pressed it against my stomach. The three of us turned toward the grainy image on the monitor. It looked like an old movie about outer space—fuzzy and black with tiny flecks of white snow floating about.

She navigated the wand around my belly for a few seconds, then a few more. She pressed harder, hard enough that, under different circumstances, I might have asked her to lighten up.

"Sorry for the pressure," she said. "I'm trying to get in there..."

"I'm okay," I said, thinking, *ouch* and *come on, baby, come on. Show us where you are.*

"I think it's too early," she mumbled after a couple of minutes, but she didn't stop. I closed my eyes.

Stop, I wanted to say. *Please stop.* But I didn't. I'd asked for this, and now, I would suffer through as my duty. No more mad libs. I was back to paying penance.

Finally, she lifted the nub.

"It's too early," she said. "Sorry."

She discharged us with a pamphlet for expecting mothers that I leafed through as we walked out, angrily noting the various lists of dos and don'ts: No-nos were deli meat, tuna, hot tubs.

Don't patronize me while treating me like an item on a checklist, I thought.

"I need to book an ultrasound," I said to the clerk at the front.

"How's Monday for you?" she asked.

It was Thursday. *Monday?* Was she kidding?

"You don't have anything sooner?"

She shook her head.

"I can drive *anywhere,*" I said. I'd rattle my busted Volvo to the most remote corner of Tennessee if she'd name a time.

"I'm afraid not," she said.

"Monday is fine," I managed to say. But it wasn't fine. My body was tingling. I couldn't wait until Monday. The urge to get my ultrasound was nothing like how it had felt to chase down the mailman when I was eighteen before he reached our house, just to see if he had my college acceptance letter because I was so eager to know. That had been full of hope, anticipation.

This was desperate, primal.

Appointment booked, Lucas and I marched across the wide lobby to the escalators. Fighting tears, I whispered, "This is a nightmare."

"It will be okay." Lucas said. "By Monday, the baby will be bigger anyway. It's probably good to wait a few days."

I said nothing, thinking, *bullshit.*

Two hours later, after Lucas had returned to work, I sat on our front porch, having called every friend I could think of to rant about the horrors of the university's maternity care. My pregnancy-enabled inner peace and purpose had evaporated, replaced by the same persistent restlessness I used to feel after eating and before purging, a mad urgency to correct the situation.

And then, just as it had in my eating disorder days, the restlessness snapped into decisiveness.

Why was I being so passive, so willing to let others call the shots? I'd relinquished my power! The university's medical center wasn't the only medical provider in town. Nashville was a city saturated with a million medical offices—there were at least five between our house and Finn's daycare—and it was barely noon; an entire half-workday remained.

Surely *someone* in the metropolitan area could give me an ultrasound.

I'd simply search until I found someone, not take no for an answer.

As luck would have it, it didn't take long. A little legwork, and I found a lab that could squeeze me in at 4 p.m.

I phoned Lucas, pleased with myself.

"I worked it out," I said, feeling resourceful. By 4:30, I'd know my baby was healthy.

At 3:55, I walked alone into a tiny office in a strip mall a few miles from our home. Since we shared a car and Finn's daycare ended at four, Lucas had dropped me off. He and Finn would return to pick me up.

I waited only a few minutes before I was called back. This time, the ultrasound tech did not face the screen to me as she performed the transvaginal, and so I asked timidly, after she'd been clicking away at the computer keyboard for a couple of minutes, "Is there a baby in there?"

"Mm-hmm," she said. She herself was quite pregnant, and in

between clicks, she draped her left hand across her pert belly.

Really? That was it?

"Does it have a heartbeat?" I pressed.

"Yeah," she said.

"What's the heartrate?" I asked.

"Your doctor will review everything with you," she said.

I took a deep breath, giving up. I would not read into it, I thought. I'd trust that this was just protocol at this lab, that she wasn't being reticent because there was bad news to hide.

"Can I get a printout of the images?" I asked. I wanted to walk away with one of those glossy strips that pregnant women style into Instagram pregnancy announcements. I didn't plan to make one myself, but photos would show that the baby was real. I could carry it in my bag. I could sear it on my soul. I could stare at it for hours and it would bring me back to trusting.

"We don't do that here," she said, peeling off her gloves and flipping on the light. "We don't have a printer. You can get dressed, and your doctor will follow up with you." She exited, leaving me behind the closed door.

I turned to the screen, which still shone brightly in the dark room. She'd already closed my patient record. How many strokes of the keys would it take to pull it back up? I stood before it for a few seconds, entertaining the idea.

Outside, Lucas and Finn were waiting in the car.

"How'd it go?" Lucas asked in his I'm-over-this voice.

"There's a baby in there," I said, fastening my seatbelt.

"Good," he said in his so-now-can-we-move-on voice. "Do you feel better now?"

"Not until I know the heartbeat," I said.

Ding.

My phone chimed—a notification from my health portal.

Your health record has been updated with a new result.

I clicked the link. There it was: the report.

Gestational age: 6 weeks 4 days.

Heartrate: 92 beats per minute.

Hmm. That was not right. I knew my cycle; it was as regular as Greenwich Mean Time, as my grandfather would say. I was definitely 7 weeks 0 days pregnant—which would mean the baby was measuring small, that it wasn't growing at the rate it should. But, I supposed, three days off wasn't *too* much of a discrepancy.

Was ninety-two beats per minute good?

I googled.

The first result read: *The normal heartbeat of a fetus at 6-7 weeks gestation is 90-110.*

"We're good," I said, looking up and exhaling. "Ninety-two is fine."

I set my phone aside and, as we glided to a stop at a red light, relaxed for the first time all day. Things were going to be better now. We were in the clear.

Three hours later, I sat in Finn's room as he fell asleep, hiding the glow of my phone in my palm beneath a blanket.

I'd gotten my ultrasound. I'd gotten confirmation of a heartbeat. The Internet had said it was normal. So why did I still feel like something was wrong?

I navigated to Google Scholar. It was time to learn from the actual authorities—academic researchers—whether ninety-two beats per minute was *really* okay.

Within a few minutes, I found a peer-reviewed study of whether pregnancies made it to full-term based on fetal heart rate at various points between six and eight weeks gestation. Perfect.

I scrolled down to the results section, where the authors had created a handy little chart titled RATES OF FETAL DEMISE that laid out the study's crisp findings in a set of clean squares.

Percentage of fetuses with a heartbeat under 100 at 6.3 weeks gestation or later to end in fetal demise: 100%.

Wait. What? That's not what the other Google result had said.

What was 6.3 weeks gestation? I navigated to the calculator, aware that it didn't matter: Either way, my baby was past that mark.

Which put me at 100% likelihood of "fetal demise."

My fingers fumbled back to the search bar to find another study. The results were the same: a heart rate of under 100 led to "demise" 100% of the time. Not 99%. Not 98%. One hundred. I'd spent the first half of my life working for 100s. Now, here was one I couldn't accept.

I was going to miscarry—it was right there, in my palm.

I took a screenshot of the chart and texted it to Lucas then tiptoed out of the room and downstairs.

"Where'd you get that?" he asked.

"A peer-reviewed paper," I said, waiting—for what, I didn't know. For him to give me an answer. To tell me the research was wrong.

He sighed.

"Well, if you miscarry, we can try again." He stood, holding his glass of wine, and said, "Come on."

I followed him to the front porch. We sat in the matching rockers, facing a thick grove of trees across the street. The moon was bright.

"What's that thing Rilke said about learning to love the questions?" he said.

"Mmm," I said, feeling anything but love for the question of whether I was going to get to have this baby. Then he tried a different tactic.

"So you have a possibility of miscarrying that's higher than you thought. That basically puts us back where we were at the beginning, right?" He was referencing the statistic that many pregnancies—up to a third—end before women even know they're pregnant. In these cases, the period might just come a little late, and they'd never know. "And you were happy when you found out you were pregnant. If you were happy then, can you be happy now?"

It felt like spin. But I liked it.

I could get on board with spin if it meant I didn't have to sit in this ickiness, this dread. If it meant that the glow would come back.

"Okay," I said.

That night, I emailed my friend Kate on our "pregnancy swagger" thread for the last time.

I wrote:

I've been having thoughts, like: If I miscarry, what a waste. I've been eating like I can just eat whatever I want. I need to start working out again tomorrow.

And I feel anger at my body. Like it's the thing that's betrayed the fetus or something. Why do I suddenly feel hollow and purposeless?

She wrote back: *What happens if/when the pregnancy moves forward?*

I never replied.

6

LOSING

BABY LOOKS GREAT! Heartbeat is a little slow, but it's still so early. Let's schedule a follow-up in ten days.

The chipper and very much not–cut–out–for–sonography nurse practitioner had reviewed my ultrasound and sent a message through the health portal.

"I'm being gaslit," I complained to Lucas, thinking of my doomsday chart. I could point to actual studies! I had capital "R" research! But gaslit about what, and how, I didn't quite know. Did I mean that I knew the pregnancy was doomed, and I was waiting for someone to tell me so? I desperately wanted to believe that the baby looked great, but I also couldn't bring myself to believe it. And so perhaps I was looking for the next best thing: somebody to confirm my worst fear, to tell me I was correct, that I was going to lose this pregnancy and go back to being old Mary, now heavier, without a baby.

Old Mary—or non-pregnant Mary—looked identical to pregnant Mary, but they were as distinct as Steve Bannon and his unfortunate resort doppelgänger, as distinct as the three Bens who lived in my college dorm freshman year: Shaggy Ben (the skater), Big Ben (the pastor-to-be), and Little Ben, who wasn't actually little but slightly smaller than his roommate, Big Ben.

If this were *The Bachelor*, contestants Old Mary and Pregnant Mary would each get their own initial: Mary O. and Mary P.

Old Mary was a hustler, a go-getter, a taskmaster. She was a goals-are-dreams-with-deadlines kind of gal who'd been on more diets or "diets" (the kind disguised as wellness kicks once dieting went out of fashion) than she could remember. Old Mary was *tired*.

Pregnant Mary didn't hustle, really. Her body was checking the productivity box for her (by building a human being from scratch), and so Pregnant Mary was allowed what Old Mary rarely took for herself: rest.

I didn't want to go back to being Old Mary yet. I was still tired.

Per the nurse practitioner's instructions, since the baby's heartbeat was "a little slow," I scheduled a follow-up ultrasound in ten days and began the long process of waiting out what I hoped would be a blip, a scary period that would wind up forgettable.

Friends and family offered pep talks while it seemed like in every room I entered, death lurked in the corner.

"Will you talk to Jill?" Lucas asked one afternoon. Jill was a former professor of Lucas's and a genetic counselor for high-risk pregnancies. He'd told her about my anxiety, and she'd offered to chat.

I found myself pacing the front yard as Jill explained to me why the online studies I'd uncovered didn't mean I'd miscarry.

"Those are most likely based on a population you aren't in," Jill said. "If women were getting six-week ultrasounds, there was already a problem, because that's so early. They were doing fertility treatments or had a history of losses. That's not you." She was right. I'd only had one pregnancy, and it had gone fine.

It was the best argument anyone had made to me about why things might turn out okay, and I tried my best to buy into it.

Then, on the sixth day of the ten, I felt an ache in my lower back like I'd perched on a stool for twenty-five hours straight. The ache was new and undeniable. Of course, I'd already googled symptoms of miscarriage and found backaches listed among them. But I'd also seen that it could be a symptom of ongoing pregnancy. And since my boobs were still sore, and I hadn't bled, perhaps the sudden ache was just the baby growing.

When Emily asked if I'd had any miscarriage symptoms, I dismissed the back pain, which had passed by then.

"Nope," I said, having swung from obsessively searching for confirmation of my fear to clinging to hope. I vacillated between doom and willed optimism and counted down the days to my appointment, at which I'd be 8 weeks 5 days pregnant.

One evening, after Finn had fallen asleep, Lucas and I were, once again, rocking on the porch at dusk.

"You know," he said, "I was thinking about how, if we didn't have all this technology, if you didn't have the option of the early ultrasound, and all this research you've been doing about miscarriage, you'd just be sitting here, pregnant. I think we've over-medicalized pregnancy."

It was a quaint and lovely idea, the thought of just sitting there, waiting, rather than reading academic papers, checking my miscarriage calculator, and counting the days till the next appointment.

And yet, later, I'd realize that I'd still have known. The over-medicalization wasn't what kicked off my anxiety; my body did. It sensed danger, and it was correct.

"It's a boy," I said. He looked puzzled. Against Lucas's preference, which was to find out the sex of the baby during standard genetic testing at twelve weeks as we'd done with Finn, I'd secretly drawn my own blood in our kitchen and sent it off in an Early Gender Reveal kit I'd ordered.

The kitchen had looked like a crime scene, me trying to squeeze a thimble of blood from my thumb while Lucas was at work. I'd paid for expedited return service, and the results arrived in my inbox thirty-six hours later—the day of our first appointment, which had overshadowed the news of our baby's sex. Who cared, if I was going to miscarry?

"I did the kit thing," I said.

"Oh, Pat," Lucas said, his nickname for me based on my middle name, Patricia, when he wanted to convey, *what am I going to do with you?* "How much did that cost?"

"Fifty dollars," I lied.

He shook his head.

"Before the expedited service," I confessed. "It was about a hundred after." Why I had felt compelled to expedite service is a question I didn't ask until later.

"So what should we name him?" he asked.

I'd been jotting down some ideas in my phone notes app, and my favorite so far had been Lucas's middle name: Day.

"Day?" I said.

With Finn, we'd gone back and forth for months, perusing lists of baby names on websites, running our favorites by friends and family, curating a finalists' list.

Not this time.

"I like it," he said after a moment. "Day."

"Did we just name him?" I asked.

"I think so," he said.

Naming him had been so easy that I wanted it to be a sign of something—that it was going to be easier from here, that he had a future, because how could he not when he already had a name?

Emily to me, 9:44 a.m.: *It's finally here. I'm sending you the biggest hug.*

Me to Emily, at 11:06 a.m.: *I mean HOW is it not even noon?*

Killing time leading up to the appointment, I cleaned the kitchen. I took a walk. I read a short story by Nabokov, "Master and Man," which really reveals my boredom, since my reading taste errs more toward this week's fiction bestseller list than the Russians.

I wore a light cotton smock-style dress that I could just pull up and didn't have to take off for the procedure. And it had another plus: The dress didn't touch me anywhere below the waist. In the wake of the dismal Internet findings, I'd weighed myself. After weeks of indulging in the French pot ice cream, I'd gained eight pounds. If we were going to return home without a baby on the way, I knew my body battle was going to come roaring back full steam; the tent dress was a gentle way of looking out for that girl, just in case.

Yet the fact that Lucas seemed optimistic about this pregnancy in spite of the last ultrasound was nearly enough to loosen my white-knuckle grip on fear. Of the two of us, he was typically the pessimist, prone to comments like, "In fifty years, the planet will probably be gone." I could recall him once confidently stating that democracy would fail within the decade, that we'd live in anarchy. And, of course, a new mole or several days of acid reflux were early indications of cancer.

So his sanguine attitude about the pregnancy was more than a little out of character, and by the time we were headed to our appointment at yet another satellite office of the university health system—one we'd also never been to but that got better reviews than the medical stadium—I'd let it rub off on me a bit. In the passenger seat, I allowed myself a happy little fantasy: Perhaps, by dinnertime, we'd have seen a new heartbeat, and Little Day would be measuring on track: 8 weeks 2 days.

We were ushered in without a wait. I lay on the table and the technician turned out the light, then inserted the wand. This time, the images were projected before us onto a large flatscreen hanging on the wall. Lucas and I could both watch along.

This next part I've gone over and over again in my mind, and I don't understand why, but it took me longer than Lucas and the tech to figure out what they saw immediately.

I saw a baby. I saw her taking measurements. The font was very tiny and red, and I thought I made out the text 7w3d, but that wasn't right, I was 8w2d, so figured I'd misread. Later, I'd learn that Lucas had known as soon as there was no movement on the screen, no flicker. Not me. I either didn't know to look for movement or was choosing not to, because when she suddenly withdrew the wand and started to pull off her gloves, I thought, *Did something happen? Did the machine malfunction?* We were just getting started.

"I have to tell you something," she said.

Why would the ultrasound tech have to tell me something?

"You remember last time the baby had a slow heartbeat? Well, today, there's no heartbeat. I'm sorry."

She'd been sitting on a stool but was standing now, her gloves balled up in one fist.

I was still lying flat on the table with my head raised, my neck strained to see the projection on the wall.

As the table lowered, I felt Lucas's hand on my arm and heard a sob come out of me.

"I'll give you some time," the tech said, leaving us in the dark.

Lucas put his arms around me as my brain short-circuited. I didn't know what to say because I didn't know what to think. This didn't make sense. I was pregnant. I was supposed to be pregnant. I was *pregnant*.

"I don't understand," I whispered, like if I spoke softly enough, maybe it could all be reversed, rewound on high speed. No one would ever even remember this part happened, we'd never have been in this moment, I'd never have said these words.

Despite my fear, I hadn't actually believed this would happen, not to me, because I hadn't done anything to make this happen…so how could it be happening? I'd done the right things: avoided alcohol, stuck to a single cup of coffee. I was used to things turning out right as long as I did my job right. I'd done my job right.

After a few minutes, the tech returned and ushered us to another room to wait on the doctor.

Eventually, my tears dried up. Lucas took the chair, and I sat on the patient table, my eyes burning and itchy, feeling as spent as if I'd run a marathon. While I waited, I figured I might as well start telling people—my family and close friends who knew about the appointment and were anxious to hear.

I fetched my phone from my purse. The top two texts in my messages were the conversation with Emily from earlier.

I hit reply.

Baby is gone, I wrote. Pressed send.

Within seconds, she was calling.

"Hi," I answered, stoic. It was the only phone call I'd answer for the rest of the day—I didn't know yet that I'd crumble hearing my loved ones' voices and shouldn't pick up.

"Oh no, Mary," she said, sounding on the verge of tears herself. "No, no, no, no, no."

"I cried in front of the tech," I said in a flat voice, no tears, no cracking. "I didn't want to, but I did."

"I'm walking into court," she said, a lawyer, "but I love you. I'll call you later."

As I hung up, I noticed Lucas looking at me, puzzled.

"Why didn't you want to cry in front of the tech?" he asked.

I shrugged, like *Oh, you know me. Just caring what people think that much.* It hadn't struck me as an odd thing to say.

I texted my mom, my sister. My other best friends.

The calls came in. I declined and declined and declined. The feelings were coming too—I felt them rising—and I had to hold it together.

I may have been a non-religious thirty-something who'd lived more of her life in New York City than anywhere else, but deep down, I was still Southern. And Southern women deal with our feelings behind closed doors. I'd been raised in a culture that prized putting on a smile in the face of heartache. I didn't know how to be sad in front of people, not even my own husband. Maybe not even in front of myself.

Finally, a woman in a white coat came in holding a stack of papers. She didn't sit.

"I'm so sorry to hear about your loss," she said. Was she talking loudly, or was it just me? She was not whispering. This was really happening. So loud. Such a harsh word: *loss*.

She very quickly laid out possible next steps: I could have a D&C, which I first heard as DNC, as in, Democratic National Committee, or she could give me medicine to bleed, or I could just wait to bleed. She looked at me, waiting. Did all women already know about these things? Had I missed some unit in sex ed on what happens when you miscarry... Speaking of which, *had* I even miscarried? The baby was dead. But I hadn't bled yet.

"What's a DNC?" I asked.

"A dilation and curettage," she said.

Oh. D *and* C.

"It's a surgery to remove the fetus," she continued. "We'd schedule you at the hospital. I'm not going to lie; many women find it pretty traumatic."

Traumatic? Okay, well, I didn't want traumatic. This was already pretty damn bad.

"What's the medicine?" I asked.

"It's four pills that you'll insert into your vagina to dilate your cervix. Within a few hours, you'll start to bleed. You'll probably bleed for a few days. That's it."

"Okay, or..."

"Or you can wait," she said. "Your body will probably figure out by eleven or twelve weeks that the pregnancy isn't viable. And you'll start to bleed then." *Eleven or twelve weeks?* That was a month away—a full month of pregnancy without actually being pregnant?

No. No, no, no, no.

If pregnancy had been a fullness, giving me a sense of purpose that I otherwise never felt, walking around with a dead baby in me sounded like the opposite.

I needed to empty my body of him soon. Now. Yesterday.

It wasn't unlike how I'd felt in my bulimic years between eating and purging. Back then, I would eat to fill the holes inside, but I couldn't fill them, so I ate more and more until I felt full— of proof. Proof of my inability to control, proof that I was more animal than civilized person and had a hunger I couldn't satisfy. Compelled to get rid of that proof, I could tell you where all the single-person bathrooms were on my college campus, a map I carried around in my head like a talisman.

After purging, I would feel clean, reset, like my grossness, my voracious, insatiable hunger had been erased. But every morning, I would wake up and my first thought would be, *Did I purge yesterday?* And if the answer was yes, I felt so sad. So, so sad.

Then the cycle would begin anew.

Walking around for another month—even another *day*—with a dead baby inside me felt as impossible as choosing not to purge after eating in my bulimic days. No one could see it, but I would know that inside me was proof that I'd failed.

"Let's do the pills," I said to the doctor.

She nodded.

"So insert the four pills, then wait. If you don't bleed enough within twelve hours, take four more. If you bleed too much, go to the ER."

I nodded, accepting the stack of papers from her, not thinking to ask what "not enough" or "too much" meant.

I looked down. It was a printout from a website that read at the top, *Patient Education: Miscarriage (Beyond the Basics).*

"Do you have any more questions?" the doctor asked. I didn't.

"Follow up with your doctor in two weeks," she said, and I thanked her while thinking, *aren't you my doctor?*

Only once in the ten years I threw up my food did someone successfully stop me.

It was my sophomore year of college. That night, my boyfriend Will and I had dinner. I don't remember what we ate, but it was more than I allowed myself to eat without purging.

That's how it usually was—a "binge" for me was just...eating. Eating food. Eating a meal. I always, *always* planned not to binge and not to purge. I always planned to eat "like a normal person," which, to me, actually meant someone on an extreme diet who consumed no more than a couple of bites of anything with carbs in it. I would allow myself a salad, for example. Maybe with half a muffin or some croutons.

But because I was hungry, I could never adhere to my own rules. I would eat a full meal: a burger *and* fries. Or an entire bowl of pasta *and* a brownie. And then, because I'd "failed," I'd think, *Well, I'm going to have to purge anyway, so I might as well eat another brownie, or ten more fries, or two hundred. Next time, I'll do better.*

Next time, I was always going to do better.

The dream was to be someone who wasn't governed by her appetite. The dream was to be someone who could run on a half-empty tank. But because I wasn't her yet, I had to erase the failure by purging.

On this particular night, hunger had won as usual, and, as we stood in my dorm room, I made an excuse to Will for why he had to leave. I don't remember what it was. I was deep into lying by this point, accustomed to making up excuses that would get me alone and near a toilet: that I needed to shower, that I had to study, that I had a phone call to make.

We were both nineteen, and Will had actually known about my eating disorder since the previous spring.

Three people knew: my mom, my dad, and Will. My mom had signed me up for therapy, which Will sometimes drove me to, although I was in the midst of changing therapists after the first one had shown me the food pyramid.

I was in that terrible in-between space, willing to tell them about my purging because I knew I needed help but was unwilling to stop. (The night I'd told my mom, my first thought after she'd left me alone in my bed had been, *Now I'll have to be even better at hiding it.*)

After hearing my made-up excuse, Will left, and as soon as I heard the door to the dorm close, I was about to venture to the private bathroom down the hall when he reappeared in my doorway.

"Are you going to throw up?" he asked. He looked crestfallen.

Ugh, I thought. I was responsible for the sadness on his face. Didn't he understand it wasn't as bad as it seemed to him? I'd thrown up hundreds of times. It was, yes, horrific in the abstract and as a lifestyle. I hated it. But a single instance wasn't something to be so sad about. I had to believe this. I had to believe it because I was still going to do it, and I needed him gone.

But I couldn't lie. I'd lied so many times—why was it so hard in this moment? Was it his face? That he'd bothered to come back?

I nodded.

"Don't," he said. "Don't do it."

"I have to," I said, my voice barely audible. Didn't he understand? I didn't have a choice.

"Please don't," he begged.

I swallowed, thinking about how I either had to let down the person I cared most about in the world or sit in this pool of disgust—a full belly—which I couldn't remember doing even once since teaching myself to purge five years earlier.

"I don't know how," I said, feeling as helpless as a small child. I couldn't make eye contact with him. It was possibly the most honest thing I'd said in years.

"Let's walk," he said, visibly relieved. He spoke with authority and confidence, like he was going to fix me. He loved walks, and we took them often. "You can tell me how it feels," he said brightly.

We set out. I was wearing a slim-fitting denim skirt that hugged my stomach and hips and made me feel powerful when I was empty and exposed when I felt bloated or full. Right now, I was the latter. That night, my gut was a hot air balloon burning, threatening to lift me off my feet.

"It feels like I'm going to burst," I confided as we walked, "like my skin is going to peel off."

"I think you need to train yourself to keep down food," he said. "You just have to practice. This is practice."

"Yeah," I said, not believing a word. Because Will didn't understand. He didn't understand that the Mary he had fallen in love with wasn't the Mary who simply...ate. The Mary who ate I'd gotten rid of long ago. She was pudgy, the last to be picked for any game at recess.

That Mary was the third grader who thought she had a boyfriend until she found out he'd asked her to be his girlfriend as a joke, which made her a punchline. That Mary was the kid in dance class who stood in her leotard, separate from the other girls as they giggled, and then one of them ran over to say, "Why does your chest look like a bird's chest?" because mine was flat and bowed. She was the eighth grader who walked into English class one day to find a note on her desk that read, *We don't want you here*. She was the Mary who dropped out of a college Shakespeare class claiming health problems, but really, she hadn't made above a B- on a single paper.

That Mary was so embarrassing that at the high school graduation party, Brandan Murdoch's dad said, "Who would've ever guessed that that weird little fifth grader would turn out to look like you?"

Deep into bulimia and sporting a tight, leopard tube dress, I'd laughed cheerfully, as if he hadn't just confirmed my deepest terror: that my calculated transformation had been vital and necessary. I'd run over to my mom and whispered the story to her, and we'd shaken our heads at his rudeness. *But he's right*, I thought. He saw through me.

Admitting my eating disorder two years later, both to Will and to my parents, had punctured a hole in the persona I'd painstakingly curated, but I didn't plan on actually shedding it. Dear God, no. The admission was more like an emergency release valve. I'd been cracking, on the verge of explosion.

But it was for one-way air flow only—no one was coming in.

Will and I eventually stopped walking and took a seat in the grass under a bronze statue of a camel. The ground beneath us was wet from the sprinklers. He leaned against the statue, and I leaned against him. Because my skirt was fitted, I had to tuck and angle my knees in a kind of chaste pose. It was dark, and the streetlamps cast an orange glow on the trees and academic buildings on Science Drive, where there was no reason to be after dark, so we found ourselves alone.

I focused on breathing, trying not to feel the sensation of the skirt waistband tight around my middle.

"I want you to get better," he said.

He had no idea what he was offering, to love a Mary who ate—what if she ate too much? What if her hunger never stopped, and she got bigger and bigger? What if?

I decided he meant that he wanted me to get better the way *I* wanted me to get better—to get better at not eating so much, so I wouldn't have to purge.

"Me too," I said, suddenly panicked that what he was saying was that he needed me to not be so needy or he wouldn't stick around. "I will, don't worry." This was already too much, letting him do this, see me like this. This couldn't become a regular thing, or he'd certainly find me too much of a downer and break up with me.

After a while, we stood, damp, and headed back to the dorms.

Nearly twenty years later, I left the OB's office clutching printouts defining miscarriage in simple terms ("the reproductive system consists of a uterus..."), still embarrassed at having cried in front of the sonographer about my own miscarriage and embarrassed to have admitted as much in front of Lucas.

And anyway, like with Will back in college, nothing Lucas said could make this better. This was beyond words.

7

SWIMMING

LUCAS WAITED OUTSIDE CVS in the car while I went in to get the medication. The pharmacist told me it would take a few minutes, so I had time to browse.

Wandering absently, I found myself in the candy aisle. Finn had been requesting gummy bears, so I grabbed a bag. Then I spotted SweeTarts. I hadn't had them in years, but if "your favorite candy" was an Internet security question, they'd win. I snatched a box of those, too. In the cracker aisle, I grabbed a box of Cheez-Its before drifting back to the pharmacy waiting area and taking a seat.

I tore open the roll of SweeTarts. Their sourness carried me back to being seven, dripping pool water, sun-spent, cross-legged in a plastic chair at the community pool, its strips leaving their impression on my tanned legs. SweeTarts were summers cannonballing off the diving board, knees clutched to my chest, and fast walking to get in line for the slide as the lifeguards yelled at us not to run. The days before it had ever occurred to me to be self-conscious about my body, before I had any idea that there was a way I was supposed to be.

SweeTarts were what kid Mary ate when the world was full of pleasure and her only care was how much more time she had to play before the whistle signaling adult swim blew.

Still waiting, I set the SweeTarts aside and opened the Cheez-Its.

Cheez-Its: more water, except this time, the ocean.

I'd spent most of my late twenties in a toxic relationship, the kind where we both tortured ourselves and each other until there was no way to go on, and when I finally ended it, I booked a solo trip to Costa Rica—my first time traveling to Central America. I had long wanted to learn to surf.

Surf school lasted a week, from 8 a.m. to 4 p.m. every day. My instructors nicknamed me "New York" based on my home state but also my extreme fear of crashing into another person with my surfboard. New Yorkers, they believed, were all wound tight.

I was terrible at surfing, but I loved failing at it. After hours of wrestling my board out past the breakers, paddling as hard as I could to catch a wave, and eating sand over and over, I'd haul my floppy body off the beach every afternoon and crash in the hammock outside my hostel room, reading Adrienne Rich poems, sipping whiskey, and snacking on Cheez-Its.

Cheez-Its took me back to that hammock, under those southern stars.

"Ms. Adkins," the pharmacist called.

"I'm so sorry you had to wait," she said when I reached the counter armed with my snacks.

"It's okay," I said, confused by her apology, since it hadn't been that long. Then it hit me: oh.

She'd filled the order and knew. She felt sorry for me.

Her kindness triggered a swell of sadness. I swallowed hard, thinking, *I don't want your sympathy. I want Day back.*

Since we graduated in 2010, my law school friends and I had maintained our ritual group viewing of *The Bachelor* every week, every season. Back in law school, we gathered in my apartment on Monday nights with wine and snacks. In the decade since, we would log on to Google chat from our four (four!) time zones, sync up our TVs, and spend ninety minutes peanut gallery-ing the show we most loved to hate on. We also, of course, caught up on each other's lives in between bungee jumping dates and rose ceremonies.

The night of my miscarriage was a *Bachelor* night. My friends floated skipping the show and FaceTiming instead, given my situation, but an hour or two watching twenty-four-year-olds cat fight over who was there for the "right reasons" sounded like exactly the distraction I needed while I waited for the pills to take effect.

And a great distraction it was, right up until the cramps kicked in. The doctor had said I'd start to cramp within four hours. Her timing had been right on point, but it was now clear that "cramping" had been quite an understatement—I'd had my period since I was twelve, and I'd also had a baby. These weren't cramps. These were contractions.

I'm gonna sign off, I typed into the chat. *Cramps are starting.*

We love you, they wrote. *Hugs. Call if you need us. We're here.*

As I shut my laptop, it felt like saying goodbye before embarking on a solitary voyage.

I sat for a moment with my computer resting on my lap. Lucas and Finn were already asleep in Finn's room, and the house felt eerily quiet.

So here it went then.

I turned on the alarm, flipped off the lights, and headed upstairs for the night. Already dressed in my sweats and wearing a pad, I didn't know what to do. I went to the bathroom and sat on the toilet, but the air between my thighs was breezy, dry. What if it took hours before anything came out? I didn't want to sit on a toilet for hours for no reason.

I grabbed the old, threadbare towel and spread it on top of the sheet on my side of the bed.

I propped myself up on top of it and scrolled on my alert-less phone, annoyed at everyone in my life who knew about my miscarriage. How long did a check-in take, for Pete's sake? Three seconds?! What was everyone *doing*? Sure, I'd declined their calls earlier, but it had been six hours since then. I opened Instagram to stoke my petulant rage at family and friends. Oh, look, must be nice to post instead of checking in with me, over here miscarrying! So glad you are enjoying *The Crown* on Netflix!

Throughout the afternoon, friends and family had texted well-meaning remarks like, "Of course it's sad. You're losing a dream," and "He's an angel now," and "You're sad because you already loved him."

None of these sat right. They all felt like a dress I wanted badly to fit but that wouldn't zip up.

Years earlier, shortly after getting engaged, I'd believed that I didn't really have opinions about what kind of wedding I wanted.

"I'm pretty chill," I'd said to my friend Haley just after telling her I was going to let the moms of the flower girls pick out whatever dresses they wanted.

She'd shaken her head knowingly.

"You don't think you have opinions," she'd said, "until people start making decisions and you realize how many opinions you have about what you *don't* want." I'd discovered she was right the moment I opened a text to a photo of a hot-pink flower girl dress.

So far, I didn't know what my feelings about my miscarriage were...but I knew they weren't any of these.

Like "losing a dream"—I'd known that heartbreak. Cue every breakup I'd ever had. Of course, I'd fantasized about the future; I'd bought the coming-home-from-the-hospital outfit, including the booties. But the grit of this loss didn't feel like a sullied fantasy. This loss was something meatier, something with mass. In fact, I wasn't sure a loss could get more physical than the "cramps" now thundering through my body as I waited for blood.

Likewise, the comment that my never-to-be-born child was an angel in heaven just left me feeling kind of...mad. *Sure, float off to be a bubble-cheeked cherub while I stay down here, depressed and hormonal and "managing a missed miscarriage,"* which, now that I thought about, wasn't a term at all, but a description. A full-blown phrase. Apparently, there wasn't a plain old word for this situation.

And the most frequent remark, the comment that I'd "already loved the baby," made me wince. How do you love someone you've never met, someone who isn't even a someone yet? Could I still be sad if I *didn't* love the baby yet? Was I allowed?

Approaching ten o'clock, I figured I might as well try to sleep. I turned out the light and lay wide awake in the dark, contracting. Waiting.

Buzz. A text from my sister-in-law Kristin asking how I was doing.

I'm hanging in there, I wrote, instead of what I was actually feeling, which was, *thank you, I've never felt this alone in my life and you have no idea how much I needed this text from you right now.*

She was headed to bed, she said. Of course she was; it was nearing eleven o'clock. Passing into the hour after which no one would be texting or calling felt like watching a horizon fade from view. It was only ocean now, as far as the eye could see, and likely I wouldn't hear from anyone till morning.

The night suddenly seemed very, very long.

It was dumb to lie in the dark if I wasn't going to sleep at all. I threw off the covers and returned to the bathroom. Pants at my ankles, I shivered, even in my long-sleeved sweatshirt, even in July with the thermostat set to seventy.

This is the most alone I've ever felt, I observed.

I thought about that short story, "Master and Man" by Nabokov, that I'd read earlier in the day, biding my time before our appointment.

In the story, the master, a selfish, cruel man, gets stuck in a blizzard while traveling by horse and carriage with his servant. The master realizes, in the middle of the night, that he's going to die. The existential crisis leads him to experience love.

Sitting on the toilet, I pictured the two men facing the night ahead, knowing it was to be unbearably cold, full of the promise of death.

Here I was, facing the same promise, but utterly alone. How long would it take to miscarry? All night?

We were to leave for a Florida vacation in two days, the first time we'd see our friends since the onset of the pandemic over two years earlier. I'd planned to announce my pregnancy there. Now I'd be announcing a miscarriage.

Finally, a contraction with consequence: Something solid fell from my body.

I swiveled around, feeling something like exhilaration. No part of me hesitated as I scooped the solid tissue from the basin, lifted it to the sink, and began my search.

It was purple and smooth like chicken liver, the parts of the whole chicken that, at some grocers, come segregated in a zip-tied plastic bag for tidy disposal.

It was slippery in my fingers, and webbed. Strong threads connected the larger pieces of tissue, threads that didn't give way easily when I tugged at them, then tugged harder. What was I looking at? A placenta? How little I knew about my own body. Other than the sac and the fetus, I didn't even know what all had been growing in there in the eight weeks I'd been pregnant—presumably the placenta, that entire organ that a woman's body generates in addition to making the baby itself.

There was so much tissue. He had to be in here somewhere. Maybe this part was him? Or this? Nothing looked like a fetus. It was all dark violet and muscular.

And then, the strangest thing—I stopped quivering. My breathing slowed, my body uncoiled and lightened, as if I'd just walked into a pool. I felt a presence. It wasn't living; it didn't have that energy. It was a placid lake, a fog lifting, the puff of smoke after the birthday candle has been blown out.

All week I'd felt death hovering in a corner of the room, but it had been frightening, a threat. Death was here again, but this time it wasn't hostile or menacing.

It's okay to love him.

The sentence passed through my mind like a message from a deeper, wiser part of me, a part of me I didn't typically have access to, or maybe one I chose not to engage.

I didn't get it. Did I love this deceased fetus but think I wasn't supposed to? Could a fetus that was never born even *be* deceased? How can something that's never born die?

Still cradling the bloody tissue over the sink, I heard myself say aloud, "I didn't know I was afraid of you."

I was talking to the tissue, talking to the remains of my would-be child. I wasn't even sure what I meant—if I had been afraid of the baby, or of death—but one thing was clear: Only moments earlier, I'd been terrified. And now, for the time being, I wasn't.

I could recognize the fear only once it had lifted, and in its place, I felt something like communion, the hush that comes over a crowd.

As I flushed the tissue down the toilet and sat back down, my phone buzzed next to me on the counter.

It was a text from Haley—my friend with the wedding wisdom, and the only friend I knew of who had miscarried—on the East Coast, where it was well after midnight.

I'd known Haley since I was nineteen. Her wisdom had always

surpassed my own. When we'd lived in the same dorm, she'd once barged into my room to seize my Olestra-filled WOW! chips (which I'd continued eating long after we all knew they wreaked havoc on our intestines) out of my hand so I wouldn't poison myself. I'd once barged into her room to find her sobbing through the final pages of *Peter Pan*. She'd officiated our wedding.

Haley and I also shared a history of late-night phone calls.

The night I'd had Finn, I'd been alone in my hospital room in the wee hours of the morning—well, half-alone. In New York City, partners were sent home so that birth mothers could share a room with a roommate. On the other side of a curtain, another new mom slept alongside her baby in a bassinet while I slept next to Finn.

At 3 a.m., a nurse had come in to check his blood sugar— protocol, given that I'd had gestational diabetes—and issued a code red: It was critically low.

Panicked, she'd held up the glucose monitor, a huge red exclamation point blinking on it, and said, "I know you're breastfeeding, but we have to give him formula *right now*!"

"Okay!" I'd said. "Yes, do it!"

I'd watched, terrified, as she'd yanked open a small bottle of formula, and when I'd asked if I could feed him, she'd hesitated.

"Is this your first kid?" she asked. I nodded.

"I'd prefer I do it then," she said. "But you can watch." She pulled a chair over and fed him while I watched. Whether it took ten minutes or thirty, I don't remember, but the entire time I watched someone else feed my new baby because his sugar had plummeted, I felt like I'd already failed. I'd already screwed up as a mother. I'd almost allowed him to die on my watch. It had only been seven hours.

When the nurse had handed him back to me, I couldn't bring myself to put him in his bassinet again. I'd decided that I just wouldn't sleep for the rest of the night. I would hold him until sunrise, until Lucas was allowed back.

In that moment, while crying as softly as I could so as not to wake my roommate, I'd received a text from Haley. Even though it was not yet 4 a.m. Even though she had her own month-old baby to take care of.

How are you over there, honey? she wrote.

With quivering thumbs, I had texted the story of what had just happened, and she'd texted back, *I'm calling, pick up.*

I can't, I wrote, *I have a roommate. I can't wake her up.*

You listen and I'll talk, she'd said.

I'd answered, and she'd launched into an impassioned lecture: I had not failed. I was allowed to fire nurses. I was going to be a great mom. It was not my fault his sugar had fallen. I listened without speaking until I felt like I could return him to his bassinet and he wouldn't die.

So, in a way, it was no surprise that it was Haley who texted me in this moment, during another wee-hour postpartum crisis.

Hi honey, was all she wrote.

I think he just came out, I texted her back.

She called.

I picked up. But I had nothing to say. I told her so.

"Let's just sit on the phone then, okay?" she said.

So, Haley and I sat on the phone again in the middle of the night, three years later. Then, I'd been holding my healthy newborn and sobbing. Now, I was quiet and giving a different kind of birth—birthing death. It was softer and sadder, and even though it was only over the phone, I sensed Haley there with me until the bleeding slowed, and I felt safe to hang up and lie down on the towel in my jumbo-sized pad.

As I fell asleep, I thought about how, even before Haley had called, I'd stopped feeling alone. The presence in that room—had it been death?

When I opened my eyes, it was light out, and the towel was dry.

8

TAILSPINNING

VACATION BEGINS! And I cut his hair again! From my aisle seat, as other passengers boarded, I captioned the photo and posted it on Instagram.

In the photo, Lucas and I are masked and Finn isn't, having just pulled his off. I'm in a straw hat and a floral sundress. Finn's hair is cut straight across his forehead, like Jim Carrey in *Dumb and Dumber*. (In the dregs of the pandemic, we were still very much in at-home haircut territory, and Finn had been a victim of my overconfidence with the kitchen shears.)

The comments rushed in.

Can we start a GoFundMe for Finn's hair?

Oh no, why didn't you just call me? my hairstylist friend wrote.

Oh my, my mother-in-law wrote.

It had been thirty-six hours since I'd spent the night in the bathroom, and we were set for Florida to meet our friends for vacation—seven adults and two kids.

It had occurred to me that I was wrong about not seeing any of them in two years—we *had* seen Jeremy and Kathleen, and their daughter Evelyn, once during the pandemic.

Jeremy and Kathleen had been Lucas's best friends long before they welcomed me into the fold. We all lived in the same Queens apartment building for years, running up and down the single flight of stairs between our places to swap eggs and gossip and vodka. Then we started having kids. When Kathleen gave birth to her daughter and found herself unable to breastfeed due to complications with her epidural, I'd rushed to the Rite Aid on the corner to get formula. A year later, it was my turn. When I couldn't breastfeed because Finn wouldn't latch, I'd shown up at her door weepy and exhausted, and on her couch, she'd pinched my nipple and coaxed it into his tiny mouth.

Still living in New York when the pandemic hit, they'd finally fled after a few months of being holed up in a 900-square-foot one-bedroom with a three-year-old, the same one we'd lived in, one floor up. They'd made the drive from Queens to Dallas, where her parents lived, and swung by Nashville on the way, putting our address in their GPS and pulling up to our house in the middle of a bright summer day.

But we were all too afraid, terrorized by the idea of hurting each other by hugging. They rolled down the windows. We stood yards away beyond the mailbox, waving, holding back tears, failing at it. They idled as we all shouted inadequate declarations.

"We love you!"

"She's so big! You're so big!" Back and forth went the trite phrases, so stupid-sounding, so insufficient to express what we were feeling. They were *right there in front of me! Here! At our house!* And they couldn't stay. It wasn't safe.

Then they were on their way.

It had been so lonely, the pandemic. I wasn't just hungry to see my friends. I was starved for it.

Under my dress, I was still bleeding, but it had subsided and was now more like a heavy period. I desperately wanted the night of the meds—July 6th, one date, one calendar box—to be *it*. I was done, *finis*. Wasn't that why I'd taken the medicine? Wasn't that the *point* of the medicine?

And so I was posting happy photos, and preparing to have a great time on vacation, and choosing to look ahead, not backward, masking far more than just my face.

Because I was still in it.

Like when a parent tells a fussy kid who's dragging his feet through a parking lot, "We're here! We're actually already here!" even when there are five more rows to go, because you need the kid to keep walking.

"The car is right there! I can see it!"

I was telling myself it was done and hoping that the bleeding was just a trickle that would cease, surely, in a few days.

We arrived in a flurry of hugs, feelings, unpacking, throwing on swimwear. Within minutes, we had congregated around the backyard pool.

In perhaps the most symbolic act of my no longer viewing my miscarriage as an ongoing miscarriage, I'd put in a tampon. A tampon, because it wasn't a baby anymore coming out, it was just period blood.

As I sat on the side of the pool in my swimsuit, Kathleen waded over and whispered, "Your tampon string is hanging out." A true friend.

I tucked it in.

"How are you feeling?" she asked.

And thus began a weekend of cognitive dissonance that wore my brain ragged, that wrung me out, then kept wringing until I was bone dry and disoriented.

I was glad she was asking me; I wanted it to be acknowledged. No, I desperately *needed* it to be acknowledged. Since we'd arrived, I'd been simultaneously overjoyed to see my friends— tearful, even—and unable to stop thinking about the fact that, a few days earlier, I'd been pregnant. It was an elephant in the room that only I could see.

I'd ridden in the Uber from the airport to the Airbnb basically praying (and I didn't pray) that, when they saw me, they wouldn't greet me with sympathy. But when they didn't, I was almost disappointed, confused. Didn't they know?

I wanted acknowledgment but not a spotlight. I wanted to be asked about it, but not expected to respond, because I didn't actually know what to say.

Really, what I wanted was for the elephant in the room to feel like an elephant to everyone, so we could all tiptoe around it, and pretend it wasn't there, and at least I wouldn't feel alone and a bit unhinged.

But my miscarriage wasn't an elephant for everyone else. It was something happening to their friend who looked like she was having a pretty good time, and—here's the irony—I was!

Later that first night, we were all boisterously making pizzas, catching up, lots of laughter, when Jeremy offered to make me a drink.

Forty-eight hours earlier, I'd been standing over the bathroom sink holding my placenta.

"Sure," I said.

A few minutes later, having taken only a few sips of the cocktail, I was spreading tomato sauce across a crust when I observed aloud, "Wow, already feeling that drink."

"Lightweight these days, huh?" Jeremy said.

The emotion surged as I said louder than I meant to, "I was pregnant until about twenty-four hours ago, so yeah!" My voice crumbled as I spoke, and as the room grew silent, I saw on their faces that the elephant hadn't been entirely invisible to them.

Jeremy grabbed me into a hug, a hug I hadn't realized I'd needed so, so much.

As the weekend went on, I lived in two realities at once: the reality of my ongoing miscarriage, which was both logistical (dealing with blood, with tampons and their pesky strings) and existential (what was going to happen now?), and the reality of my vacation, which was water to parched souls for all of us.

We stayed up late playing games, took long walks on the beach, swam in the ocean with our kids, swapped stories of how the pandemic had *really* been for us, the kind of honesty that rarely comes out over FaceTime and Zoom.

Except for one-on-one with Kathleen, my miscarriage didn't come up again on the trip, and I was half grateful for that and half bothered by it. While the fact of it was eating up at least 80% of my brain every day, I didn't want it to.

I kept thinking about an incident a few years earlier, after Haley had miscarried. Lucas and I had attended her birthday party at a bowling alley, and I'd been surprised when, as soon as I'd hugged her hello, she'd started to tell me her miscarriage story. After she told me, she told Lucas. As I bowled and chatted with others, I could hear the two of them discussing it.

She's spending her birthday talking about her miscarriage, I remembered thinking. *It must have really affected her.*

And the part my brain kept returning to now was my surprise at this. I hadn't realized that miscarriage was a big deal.

Now that I got that it was an asteroid crashing into a life and leaving a crater visible from space, I was stunned. How clueless I'd been. How deeply ignorant, to be surprised that my friend was having a reaction to her own miscarriage. What on earth kind of culture did we live in that I'd made it to thirty-nine believing such a lie about miscarriage, that it was a breezy blip, a dish that had to be sent back, mail delivered to the wrong house? What an extraordinary misunderstanding. What a mind-boggling blind spot.

How had I failed her as a friend? I cringed, thinking of what I didn't say, what I didn't do.

One night, the group went out to a seaside restaurant. The diners sat on the same dock where the fishermen unloaded their loot. We were gathered around a picnic table, picking at Saltines and shrimp cocktail, when someone said, "Mary, your book is out so soon!"

My next novel would be published in less than a month.

All eyes on me, I felt utterly incapable of conversing about the book. Everything I could think of to say sounded stupid in my head: *Yeah, I'm excited!* No, I wasn't. I was devastated. My brain had no space for my upcoming book launch. *I love the cover, here's a pic.* I was still bleeding. What had the doctor said about bleeding too much? *I can't wait for you all to read it.* There was one thing I couldn't wait for: to stop bleeding so I could get pregnant again. Everything else faded into the background.

When another friend asked, "What are you working on now?" I needed to get away and used Finn as my excuse. He'd been begging to check out the fishing boat that had moored at the end of the dock.

Finn and I ambled past all the diners to where thick-handed men tossed silver carcasses into a glistening tub.

What *was* I working on now? Trying to make it through this miscarriage without seeming like anything was wrong.

And why? Why save face in front of friends who didn't care if I was a mess? Partly habit, a lifetime of curated responses.

But there was more: My grief felt dangerous.

After a lifetime of deeply internalizing what people thought of me, I was struggling to figure out what my honest reaction to miscarriage was. I filtered the experience through what I was supposed to feel, what others expected of me, what the "right" way to view a miscarriage was. Problem was, that was context-specific.

Some friends were strictly scientific about it. This view I was most tempted by, as it promised the least complication, the least pain. The fetus was a ball of cells that my body recognized as unviable. No more, no less.

Family members took more of a departed angel approach, treating it as a soul ascended to heaven.

And my friend Nicole had explained her theory that souls have free will and must agree to become human. Sometimes, she believed, that isn't the choice they make.

In the triangle of these views, I tried to locate myself. It was embarrassingly difficult.

I am someone who has, tattooed on my arm, a gecko that's twice the size I wanted because I didn't want to ask the tattoo artist to redo his sketch. I once let an extremely stoned nail technician finish a manicure that involved painting the full tips of my fingers, skin and all, a bright poppy red, because I didn't want to make her feel bad. My brother-in-law Josh regularly says, "Is this a beef-in-the-queso moment?" because once, at a Mexican restaurant, he asked if everyone was cool with beef in the queso, and even though none of us liked it, my entire family said yes. When the queso came, we ate around the beef.

"Why didn't you just say no?!" he very sensibly prodded. But we were just trying to be agreeable.

When it came to my miscarriage, I didn't know how to parse what I believed or felt from what I thought I was supposed to believe or feel.

I was pretty sure there had been a life, for two reasons. One, there had been a heartbeat. That, to me, signified life. Sure, a life that couldn't exist outside of a womb, but a life nonetheless. And two, more mystically, because I'd felt death's presence in that bathroom, and to have a death, there must have been a life.

This bothered me politically. Did believing there to have been life make me unsupportive of women and families who choose to terminate? Because the right to choose was something I would never want to call into question, even in the privacy of my mind.

Feeling like I was tiptoeing around landmines in my own thinking, I texted my friend Jenn to ask if I could still be pro-choice if I believed a life existed at six weeks. She said I could. I felt relieved, but also like I should keep quiet, lest I inadvertently supply fodder for taking away anyone's autonomy. (Were miscarrying women collateral damage in the surge to strip away reproductive freedoms? Grieve, but not too loudly, lest your grief be used against you.)

Grieving also daunted me because I was hesitant to surrender to something I didn't at all understand. I'd lived my whole adult life believing that pain can and should be turned into a lesson, a takeaway.

Lesson from a bone-shattering car accident at eighteen: Even just driving to Blockbuster two miles from home, seat belts *are* critical.

Lesson from a relationship that sucked out all my joy and frequently left me in tears: Look for red flags of narcissism.

Lesson from a lost package that cost me several hundred bucks I didn't have: Avoid UPS; stick with USPS or FedEx.

Even my eating disorder I'd managed to understand as a kind of course in how *not* to live: Don't get so obsessed with thinness that you self-destruct.

But this time, there seemed to be no reason for my suffering, and without one, I felt as unfinished as an essay without a conclusion, all while the *main* thing I wanted was for this to be finished. Completed. You get a pass, a credit. You can move on to the next semester.

One morning at the beach, while my friends played spike ball and I sat shaded by an umbrella, I picked up my phone to search for memoirs on pregnancy loss. Perhaps someone who'd gone through this had insight to share.

My search turned up self-help guides on how to grieve, many of which had golden-winged cherubs adorning their covers and titles like *100 Practical Ideas*, *A Bible Study for Miscarriage*, and *In the Arms of Angels Now*.

No, no, no. I scrolled, growing increasingly cynical. Where

were the actual *memoirs*? Where were the stories?

I didn't even understand my grief yet, or even fully accept it; I wasn't ready for eighteen prompts or twelve principles for navigating it. (Later, multiple publishers would tell my agent that fertility is a "hard sell." Talk about the power of a cultural taboo. Even searching "miscarriage memoir" led to memoirs that happened to have a miscarriage in them but were about something else entirely, as if that's how much space and attention miscarriage warrants in our society: A book that devotes one paragraph to the subject constitutes a "miscarriage memoir.")

I did find *I Had a Miscarriage* by Jessica Zucker, which I devoured in three hours and then wished I hadn't read so fast.

Finally, there was the fact that miscarrying had shown me how little control I had. And if I couldn't control fertility, what else couldn't I control?

What others saw when they looked at me?

My own happiness?

Life?

I'd spent almost three decades believing I could curate a life I wanted. Accordingly, I gave myself credit for what I'd done, for who I was, for what I'd accomplished. *I* made those things happen: *I* wrote those books, *I* grew and birthed Finn, *I* ran those marathons, and *I* cultivated these friendships.

But I'd done all the right things for this pregnancy, and now it was just...gone. Poof.

"Unfair" doesn't capture it. I knew life wasn't fair.

This was existential. This grief threatened to shatter my whole way of living.

It wasn't the first time my illusion of control had been rattled in the realm of parenting.

At Finn's one-year check-up shortly after we'd moved to Nashville, I shifted nervously in my chair as the doctor read aloud questions from a lengthy questionnaire.

"Does he know his name?"

"I don't know…so I guess no."

"Does he know your name?"

"Hmm. No."

"Does he engage in imaginary play?"

"No," I answered, then backtracked. "Wait, what counts as imaginary play?"

"Like with dolls," she said.

"Then no," I said, eyeing the number of ticks she'd penned on the sheet.

She'd diagnosed him with a significant speech delay, qualifying him for at-home therapy sponsored by the state.

I'd felt responsible—both for it and to solve it. I wondered if the occasional glass of wine I'd had during pregnancy was to blame or the fact that we'd let him watch *Sesame Street* in his highchair.

So did Lucas, who was deep in his graduate program, spending all his time studying the symptoms of chromosomal abnormalities in children. Every child he read about was his own child, every symptom, something Finn once exhibited or might exhibit.

Lucas would be off studying at his desk and then suddenly appear in the kitchen, squatting to peer into Finn's face.

"I'm checking his gaze," he'd say. Or his gait. Or the shape of his forehead.

I observed these moments with a racing heart, a scary ferocity rising as I read into his worry, that Lucas was putting strings on his love for Finn.

Make me choose between you and him, and I'll choose him, I thought, my heart rushing so far ahead of me that I couldn't keep up with it.

The government-sponsored therapist who showed up was kind and patient, but when I didn't see Finn making observable progress, I booked additional weekly sessions with a second therapist across town. By the time the pandemic hit, Finn was seeing two therapists for a total of four days a week.

In the world of COVID, speech therapy turned into a comedy of errors. I wasn't sure which was a more absurd solution: a masked speech therapist attempting to demonstrate muffled words from behind an opaque piece of cloth or trying to get a toddler to engage in a Zoom therapy session.

We opted for the former. I'd sit across the room while Finn and his therapist, both masked, worked to help him speak.

Since we all knew therapy could only be so effective with masks, I'd take notes or video with my phone, and, back home, Lucas and I would do the same exercises with him, unmasked.

One morning, his therapist proposed a hypothesis.

"I think he's being perfectionistic," she said. "If he can't say it right, he doesn't want to at all."

She proposed an idea: Since opening consonants were his struggle (like the "d" at the beginning of "dog"), what if we gave him permission not to use them? Let "dog" be "og." Let "water" be "ater."

Overnight, Finn became a talker—just a talker without opening consonants. Others had to be taught to understand him, but once we explained it to them, they could. It was like Pig Latin, an entirely comprehensible made-up language with its own simple rules: Finn Speak.

As we gradually started adding consonants, a "p" here, an "m" there, it felt like a miracle. Lucas and I got along better. The energy in our house grew calmer. And Finn's vocabulary was growing daily.

I credited his brilliant therapist. *If we hadn't found her...* I thought.

It felt like a near miss—as if, had I failed to make the right choice at the exact right time, my child might have been forever scarred by my oversight.

On the other hand, Finn had been understanding all along.

So sometimes I wondered…what if he'd just been figuring out how to talk on his own timeline? What if we only thought that our adult tests and milestones and intense interventions had been the reason he'd started to speak?

In truth, the idea of having had no control over the situation was scarier than the idea of it having been a near miss.

And I could say the same thing about the miscarriage, which wasn't even close to over.

9

BLEEDING

I BLED FOR FORTY DAYS.

It was biblical, brutal, and infuriating. All I wanted was for it to stop so that I could try to get pregnant again.

Then there was the weight I'd gained. My body revulsion had resurfaced within days. At the beach, I refused to take my cover-up off, horrified by the extra rolls that had appeared in my midsection over the previous six weeks and horrified that I was horrified (*You were just pregnant three days ago, Mary. Be nicer to yourself!*). But my pep talk was inadequate in the face of my deep, longstanding dissatisfaction with my flesh—and even the pep talk itself was rooted in my belief that only pregnancy justified weight gain. (God forbid a woman has soft rolls of flesh just because she's a person with a body.)

And there were the complicated thoughts I struggled to understand or even name. The vocabulary of pregnancy loss failed to describe what I was feeling. Did other women also flounder in the pool of common terms—the talk of angels, or the politically charged insistence on personhood or petri dish specimen? Did they feel comfortable using the word "baby," or did it give them pause as well? Did they also hunt and come up empty-handed from the swamp of ill-fitting options: son, daughter, embryo, fetus, unborn, unviable. Unsolvable. Unfathomable.

Un-, un-, un-.

The way I saw it, if I got pregnant again, that would solve, well, everything. I wouldn't care that I'd gained weight. I'd recover my sense of purpose, and I could set aside the troubling existential concerns that miscarriage had churned up for me. Most importantly, the miscarriage would just become something that happened to me that was unfortunate but not dispositive—like a flu or a fender bender. It wasn't going to change my future permanently in any way; it certainly wouldn't mean that I wouldn't have another kid.

I was trying to move on with my life in a world that also seemed to want me to move on with my life. I still didn't know how to talk about miscarriage, but neither did anyone else, which made us all excellent bedfellows when it came to me suppressing and them dismissing the gravity of the event. Lines like, "At least it was early," "You clearly get pregnant easily," and, "Oh, you guys weren't even trying? Well, that's good" stung while also affirming my determined attitude that this wasn't going to be a big deal.

Except my grief wasn't on the same page as the rest of us. Rather than playing by our rules, it kept rising up and bubbling out of me when I didn't expect it.

One afternoon in the kitchen, Finn was sitting eating his after-school snack and watching cartoons while I cooked dinner. Standing over the cutting board before a mound of onions, I collapsed in sobs.

"Mama," he said, "are you sad?" He came over and put his small hands on my cheeks.

"I'm okay," I said. "But, yes, I'm sad."

"Are you sick?"

"No."

"Do you have a boo-boo?"

"Yes, I have a boo-boo."

"Do you need me to get you a Band-Aid?"

"I'm okay."

"I'm going to get you a Band-Aid," he said, and opened the pantry in search of one.

Another day, I was meeting with a friend to plan my upcoming book launch party.

She'd arrived before me and was waiting in the warehouse space I'd rented for the event. As I approached, I noticed she looked anxious and asked what was wrong.

"I'm pregnant," she said. "I just found out." It was evident that she wasn't thrilled. She regarded me wide-eyed, waiting for me to respond.

"I'm miscarrying," I said. She blinked.

"What?" she asked.

"I'm miscarrying," I repeated. "Wait, so you don't want to be pregnant?" I turned the conversation back to her, thinking, *Mary, what is your problem? Responding to someone's pregnancy news by telling them you're miscarrying?!* But the words had popped out of me, awkward and, frankly, pretty rude.

My body was also not letting me forget.

Another morning, I was chatting with our new nanny whom we'd just hired—it was her first day. She and I stood in our living room discussing the merits of local kid attractions when Lucas walked in, and I watched his face register alarm.

"What?" I asked.

He looked down at my feet. Underneath me was a puddle of blood. Finn's nanny politely averted her eyes.

"Sorry, let me just clean that up," I said, then proceeded to do so without mentioning it again. "So, yeah, he loves the zoo!" I rattled on while mopping up blood with a paper towel. Six months later, she'd show up tearful while suffering a miscarriage herself, and as I'd hug her, she'd do the exact same minimizing: "It's just the hormones. I'm okay. Sorry. It was only six weeks."

"It was only x weeks," we say, as if this makes any sense at all.

Why do we do this to ourselves? When someone loses a child, they don't say, "Well, she was only in kindergarten, not even middle school, so I don't know why I'm so sad."

Yet every woman I've known to miscarry has qualified her miscarriage to me by how early it was, as if to tell me and herself that she doesn't deserve to be sad.

Six to twelve weeks? Well, you weren't showing yet.

Twelve to eighteen weeks? Sucks, but listen, you can try again. Good news is that you can carry a pregnancy! (Yes, people say these things.)

Eighteen weeks or beyond? Okay, you get to be sad. Maybe even for a whole week. (A friend told a story of miscarrying and sitting among loved ones as they planned a meal train for her. One said, "I'm so sorry, I can't make a meal this week. I'll be gone," and my friend said, "Oh, don't worry, I'll still be sad next week, and the week after that.")

I was especially careful to hide my grief from Lucas—Lucas above all. Lucas held a power that was dangerous to me. He could keep us from trying again. I knew how he took on my pain, how much he cared. If he saw that I'd been wrecked, he'd not want it to happen again. And I couldn't risk that.

If he thought that I'd just bounced back, though, well, then he was more likely to be down for trying again as soon as we could...as soon as I fucking stopped bleeding.

But the bleeding went on and on and on. The misoprostol, the medicine I'd taken to accelerate my bleeding, seemed to have accelerated nothing.

At one point, thinking it had stopped, I recklessly attended an out-of-town wedding sans tampon or pad. Wearing an emerald green satin dress that I actually felt pretty in, I was listening to the bride's father's speech when warmth crawled between my legs.

No, I thought. *Not now.* I couldn't wait; it wouldn't be wise. I stood and exited in the middle of his speech, drawing a concerned look from Lucas across the table, to find that a stain the size of a basketball had bloomed on the seat of my dress. There was absolutely nothing to be done—the hotel was several miles away, and I hadn't brought a backup dress.

Relying on the fact that the color of the dress was deep, the lighting was dim, and the dinner at hand would allow me to remain seated, I self-consciously sidled back to my table, cringing for the employee who would later discover the pink-stained chair cushion.

When we returned to Nashville, I phoned my old OB—the one from New York whom I trusted but who was out of network for our insurance.

"It's possible your miscarriage has segued right into a period," her nurse told me. "But there shouldn't be anything to worry about unless you're filling more than a pad in an hour."

Segued into a period?

"Jesus, your body is *really* letting you know you're not pregnant," Emily joked.

But I wasn't filling more than a pad in an hour. So I guessed...I was fine?

I wasn't fine.

Every day, that became clearer. All I could think about was getting pregnant again. I was irritable, prone to tears or angry outbursts, uninterested in anything other than when I would stop bleeding.

And I loathed my body, was furious at it for being heavier *and* losing the baby—both sins warranting shame for women in

America. Even as I was still bleeding, I'd tried dieting, but then didn't care enough, got annoyed at myself for spending money on a weight-loss app, and canceled it. Abandoning the diet hadn't been an act of self-care; it had been giving up—caring so little that I couldn't summon the energy.

I needed to talk to a professional, but it had been years since I'd been in therapy, and my old therapist, whom I'd seen in person, was also back in New York.

I recalled seeing ads for an online therapy service on the subway back then. I googled it and found that there were providers in my area. On the intake form, I wrote that I was signing up to process my miscarriage and requested the first available therapist.

Of the various preferences I was asked about (gender, age, religion), my single request was that the person be non-religious. I didn't want to wonder if the therapist was secretly thinking that God had a plan and that this was part of it. True or not, neither of those ideas comforted me.

One afternoon in late July, I sat on my front porch with my laptop balanced on the armchair of the rocker. On the screen, my new therapist Elizabeth didn't know how to position herself so that the lower part of her face was in camera view. I could only see her from the nostrils up, her dark-rimmed glasses and a shock of white hair. She was like Dilbert, the cartoon with no mouth or chin; he's just hair, glasses, and nose.

"Tell me what's going on," the top half of her face said.

"I had a miscarriage a few weeks ago, and I'm not doing well." I spoke in a professional, efficient tone, like I was leading a meeting and wanted to respect everyone's time. "I'm desperate to get pregnant again or lose weight—or both. Like, obsessed. And so that's why I'm here, to figure out how to have a healthier mindset around my fertility and my body."

Now it was in her hands. Make me well. Fix me.

"What are you doing to try to lose weight?" she asked.

"I tried this app that worked for me after I had Finn, but it felt overwhelming, so I gave up. Now I think it'll be easier just to get pregnant again, because if I lose weight then immediately get pregnant, there was no point to losing it in the first place…"

She nodded.

"So what are you doing to get pregnant again?" she asked.

"Well, that's more complicated…" I sighed.

My bleeding had reduced to a trickle, and I'd read that one could ovulate even while spotting. I'd purchased a digital fertility tracker and was closely monitoring my estrogen and luteinizing hormone (LH). The day they both spiked, we would have sex…more than once if, you know, physics allowed. I explained this to her.

"Do you think all of this control you're trying to exert is to avoid feeling your feelings?"

What control I was trying to exert? I *had* no control. That was the problem.

"Am I?" I asked.

"You're trying to control your body by making it smaller. You're trying to decide when you'll get pregnant again."

I considered this.

"And your energy when we started this session was kind of a lot," she said.

"Wait, it was?"

"Yes." She chuckled. It was coarse, gritty, the kind that threatens to erupt into a cough.

"Okay…" I consciously tried to let her words sink in: I was trying to control in order to avoid feeling my feelings.

"What are you feeling?" she asked.

"I'm getting it," I said confidently. "I see what you mean."

"What are you feeling?" she asked again.

"Clarity now."

"No, *feeling*," she said. "Not thinking." Then, forcefully, as if

I was failing to see the obvious, "You're *sad*, Mary."

Oh. Oh, right. Sad is a feeling, and that's what I was.

My eyes began to burn, which seemed to confirm her hypothesis. Once the tears started, they wouldn't turn off. By naming my sadness, she'd turned on a hose.

As we approached the hour mark, I said, summing up the session, wiping my eyes, "So the takeaway is that I need to stop avoiding my feelings."

"Well, I didn't say you were *successfully* avoiding them," she said. The woman was brutal. "But maybe you don't need to try so hard to fill the hole."

How strange that she'd used that phrasing.

Fill all the tiny holes.

I nodded.

"I should just let the hole be empty for a while," I said.

She raised her eyebrows. I still couldn't see her mouth in view, but I could tell she was smiling by the way her temples crinkled.

"Nope," she said.

Huh? I waited for her to clarify.

"You don't get to decide when the hole fills," she said with the same witchy chuckle.

Whoa.

Had I made it to thirty-nine without knowing how feelings work? Or at least how grief works? I thought I could contain my sadness, relegate it to when and where it was convenient for me. Wipe my cheeks and show up. Release the sadness like letting a dog out to pee, then putting it back into its kennel.

But maybe my grief had been popping out at inconvenient times because that wasn't actually true. And if I didn't get to decide when the hole filled, could it be there *forever*?

I recalled a friend once telling me that after he'd gone through a bad break-up, a therapist had said, "You may always be sad about this." At the time, I'd thought, *how unhelpful, he should find a new therapist!*

Was mine now essentially saying the same thing—that I may have a hole that never fills? That I *can't* fill?

"Shit," I said.

I could see in the way her (upper) face relaxed that this was probably the most honest thing I'd uttered the whole session.

Thirty-one days into the bleeding, my third novel was released. I wanted to care. I threw a launch party. I packed my calendar full of virtual events.

For the party, at an airy and bright women's co-working space in Nashville, I wore an outfit that matched my book cover: yellow suede heels, pink chandelier earrings, and a white floor-length dress I'd bought during one of those outlandish pandemic clearance sales. Ordinarily, dressing to match a book cover would totally delight me, because I'm that much of a nerd. But checking out my ensemble in the mirror, I felt none of the expected effervescence, no zest. I felt as flat as a forgotten soda.

Lucas and I, along with our friend Lily, decorated the event space with custom swag that my mom had ordered—totes, mugs, and beach towels splashed with my joyful book cover, bright pink and yellow. My friend Kate (of the pregnancy swagger email project) flew in from New York to interview me about the book. It was a group effort, my friends and family rallying to make it a special day.

I smiled and signed books, going through the motions.

As the night drew to a close, I was chatting with a loquacious (and quite drunk) partygoer when I looked over to see Lucas, Lily, and her husband hauling service platters and boxes of decor from the venue. *These people are doing this because they care about me,* I thought. Yet instead of loved and full, I felt mostly guilt that their generosity was failing to penetrate my numbness. It was supposed to be a day of celebration, and all I felt was tired. Under my white dress, I was still bleeding.

I was barreling toward something, a reckoning—the unresolved questions raised by my miscarriage, the feelings I still wasn't allowing myself to feel. It wasn't as simple as my therapist had made it sound, to feel my feelings. Because to feel my feelings about this meant to entertain the questions as well.

It's okay to love him, the phrase I'd downloaded from somewhere—my subconscious, the great beyond, a grandmaster puppeteer—nagged at me.

If it was okay to love him without his earning it by becoming human, then what did that mean for me? Did I also not have to earn love? And if I didn't, what on earth had I been doing all this time, and did I want to keep doing it?

The one thing that could swipe me out of thin air, that could save me from this coyote-style freefall before I hit the pavement with a splat, was double lines.

PART II

EMPTY

10

DOUBLE LINES

THE BLUR OF A WISH COME TRUE—I stood at the stove holding the test under the bright oven light. I'd been waiting seventy-eight days, and now the universe had thrown me a lifesaver; I would not drown.

"I'm pregnant," I said to Lucas from across the room, my voice level.

"Oh," he said from the kitchen table, looking nervous. "How do you feel?"

I shrugged. Could he not have asked an easier question?

My limbs were lighting up like I'd had four cups of coffee. I felt like my whole body was conducting electricity, like I was wrapped around one of those balls at a science museum. Static hummed through me as I made Finn's lunch and helped him put on his shoes.

The moment Lucas left to take Finn to school, I texted Emily. She called. I answered and burst into tears.

"I don't want it to happen again."

"You're so brave," she said. Was I? I felt desperate and

terrified, not brave. "Think of it like a really good first date," she said. "No one's making wedding plans yet, but you get to be hopeful."

A really good first date, I thought, trying to imagine a world where I could hold it that lightly.

As soon as I had to pee, I took the other two pregnancy tests I had in my possession, back-to-back, using the same urine. Both were positive, but barely.

I couldn't stay in the house with a body aflame. I threw on a bra, grabbed my keys, and climbed into the car.

After my miscarriage, a cousin of mine who had miscarried years earlier then later birthed two children, had said to me, "When you get pregnant again after miscarriage, get ready. It's a doozie."

I'd assumed she meant fear, and I hadn't asked her to elaborate.

Was this the doozie? I'd just received the best news, the exact thing I'd set my eyes on for months, but the storm brewing in my chest felt like the opposite, like something terrible was underway.

This is good! my brain cried as my body responded like it was fleeing wildfire.

I needed to return some packages, so I drove in the direction of UPS, but UPS was too close. I'd be there in four minutes. I needed to drive for more than four minutes. I needed to drive and drive; I didn't care where.

This is happy news! I thought over and over. This was what I'd wanted.

But my body was revolting. It passed UPS without pulling in. I drifted from red light to red light, following the tide of Nashville traffic, tracing the yellow lines through downtown.

Eventually, I made my way back to UPS and parked.

It was only 8 a.m. and late September, but the day was already hot.

I opened the door but didn't climb out. I was due to teach a creative writing class later in the day. In the two years I'd been teaching, I'd never canceled a single class. But I'd never felt this incapable of coherent thought. My mind was a mush of terror and other feelings I couldn't name that my therapist possibly could— probably sadness, and maybe some rage? Melancholy, perhaps.

I grabbed my phone and dashed off an email to my class: *Dear class, I have a migraine and am so sorry, but I won't be able to teach today.*

Within seconds, my mom, who was in the class, texted asking if it was really a migraine.

Are you having another loss? she wrote, oddly.

"Ha!" I laughed aloud. The irony. But my chest tightened. The suggestion tapped something: It did feel like a loss. These sensations were familiar, the jolts of energy, the restlessness. These were how I'd felt in those days between the two ultrasounds over the summer: panicked, with a sense of death crouching in the corner of the room.

But I was pregnant! The start of something, a great first date! So why did it feel more like an ending than a beginning?

I took the packages inside and dropped them off, then climbed back in the car to drive home.

Are you okay? Haley texted. She was also in the canceled class.

At a red light, I wrote back, *I keep thinking about the other baby.*

As the light turned green and I turned to the road ahead, I wondered why I'd written that. It wasn't true. I hadn't been thinking about Day at all.

A good first date.

Here's a first date I once had:

We'd been walking the streets of New Haven at dusk. I was twenty-six. We were standing at a bus stop waiting for my bus home under an orange streetlamp when he asked me to come up with a six-word story like the famous one misattributed to

Hemingway: "For sale: baby shoes, never worn."

"Don't think too hard," he said, flirting.

"Three words, too scared, too late," I said after a minute.

The bus came before I had a chance to explain to him what they meant, and, riding home, I couldn't believe that's what had popped out of my mouth. I hadn't thought about Joanne in years.

When I was ten, we'd moved from Georgia to South Carolina, where my parents began working at a new church. As ministers on staff, they both sat behind the pulpit on Sunday mornings, which meant my six-year-old sister and I needed someone to supervise us during the weekly service.

Enter Joanne, a fifty-something Golden Girl in fuchsia lipstick, a never-not-perfect manicure, and a silver, Snow White coif.

She'd perch, a queen, between my sister and me on the seventh pew back, passing us quiet candies (never loud candies), patting our restless hands with her soft ones, and winking when she shushed us so that we felt in on a secret. After church, while my parents chatted with congregants, she'd take us to lunch at Red Lobster and let us eat as many cheese biscuits as we wanted.

When we had overnights at her house, she'd tuck us into a large canopy bed in her guest room and sing us 1940s tunes, including the World War II–inspired "White Cliffs of Dover."

The white cliffs, she explained, ran along England's east coast, turned white by algae on the limestone. Legend held that when soldiers returned home by sea, they'd spot white in the distance and know they'd made it. I'd fall asleep imagining the cliffs and how I would one day go there and see them for myself.

One Sunday morning when I was in tenth grade, as I stood next to her singing a hymn, Joanne whispered, "There's a lump in my breast." I couldn't tell if she was worried, but I decided not to be. Both of my grandmothers had had breast cancer in their fifties and recovered. I assumed Joanne would too.

But as the months passed and Joanne lost her hair and stopped driving, and I got my license and began driving her around, I noticed our conversations changing. She started telling me stories that I was surprised a grown-up was willing to share with a teenager: about her first marriage and what had gone wrong, why she'd gotten divorced. About her next marriage and her sex life and how important it was to keep up sex in a relationship. Though it dawned on me that she was teaching me what she wanted me to know before she was gone—things she ordinarily wouldn't tell me for many more years, like how to sustain a marriage—I pushed the thought away.

It wasn't until I sat in her hospital room, her cheeks purple and bloated, her eyes swollen shut, as she croaked out sounds that weren't quite coughs and weren't quite snores, that I understood. And even then, it was only because her husband, crumpled over his cane in the chair next to me, whispered, "They won't say it, but I know that sound. That's the death rattle."

"If you have anything you want to say to her, you should do it now," my mom instructed. My sister, then twelve, had always been at ease around love, more comfortable with its display than I. By the time I was twelve, I'd stopped cuddling with our parents. Even when I wanted to, it seemed childish, and I wanted to appear mature. But even as a middle schooler, my sister would still plop her head in my mom's lap and say, "Will you play with my hair?"

So the younger of us approached the bed, took Joanne's puffy hand, and said without flinching, "I love you, Joanne. I'll miss you."

I said nothing.

The next morning, after learning that Joanne had died in the night, I grabbed the car keys and drove to the pharmacy down the block, where I headed for the aisle with the hair dye. I grabbed a box, returned home, and spread it over my scalp, doing my best to follow the directions. But when I rinsed, to my horror, I wasn't a bright blonde like the woman on the box. Orange splotches covered my head.

I started to cry.

My mom appeared in the bathroom doorway, just home from the hospital, where she'd been gathering Joanne's things.

"What are you doing?" she asked.

"I look like a giraffe!" I screamed, with full-blown sobs. "Please make me a salon appointment! I have to find someone to fix it. I can't go out like this!"

"Today?!" she said, her eyes ringed with clouds of mascara. "This is what you decided to do *today*?!"

Today, yes, because today was the day Joanne had died, and I couldn't fix that. But my hair, I could fix—I just had to ruin it first.

On the first date at the bus stop, having not thought about Joanne in years, I found her there, hovering beneath the surface. Apparently, just because I hadn't thought about her death didn't mean it wasn't lurking.

Three words, too scared, too late.

"Clever," my date had said approvingly. I don't remember his story, and we didn't go on another date after that.

11

SEA NETTLES

THE MORNING AFTER I TESTED positive again, Lucas and I took Finn to Atlanta to visit Lucas's dad and stepmom and the Georgia aquarium.

As we marveled at the belugas and whale sharks and playful otters, I drifted, in a stupor. I'd hovered as I'd packed a bag for myself and Finn, ridden south over the mountains while Lucas drove, and wandered into the darkness surrounded by iridescent sea life.

When we reached the sea nettles—a species of jellyfish with a bell that glows different colors, its long tentacles trailing behind it like a bride's train—I was mesmerized by its steady beat. I encouraged Lucas and Finn to go ahead.

How long did I stand there? I don't know, but by the time I walked away, Finn and Lucas had seen most of the rest of the aquarium.

Earlier that morning, I'd peed on another stick, and the line hadn't been much darker than the day before. I told myself it was fine, that twenty-four hours wasn't very long, and packed a fresh box of three pregnancy tests I'd picked up at the pharmacy. Surely, they'd get darker.

But the next day, when I awoke early in our hotel room and quietly made my way to the bathroom, the line barely registered against the white background of the window. It was a pale peach, as washed out as the day before. Not even a baby girl pink. "Sheer" in nail polish land.

Shouldn't my line be getting darker?

Could it be a chemical pregnancy, I wondered, the kind that starts but doesn't stick? I'd heard of them—they're not even detected most of the time. Fertilization takes place, but the embryo never implants, and a period then comes, maybe on schedule, maybe late.

Don't do this to me, I thought at the universe. *Don't do this to me.* The plea ran through my mind as I climbed back into the hotel king where Lucas and Finn remained asleep.

But by the time Finn stirred twenty or so minutes later, as light seeped around the edges of the drapes, the line on the test next to me on the side table had darkened.

Huh.

Confusing.

I offered to take Finn down to breakfast. While he ate cold eggs from a carton and wolfed down microwave sausage, I stuck the iPad in front of him and hunched over my phone.

From a handful of internet forums, I learned that first morning urine ("FMU") often produced only a light positive because of proteins that accumulated during the night and "ate up" the hCG, which is the hormone that produces the "you're pregnant!" line. Testing with the second or third pee of the morning, therefore, was more reliable if you didn't want to get a false negative. I also learned that after about twenty minutes, the darkness of the line was more likely due to evaporation than a real indication of hormone levels.

Scrolling through these forums, I uncovered the same photo, over and over again, from newly pregnant posters: pee sticks—anywhere from six to twenty or more—positioned in a clean stack and scribbled with dates and times. These were captioned *My progress!* or *Do you think this is a chemical???* or *Here was my first week—now I'm at seventeen weeks!!!!*

Sometimes, the same date would appear on multiple sticks:

2/11 @ 6 a.m.

2/11 @ 9:30 a.m.

2/11 @ 4 p.m.

Under the photo, comments would mostly advise the woman to keep testing or wait, then test again, or they were cheerful appeals to positive thinking: *You got this, mama!* and *Any line is a line!*

When the occasional commenter chimed in to say, "None of this is reliable. Call your doctor to get a blood test," everyone roundly ignored them; these naysayers' singular remarks faded into oblivion as the threads asking and answering the question we all had reached into the double-digits of pages—the Internet equivalent of outer space: Was this baby going to make it? Was the pregnancy going to stick?

The original poster never returned to update the thread on the ultimate outcome of the pregnancy. Many of the threads had been started many months earlier, sometimes years.

Somewhere, they were either nursing babies or chasing toddlers, or not. But we, the pregnant or soon-to-be-pregnant or hoping-to-be-pregnant, would never know.

Second morning urine then.

After the sea nettles, I drifted to the aquarium restroom, where I took another: second test, second morning urine.

The shade of the line wasn't much different from the hotel test, but also, I hadn't really had to go, so there was very little sample. I wondered if that mattered. There had been enough pee to trigger the control line. Surely that was enough.

When we arrived at my in-laws' house bearing takeout lunch a couple hours later, I finally had to pee again and snuck off.

Aha!

Third morning urine! TMU, baby. The line that was downright *pink*. Not hot pink. Not mauve. But a faded, bubblegum pink.

Hope, it turned out, was the color of Barbie. *Hope.*

I returned to the living room, my hope hidden in the pocket of my sweater, and joined Finn on the floor, where he was working an ABCs puzzle while the adults chatted around him.

Lucas's stepmother, also named Mary, had recently been diagnosed with advanced stage lung cancer. She was in good spirits, but she got winded easily and preferred to stay seated.

As Finn and I placed the F and G pieces together, the adults chatted about the work Lucas was doing, counseling families with genetic illness. I half-listened until Mary said something that caught my attention.

"Well, you know, I lost a baby once she was born. SIDS. And I lost another at nine months pregnant." I looked up. I'd known she'd lost an infant, tragically. But I hadn't known that she'd also lost a pregnancy—and at nine months.

"What?" I said.

As she described what happened—tumbling down a flight of stairs—I held my breath. It was upsetting in a familiar and visceral way, as if my body was remembering. But remembering what? I hadn't gone through anything nearly as terrible. Losing a baby at nine months would be so much worse than what I'd gone through at only eight weeks.

What you went through was nothing compared to what other people endure, I told myself for the millionth time.

It was almost embarrassing that my breezy little miscarriage— my "early loss"—had been the worst thing that had ever happened to me.

"That's terrible," I muttered, fingering the pregnancy test in the pocket of my sweater.

Several hours later, we were back in the car headed west, home to Nashville. The drive through eastern Tennessee is beautiful in the fall. We curved through mountains drenched in orange.

Every few minutes, I would reach down to the bag at my feet and pull out the three pregnancy tests I'd taken over the course of the day. I'd line them up in my palm and peer into them like a fortune teller, searching for the future in their varieties of pink.

"What are you doing?" Lucas asked from the driver's seat the third time I did it.

"I'm seeing if the lines are getting darker," I said. That I'd already learned the darkening was due to evaporation didn't matter. I was, I told myself, checking to see if they already *were* darker, and perhaps I'd only missed it because of bad lighting…or something. I didn't need to clarify this distinction for Lucas; we both knew it didn't matter.

"Are they?" he asked.

That he was seeming to take whatever pseudoscience experiment I was conducting on my side of the car at face value—actually humoring me—was telling. Normally, we were fairly quick to call each other out on things. In a real exchange we'd once had, I told him that when he chews gum, he looks rapey, and he responded that at least his breath didn't smell like a garbage disposal met a cup of coffee. And we'd both cackled.

An "uh, why do you keep doing that?" would have been more our vibe, but he was politely asking me if my lines were darkening, which meant he thought I was fragile…and he wasn't wrong.

"I think so, but barely," I said, dropping them back into the bag at my feet and telling myself I wouldn't pull them out again.

When we reached Chattanooga, we pulled into a car-charging station that abutted the city's tiny airport. Lucas had gotten a new car, electric. *I got a miscarriage, and you got a new car,* I would "joke."

It would take about half an hour to charge, and Finn wanted to watch the airplanes, so I waited as he and Lucas strolled hand in hand across the parking lot to a spot where they could get a better view.

The instant they were out of sight, I yanked out my three tests, addict-style. I stepped into the sunlight and lifted them high, searching for something, though I no longer knew what.

"This is no way to live," Lucas said, seated at our kitchen table. I stood across the room from him, clutching the counter between us for protection. It was late Monday morning. We were back from Atlanta, and while I knew what he was referring to, I also suspected that he had no idea how much worse it had gotten since our return twenty-four hours earlier.

The number of tests I'd taken since arriving home had skyrocketed from three to somewhere in the high teens; I'd fled to purchase more as soon as we'd pulled in.

Whenever I had to pee, I took a test. Whenever I didn't have to pee, I drank water so I could pee.

"What do you mean?" I cooed in my falsest voice, wondering how much he knew. Had he noticed me sneaking away, heard the crackling of the foil behind the bathroom door as I tore open each individual test? Had I failed to sufficiently bury the telltale, hot pink wrappers under non-incriminating garbage in the trashcan: crumpled tissues, empty yogurt pouches, a gnarled tube of toothpaste?

If I pinned him down to specify a particular act, I could perhaps agree with him that it was a problem and assure him I'd stop doing that one small thing, convincing him—and perhaps myself—that I was fine. JUST FINE!

He studied me for a moment before saying, "You pulled out pregnancy tests every few minutes to stare at them the entire drive back from Atlanta."

"Not the *entire* drive," I mumbled, remembering how hard it had been to resist reaching for them as often as I'd wanted to during the three-hour journey. I sighed. "I know," I conceded. I wasn't okay. This wasn't okay.

"Have you talked to your therapist about this?" he asked.

In fact, I had, having requested we move up our regular Thursday appointment given my sudden test addiction. We'd met earlier that morning.

"I feel like Gollum," I'd told her, whose dark obsession makes him grotesque: eyes bulging, shriveled.

That was me: the Gollum of pregnancy tests.

My therapist, whom I'd now been seeing weekly for a couple of months, had given my behavior a name: obsessive-compulsive, which she defined for me as doing the same thing over and over, hoping to ease anxiety but, instead, worsening it.

"Wait, do I have OCD?" I'd asked her.

"I'm not diagnosing you. I'm describing the behavior," she'd said, then encouraged me to talk to my doctor if I was really that uncertain about the pregnancy, since the tests weren't providing the reassurance I craved.

"She told me to talk to my doctor and stop taking tests," I told Lucas.

"Good," he said. "Have you?"

I shook my head. He sighed.

"But I mean, I will," I said unconvincingly. It was still before noon. The day had barely started.

"You're not the only one affected by your behavior," he said. "We all feel it."

I winced. Lucas didn't even know the bulk of it—but Finn did. I hadn't bothered hiding my full crazy from Finn, relying on the fact that, at three, he didn't *really* understand what was happening. Finn accompanied me on my pregnancy test splurges, stood by my side in bathrooms as I peed on them over and over again, asked me what I was doing. He now thought of pregnancy tests as "Mama toys." His little eyes had a front seat to my preoccupation. He waited me out, sweet and curious.

"Can I see it?" he'd ask, peering over the test window, both of our eyes tracking the blooming control line.

"I understand," I told Lucas. It wasn't just about me anymore; I needed to find a way to loosen my grip on this pregnancy for all of us.

That afternoon, I made two phone calls.

First, I called our health insurance company and asked for an estimate on what it would cost not to have the baby at the university hospital but with the OB I'd seen in Nashville prior to getting pregnant. I liked her.

"From start to finish," I asked. "The entire pregnancy."

Turns out she wasn't actually out of network, just not part of the free maternity "bundle." In any case, the "bundle" had not turned out to be so great after all, as it had "unraveled" (once again, the insurance plan's word) when I'd miscarried. The bills had come in shortly after I'd started to bleed.

"Unraveling the bundle" as a phrase was not lost on me. Someone at the insurance company thought of that. Someone named it that.

Women-friendly policy, indeed, I thought, a stack of ultrasound bills next to me that would have been free had I not miscarried. There's America for you.

Now, after waiting on hold for a few minutes, I got my answer: It would cost $2,700 to have the baby with the local OB I liked.

Worth it, I thought. Immediately, I called my new-old OB's office and reached the nurse line.

"I'm like a week pregnant after having a miscarriage earlier this year," I told a nurse named Melissa, "and my anxiety is very high. I keep taking pregnancy tests. Do you have any suggestions?"

"Why don't you come in for a blood test," she said. She explained that my hCG should be doubling roughly every forty-eight hours, so we'd test me every couple of days.

I breathed a massive sigh of relief, proud of how I was taking my therapist's advice seriously. I was in the doctor's hands now.

1 2

ALPINE SLIDE

SEPT. 27 | 4:19 P.M. - *ME: HI!* *Just wondering when the lab results from this morning will be ready? Thanks so much, sorry, just anxious haha.*

Sept. 27 | 5:07 p.m. – *Nurse: They aren't back just yet.*

Sept. 28 | 7:49 a.m. – *Me: Just checking in on labs, thanks! ☺*

Sept. 28 | 8:14 a.m. – *Nurse: I don't see them yet, but we will send them your way once we receive them.*

Sept. 28 | 5:32 p.m. – *Me: Hello, I think the office is closed, and I didn't get lab results. Do you know when I can expect those? I came in yesterday morning. Also, should I plan to come in tomorrow for another round? Every 48 hours was mentioned. Thanks, Mary*

Sept. 28 | 6:10 p.m. – *Nurse: Mary, Your Beta hCG level is 51, which is consistent with a very early pregnancy. Let's have you come in tomorrow so we can recheck that level. Your progesterone level is 18, which is great. Yes, come in tomorrow.*

Sept. 29 | 7:03 p.m. – *Good morning, I just went in for labs first thing. I wondered if labs ever return same day or if I should expect them tomorrow? (Just asking out of sheer anxiety here, sorry, I know this is annoying.) Thank you!*

Having merely displaced my anxiety from pee tests to blood tests, I received my second lab result just as I was packing to spend a weekend in Utah with my law school best friends—the same crew I watched *The Bachelor* with the night I miscarried. It affirmed that my hormone levels were right on track.

Assembling my toiletries, I dropped two pregnancy tests into my bag, then paused. What if I didn't? What if I could just have fun?

"What if you kept this between you and your doctor?" my therapist had suggested.

I took them out, feeling subversive and brave for daring to go a whole weekend without a single test on hand. Look at me and my mental health!

At the airport in Salt Lake City, awaiting the arrival of my friends' flights, I wandered into a gift shop and stumbled on a box of prints for sale, including a handful of classic children's book covers—*Alice in Wonderland, Peter Pan, Huckleberry Finn.*

When I'd first found out I was pregnant with Finn, Lucas and I had been days away from a long-planned trip to Europe, our first together. By the time we made it to Paris, I was six weeks pregnant, and though I'd felt a little superstitious about purchasing anything for "the baby" yet, I'd been unable to resist doling out forty euros for some vintage prints of *Babar*, the French children's cartoon, sold by a charming bookseller on the bank of the Seine. Those prints had hung in Finn's room in New York as an infant, and they still hung in his room in Nashville.

That I now stood before a similar set of prints felt like an invitation to trust.

I purchased three for the new baby's room.

See, universe? I thought. *This is me trusting.*

Because Finn—and therefore I—woke up at 5 a.m. most mornings, and because I'd traveled from a later time zone, I couldn't sleep past 5:30 a.m. Mountain Time.

That first morning, I tiptoed downstairs in our rented cabin, made myself a pot of decaf, and waited for someone else to wake up.

These were my best friends from law school, my crew ever since, fourteen years earlier, we'd made it through that first, grueling semester together, and then five more after that. Since then, we'd supported each other through the bar exam, starting and leaving jobs, breakups, cross-country moves, childbearing, and now, child not-bearing. Child attempting and failing. Child hoping.

One of these three friends was Emily, with whom I'd celebrated gleefully in the Walmart parking lot six months earlier, before I'd even told Lucas. Back then, we were both pregnant and expecting to be *more* pregnant together on this trip, which was already on the books, giddy about the photos we'd take together in October with our bellies.

Here we were. October had arrived. Neither of us with a belly, neither of us sustaining our pregnancies from May.

When I heard rustling and spotted Emily creeping down the stairs just before six, I was glad to see it was her.

Of everyone in my life, she was the person I had spoken with most over the prior months. I didn't feel like I was speaking gibberish when I talked to her, not like I often did with other people. Even with people I was close to, it was almost like I was speaking in a language they'd studied in high school but didn't quite speak. They'd scrunch their faces, listening hard, then say something that revealed they hadn't *quite* gotten what I'd said. Except that we were both speaking English, like we always had, so I constantly gaslighted myself. Why couldn't I communicate better about this? Why did it seem like no one got it?

But Emily got it.

We looked at each other for a minute. This trip was the first time we'd seen each other in person since life had taken a dark turn for us both.

"How are you?" she asked. I shrugged. She pretty much knew—we talked every day or so.

Nonetheless, I asked her the same thing, too, and soon we were talking about our lives now in the language we both spoke, the language of people who, for lack of a better way to put it, have been through fertility shit. Foul-smelling, toxic *shit*.

At thirty-nine, both of us were still on the fertility train—I was newly pregnant, and she was still trying—but gone were the proclamations about the future, gone was the naïve optimism of our former selves.

Only months earlier, we'd been bubbly, gabby, making long-term plans for our pregnant bellies and the children inside. Maybe our kids would date! They would come on vacations with us, and we'd teach them how to make gin martinis for us, their aunties. The things women say all the time when they're excited about pregnancy.

And it wasn't just the optimism, it was the language of control, of planning out fertility on a timeline like it was a college major or house renovation. I'd once overheard a woman in the waiting room of my OB's office talking about how she wanted to get pregnant right then so that she wouldn't be pregnant for a wedding she had to attend in the spring, and another woman talking about how she was pretty sure she could knock out three pregnancies before she hit forty; that way, she wouldn't have to resort to IVF.

Once upon a time, these comments wouldn't have registered as misguided to me, because I, too, believed that fertility was human control, that it would bend to the will of the wisher. After all, science was both advanced and on our side, right? Worst-case scenario, you just got reproductive technology involved.

But Emily and I now spoke the language of women who'd been burned by the truth: that absolutely nothing was guaranteed, and that a seemingly healthy pregnancy could turn in an instant.

Speaking to a friend who now spoke my language was like setting foot on familiar soil after a lengthy bout of homesickness.

I was pregnant again, but we weren't giddy about it—we reserved our giddiness for making fun of how many pregnancy tests I'd taken.

The *Alice in Wonderland* print was in my suitcase, but I wasn't buying a frame yet.

On our last morning of the trip, we decided to do the Alpine Slide—you ride a ski lift up to a peak, then get in your own little sled to zoom down a curvy track that traces the mountainside.

Peeing over the weekend, I'd felt like I was missing something, like I was *wasting* the pee. But without tests to line up and compare, without a progression of lines to preoccupy me, I'd managed to actually have fun with my friends. We took long walks around town and wandered into thrift stores. We made enchiladas and compared worst-ever boyfriends in the hot tub (I perched on the side).

It helped that, without a car or a pharmacy nearby, I had no choice. Only once did I entertain a fantasy of sneaking off to the 7/11 in walking distance to see if perhaps, they had a test. But it passed, and I didn't.

The last morning was chilly, and, as we approached the ticket booth for the Alpine Slide, I slid my hands into the pockets of the cardigan I'd thrown on. There was something in one of them.

I reflexively pulled it out.

"Is that a pregnancy test?" Emily asked. "Oh my God, Mary."

Other people find dollar bills or receipts in their pockets. I was now finding old pregnancy tests.

At the top of the mountain, I handed my ticket over and climbed into my sled. Of course, I'd already done the calculus of whether this activity could possibly harm the baby, because I thought it a hundred times a day. *Will this food kill the baby? Will this scent that just wafted over this way kill the baby?*

But it looked fun, and I needed fun. Besides, really old people were doing it. It couldn't be that dangerous.

The teenager manning the entry point showed me how to accelerate and how to brake. I watched my friends take off first, then started my descent.

I meandered down the mountain, gripping the brake bar with both hands, holding it tightly. I wasn't about to go zipping down, not with this pregnancy on the line. My fists remained clenched around that plastic handle, my knuckles white. As long as there was friction, I knew the brake was working, and if the brake was working, I could control my speed; I wouldn't suddenly ricochet toward a crash landing.

As I approached the bottom of the slide, my friends grew from small silhouettes to humans I could tell were smiling. Gliding to a stop, I saw that my friend Karen was cracking up and videoing me with her phone.

"What's so funny?" I asked.

"Did you brake the whole way like that? Could you have gone any slower? We've been down here for like half an hour."

"I think I went a normal speed," I said, embarrassed. "It's probably because I left a few minutes after you."

As I crawled out of my sled, I didn't say what I was thinking: that even braking the whole way, it had felt far faster than was safe.

And then I was back home and off the wagon.

I stood frozen before an empty shelf in Target where the pregnancy tests were supposed to be. I couldn't believe it. Fucking Target was out of tests.

The shelf wasn't totally empty—there were "cheapies," the off-brand tests that don't show a positive as early and cost half as much as the real deal. But I needed First Response, the brand of tests already dated and time-stamped in red Sharpie: 9/27 @ 7:30 a.m.; 9/27 @ 9:30 a.m.; 9/28 @ 6:20 p.m. Too much variation was possible if I suddenly switched brands, and tracking the darkness of the line was already a tricky game.

I'd just have to find the tests elsewhere.

As I crossed the Target parking lot, I pondered where to land my next stash. Walgreen's up-charged them almost 100%; they were $22, not $12, and I still had a *tiny* bit of dignity. Twenty-two? Come on.

I climbed into my car and pulled up my Amazon app.

But no. I'd already placed three separate orders for same-day delivery that had all been canceled by the company. Even Amazon, apparently, was out. I doubted that had changed. I dropped my phone onto the passenger seat, cursing supply chain issues. I started the engine but didn't put it in reverse.

Clinging to the wheel, I started to cry.

Goddammit.

For so long, I'd believed that hard work earned me what I wanted.

College: check.

Law school: check.

Publish novels: check.

Make enough to live *and* take vacations: check.

Have baby number one: check.

Years earlier, some friends and I, in our early thirties at the time, read a book called *Designing Your Life* together and met for brunch to talk about it. The book was written by two Stanford professors who taught a massively popular course by the same name, and the idea was to apply principles of tech design to create "a life that is both meaningful and fulfilling."

Over eggs Benedict, we four young, white adults with college degrees living in New York City discussed the book. None of us questioned the fundamental assumption of it—that we could, in fact, design our lives. Of course we could, wasn't that a given? I can imagine an amphitheater full of Stanford kids in name brands taking notes on their Macs and feeling, likewise, utterly in control of their fates; it isn't even a question.

But miscarriage was holding up a mirror to my entitlement.

What if the life I had designed in my mind years ago—a family with two kids—wasn't possible? What if all the prenatal vitamins and positive thinking in the world didn't make a difference, and I lost this baby too? What if my body wasn't a machine that I simply operated to achieve goals A, B, and C but a creature over which I had zero control? What if my *body* decided whether I had another kid or not?

I didn't know what that would mean; I just knew it scared the shit out of me.

And so, this pregnancy had to stick.

I took a deep breath and wiped my cheeks.

Walgreens, with its $22 price tag, it was. I put the car in reverse.

I needed this pregnancy to fix me. I didn't know what being fixed looked like, but I knew she wasn't who I'd been before I had gotten pregnant in Mexico, and she wasn't who I was now, either. She wasn't hustling to reach the next milestone to fill the emptiness inside, but she also wasn't frantically taking so many pregnancy tests they wouldn't fit in the bedside table drawer. She was someone I didn't know yet.

Fix: a verb and a noun. For me, this pregnancy was both.

I'd already begun measuring this bud of a life by the same breed of standards I pegged on myself. Already, I was full of requirements:

Produce a darker line.

Give me a "good" sonogram.

Yield a genetic test with the right outcome.

Live up, live up, live up. Perform, perform, perform.

Through hard work, we can create a life that is both meaningful and fulfilling.

Show me that's still true, little one, show me.

Make my life mean something.

13

MAGIC EYE

LEADING UP TO THE MORNING OF my eight-week checkup (at which I'd confirmed there would be an ultrasound), I told myself that it would be fine—very few women have two miscarriages in a row. Statistics were in my favor.

"I don't think ovaries work that way," my therapist said, and I blinked at her, thinking, *well, I got an A in college stats, Dilbert, and I disagree.*

Like I had with my last pregnancy, I was living for the checkup, convinced that if I could just make it to that appointment, I would be able to relax. If I could only see the heartbeat... I just needed a heartbeat to calm my nerves.

I was working on the couch one morning, Finn already at daycare, when Lucas, who'd been on a run, charged through the back entrance. He marched past me to the front door, alarmed.

"I just heard something weird coming from the front," he said.

Barefoot, I followed. He jogged to the road, heading toward the busy intersection at the end of our street, then disappeared over the small hill that led to the highway. I crested it to find

Lucas, bewildered, before a three-car traffic jam. At his feet, a toddler, naked from the waist down, was crying. As it registered that Lucas was guarding her but wasn't picking her up because she was a naked little girl, I hurried to grab her.

The cars passed, and the three of us were left alone. There wasn't another adult in sight.

When I saw a man in a baseball cap hurriedly approaching, I thought, *Thank God.* I walked his way, prepared to hand over the screaming little girl, when he hollered, "Do you know whose she is?"

"Okay, um, let's go inside and get a diaper on her," I said. She was much smaller than Finn, but he was still in diapers. Lucas and the man followed me back to our house. The little girl had stopped screaming and was just whimpering.

Lucas fetched her some milk, and a second neighbor appeared in the doorway with a box of doughnuts.

"Do you think she's hungry?" he said cheerfully. The doughnuts had pink frosting, every single one. We all stared at him. Lucas finally took the doughnuts and put them on the coffee table—this would be the detail we'd revisit later for giggles.

"We should call social services, right?" my neighbor said. The men looked to me for what to do, deferring to my judgment.

"We should find where she lives, I think," I said. Surely there was an explanation. She'd escaped before someone had realized she was gone.

Once, shortly after Finn had started walking, I'd been folding laundry in the Florida condo where we were staying when I'd noticed that it had grown suspiciously quiet. I'd searched the apartment and, finding Finn nowhere, put together that he'd figured out how to open the condo door. I'd found him in the hallway of the massive building, which had fourteen floors with over a thousand units. We were on the eleventh floor. If I'd been a few seconds later, he easily could have wandered to the elevator, pressed the button, and disappeared.

It would have been my worst nightmare.

What if this was someone's worst nightmare?

But what if she *wasn't* safe? Why wasn't a parent out looking for her by now?

Then we heard it: wailing.

It was coming from down the street in the opposite direction from where we'd found the girl, the sounds of a parent in agony.

We rushed out. I was still carrying her.

When the mother saw us, she clutched her chest and collapsed in the grass, sobbing. She couldn't speak for several minutes. I squatted next to her and awkwardly rubbed her back, hoping she wasn't having an actual heart attack. Her eyes, when we made eye contact, were full of terror. Was I here to ruin her life?

"I can't lose my children," she was begging over and over. "Please, I can't lose my children." When she caught her breath, she explained that her nine-year-old had been watching the two-year-old. But, you know, he was nine.

As we walked back to our house a few minutes later, I remembered when, a few days after Finn was born, my sister found me crying in my bed while nursing.

"What's wrong?" she'd asked.

"I just realized that I've willingly created a being with the power to destroy me," I said.

My sister had raised her eyebrows and reached for Finn.

"Okaaaaay, I think you need a nap."

Your children do not belong to you, my OB had quoted to me the night of Finn's birth. An understatement, it now seemed. Even before they were children, they were entirely out of our control— from the moment they were conceived, we could not save them.

Here I was, waiting for the next ultrasound to alleviate my fear. But even if it did for a moment, even if my pregnancy proceeded perfectly and the baby was born without issue, the fear would always return, because being a parent meant being afraid.

Pregnancy just gave you an early start.

On the drive to our appointment, I turned on "Let It Be" to calm my nerves. I did not hear the lyrics as an invitation to "let it be" should I miscarry again. I heard them as an invitation to be patient and calm during the long minutes that stood between me and my precious sonogram.

Since Lucas would be coming from work, we drove separately, but because he had never been to my new-old OB's office before, I met him at his office first so he could follow me. This way, we could park together, and he wouldn't have to navigate his way through the maze of buildings and offices.

Lucas's workplace was only a few blocks from the appointment, in a neighborhood that I had driven through a million times to take Finn to daycare—but somehow, I still got lost. Between his office and my OB's, I drove in circles with Lucas tailing me, feeling rattled and sheepish as I glanced in my rearview mirror at his unreadable face in sunglasses. Where was the entrance to the parking lot? Was this the right lot? Was this even my OB's building?

I'd been there at least five times for bloodwork within the last few weeks, so why was this so confusing?

Finally, we parked.

"Sorry," I said, climbing out of my car.

"Oh, Pat," Lucas said. "Are you nervous?"

I nodded. Yes. He took my hand.

Inside, I finally met Melissa, the nurse I'd been messaging. She was tall, with a blonde ponytail and a thick Tennessee accent.

"How have you been feeling?" she asked.

"Pretty anxious," I said, thinking of my mind, not my body.

"Nauseous?" she asked.

Oh, that's what she'd meant. I shook my head.

"But a lot of fatigue," I said quickly, to assure her I wasn't *entirely* symptom-free—as if, for this pregnancy to be healthy, I needed to convince *her* it was healthy.

She procured a sheet of paper with a yearly calendar on it, then highlighted every fourth week through June pink.

"When you leave, you're going to go ahead and make all of your checkups now for your entire pregnancy," she said, handing it to me. "Give this to the girls at the front."

I took the paper.

"Anything you want to talk about with Dr. Morrow today?"

"Just want to see the baby," I said with a forced chuckle.

"Of course," she said. Then she handed me a plastic cup, told me to pee in it, and, while I was in the bathroom, to weigh myself.

I hadn't weighed myself in a couple of months. After I hadn't been successful at even *trying* to lose the weight I'd gained in my last pregnancy, I'd performed the smallest, most half-assed act of self-care ever and stopped weighing myself. I was already miserable in my skin; I didn't need to torment myself further.

At least the scale was in a private bathroom.

It was two days before Halloween, and I was wearing Uggs and a heavy sweater. I shed both, accustomed to the practice of eliminating every extraneous shred of weight before facing down a scale.

I stepped.

Well, *damn.*

I'd gained eight *more* pounds.

I grimaced. This pregnancy, I hadn't even allowed myself the ice cream, thinking of the worst-case scenario: What if I gained *more* weight, and the baby didn't stick? I'd be in it even deeper.

I've gained sixteen pounds and haven't made it through a first trimester yet, I thought.

It's alright, we're growing our second human this year! another voice chimed in.

I had a baby coming. And this baby would make it all worth

it.

My OB, Dr. Morrow, rolled the machine into the room with the most comforting words I could hope for: "Why don't we start with the ultrasound, since I know you're anxious?"

This! This was the kind of bedside manner a woman needed!

I lay back as she flipped off the light and instructed Lucas to stand on my left side so we could both view her computer monitor.

I wondered if his heart was racing too.

It's going to be fine. Breathe.

"There's the gestational sac..." she said quietly. And then she said nothing more.

We were looking at space. There was nothing in it. The sac had a clear, ovular border.

Lucas touched my arm, but I couldn't turn away from the screen; my eyes were locked on that blob. I sensed that Dr. Morrow was searching for a fetus longer than she, with her expertise, knew was reasonable. Her warm arm rested against my leg, her face only a foot from mine, and I felt her wanting the situation to be different too, wanting to disbelieve what we all saw in front of us.

"Okay, let's stop putting you through this," she finally said, pulling out the wand.

Putting me through what? I thought. The ultrasound? I didn't want the ultrasound to end. I wanted to keep searching. Maybe it would be like a Magic Eye, all abstract patterns until: a leaping dolphin, a castle, a sailboat.

Would it appear?

After a few seconds or minutes, I sat up, aware of both Lucas and Dr. Morrow watching me. But I had nothing to give them. Not tears. Not surprise. Not anger.

When I was eighteen, the driver of an oncoming car hit the driver's side of mine while I was at the wheel, and the first memory

I have after pulling out of Blockbuster is of sitting in an ambulance as an EMT rapped on my collarbone and asked if it hurt. It did. The sting of that man tapping my collarbone is where my memory clocks in.

In the office that day, I know that Dr. Morrow explained to me what I already knew: that the baby was not viable, that I'd had another "missed miscarriage," that my body hadn't recognized it yet and would in its own time, but that I could also take meds to accelerate the bleeding. But I don't remember any of this taking place.

My memory clocks in with Dr. Morrow lifting a gray envelope. Had a nurse brought it in? Was it in a drawer?

"I'm giving you the medicine here because some pharmacists have been giving women a hard time. They think they're using it for abortions."

"Are you kidding?" I said. I remembered the last pharmacist's kindness as I'd put my SweeTarts and Cheez-Its on the counter. Why couldn't everyone be like her? I'd hated her pity, but pity was preferable to cruelty. I took the envelope and peeked inside. Along with the pills, it contained a small, black card with white print that read, *We are sorry for your loss.*

"We're flying to Dallas tomorrow," I said. We were taking Finn to spend Halloween with his cousins. It would be his first year trick-or-treating. He'd picked out his costume—a squid that he insisted was an octopus.

"No need to take it until you come back then," she said. "But take it with you, because if you start bleeding in Dallas, taking it will make you bleed less."

I tried to get my head around the logic: It makes you bleed, but if you do bleed, it makes you bleed less. Magical bleeding medicine. It just did whatever you needed it to do. Could it bring the baby back?

As we stood to leave, I noticed the calendar, highlighted in pink, on the table where I'd left it. Walking away from it felt like walking away from the baby. I wanted to grab that piece of paper and hold it to me.

"Can we test the fetus?" Lucas asked.

"There is no fetus to test," she said. "It's just a sac."

Empty.

A hole.

14

MOTHERING

IF THERE WAS SOMETHING FUNDAMENTAL missing in me, was it also missing in everyone? And if pregnancy couldn't fill it, what could?

I was never someone who looked down on religious people. I was the daughter of ministers, and I respected my parents' faith. If anything, I was envious of it. To wholeheartedly believe in something, to feel as if you understood the workings of the universe—how calming that must feel.

"All you have to do is accept Jesus into your heart," was the phrase uttered by Christians throughout my upbringing, but, for me, it hadn't turned out to be that simple. I'd been baptized. I'd accepted Jesus. I'd sung the songs and prayed the prayers.

But as with other belief systems I had tried on over the years— the allure of thinness, the numbing power of wine, the vainglory of workaholism—my trust in the thing, whatever the thing was, would start to crumble, big chunks falling away until there was only space again. I'd still wake up under a pressure to prove something without knowing why, and another day would begin, and another day would end.

In 2020, during my pandemic wellness craze, when I cut out meat, caffeine, and alcohol and set up a meditation chair in my closet to be more like Glennon Doyle, the sense of still not being enough, of having so much further to go before I got *there,* wherever there was, nagged at me. Over evening lavender tea, I read a book on "the perils and promises of a spiritual life" through meditation, and rather than making me feel grounded, the author's assertion that a spiritual quest is never complete made me feel tired. *You mean I'm never done?* I thought.

I was still waiting to arrive…somewhere. I wanted to feel not just alive, but like I got it, the point of living, for me. I wasn't looking for anything as grandiose as an answer to *everyone's* existential questions, nor did I believe such a thing even existed. I just wanted to find my own way to be—as the Bible verse I'd memorized as a kid put it, "in this world but not of it." Or maybe I just wanted to not loathe my body.

Surprisingly, in the midst of my second miscarriage came a fleck of light.

It started when I got home from the ultrasound where we'd seen the empty sac. Lucas had gone back to work. Although I'd joked that we should just go get drunk and call it a day, I'd assured him I was fine, and we made a plan to eat dinner out that night.

Alone in the house, I went out to check the mail.

Inside the mailbox was a package. When I saw Poshmark in the return address, I knew what it was: a pair of thrifted maternity jeans I'd ordered weeks earlier.

What timing.

I took them inside and opened the package. I'd ordered them because they were the only maternity jeans I'd ever seen that didn't *look* like maternity jeans; if you weren't really paying attention, you'd think they were just regular jeans. They had very thin denim panels at the seams that would stretch as you grew, unlike the standard maternity jean, which is essentially denim leggings attached to a giant spandex tube from the crotch up.

I unfolded them, thinking they were even better in person than I expected.

Might as well see what they looked like.

I took them up to my room and pulled them on, then stood in front of my full-length mirror.

A woman who was no longer pregnant but wearing maternity jeans looked back at me.

She was noticeably bigger.

But instead of grimacing, instead of shifting my gaze away with a familiar disgust, I found a swell of tenderness rise in my chest— as if the motherly instinct, that creature of my hormones, had shifted its focus from the baby inside me to the reflection before me.

To *mother* as a verb can mean two things: to create—be the origin of—or to care for and protect. In one sense, I'd now mothered three beings; my body had created three sparks of life. In the other, I'd mothered one: Finn. Had I ever mothered myself? What would that even look like?

Then I remembered. I was nineteen years old and five years into bulimia when I finally told my mom I needed help. It was the middle of the night. I was lying in a guest bed at my grandmother's house and doing a hundred butt clenches to counter the few bites of pizza I'd been unable to purge that day, though I'd managed to get rid of most of it (how I thought about it—*get rid of*), when the thought passed through my mind: *You're killing yourself.*

I was purging at least once a day, often more. A low-grade burn stung my throat for most of my waking hours. I'd trained my gag reflex so effectively that, sometimes, I didn't even need my hand. I could just bend over. To this day, I struggle to brush my tongue.

I'd become so successful at bulimia that my survival instinct was kicking in. *You're killing yourself,* the voice kept insisting as I lay there, squeezing my glutes and counting.

When my mom appeared in the doorway in her gown—for no reason, as far as I knew—I said, "I have to tell you something." She sat on the edge of the bed. "I think I have—" I started, then corrected myself. "I *know* I have an eating disorder," I said, "and I don't know what to do."

She told me it would be okay, that when we got home, we'd find a therapist. But in the meantime, there was the rest of our trip to deal with—we had almost a week to go visiting our big, sprawling Louisiana family.

Over the coming days, my mom became my co-conspirator in seeking out foods I wouldn't feel the need to purge. It wasn't a solution, we knew; it was temporary, a tourniquet to stop the bleeding. She invented an excuse for why we couldn't meet the family for lunch at a burger joint and drove me across town for a fruit-only smoothie. I was remarkably high-maintenance—rather, my eating disorder was—and we indulged it without question. Anything to keep me from purging.

But on the last night of vacation, my step-grandfather made ribs. They were piled high on the counter buffet, a towering tray. He was the kind of man who liked to comment on how much food remained on each person's plate at the conclusion of a meal, and so my mom and I shared a glance as I tentatively tonged two ribs onto mine and found a seat at the long dining room table.

In the chaos of cousins and aunts and uncles serving themselves, amidst the chatter and clinking of silverware, my mom sat next to me and snatched a rib from my plate. She sank her teeth into it, ripping into like an animal, frantic, manic. She grabbed the other and did the same. It was barbaric and crazed. The meal hadn't started yet! People could see her!

By the time my step-grandfather was bidding us to bow our heads in prayer, my plate contained scraps of meat bones. No one said anything.

I didn't purge that night, and I don't think it was because of how much I had or hadn't eaten. Watching my mom do that for me—the love. Holy shit, the *love*.

I looked at my reflection now, and I saw my mother's child. I saw a little girl who was hurting, who wanted to be able to wear these jeans and now believed she couldn't because they weren't for her.

Oh, honey, I thought, *you can wear these jeans if you want.*

On the floor of that stadium at sixteen, broken, I'd stopped fighting what I knew to be true.

Now, I saw the woman in the mirror, and I didn't need to change her.

Then it struck me—I was still pregnant.

I'd never thought of pregnancy this way, because no one talked about it this way. Pregnancy meant having a baby-to-be that everyone would get to meet, that would cry and be a human and get a birth certificate and poop.

But I was as pregnant as I'd ever been during this pregnancy, given that all that was inside of me was a gestational sac, and the hormones of pregnancy still coursed through me. My body still believed itself to be pregnant. It was sending blood and nutrients to a placenta, nurturing a life that it believed to be there.

In fact, it was October, which meant that, except for about three weeks after the end of my first miscarriage, I'd been pregnant for six months. Indeed, much of that time I'd been pregnant with death, ushering lives out of this world, not in...but pregnant all the same.

I walked around the house wearing the jeans, feeling like I'd just uncovered something important, something essential for me to understand if I ever wanted to find the peace I craved.

If pregnancy wasn't a means to an end but rather a state of being, what did that mean for how I viewed my body? For how I would proceed from here?

I didn't feel the same urgency to purge my body of the pregnancy as I had the last time. I'd been here before—for forty days, in fact. I knew it wasn't going to kill me. Packing for Dallas, I'd included the pills, but I didn't expect to use them until I got back. I'd decide then.

The moment in the mirror seemed to have shifted something. It was a sliver of kindness, a peek into an alternative universe in which I was kinder to myself. I let my imagination slide into it.

What if I just allowed myself to be pregnant, still? What if I didn't subscribe to the world's definition of what pregnancy was, and I did all the things I'd do if there *were* a baby with a heartbeat—let myself sleep if I was tired, wear the clothes that felt most comfortable, refuse to start exercising right away, because fuck that?

It felt radical, subversive, ridiculous.

It felt kind, necessary, and overdue.

Still wearing the maternity jeans, I went to my computer. There didn't seem to be a way to message the seller of the jeans directly, so I typed an email to Poshmark customer service:

Hello,

I don't know if you can pass this on to my seller, but if you can, I would appreciate it. Her package arrived at a valuable moment for me today. I am having a miscarriage. When the jeans arrived, I tried them on anyway, and they fit my still-pregnant body perfectly. It was a blessing in disguise because I needed the reminder that I am still pregnant, even if the baby isn't on its way, and I can treat my body gently with clothes that fit.

Thank you.

Poshmark wrote me back that they couldn't get the message to the seller, so it never reached her.

I started to bleed in Dallas on Halloween. No medicine needed.

This time, I sat in my sister's guest bathroom. A doily hand towel splayed from a ring on the wall.

It was around 9 a.m., and everyone was awake—my nephews and Finn were eating Cheerios and watching cartoons; my brother-in-law was on a ladder just outside the bathroom working to fix the sound system before a party later; my parents were on their way over from Louisiana.

I didn't feel death in the room. I felt no presence, no sense of loss. I felt annoyed.

"Dammit," I said. I didn't even have a pad on me. How had I not even thought to bring pads?

"Katie Beth!" I yelled for my sister, like I had when we were teenagers. "Can someone get Katie Beth!"

I was supposed to take the magic medicine to make me bleed less. I opened the packet. The instructions on this set of pills didn't say to insert them into my vagina but in front of my lower gums.

My *mouth?* Okay…

I lined up the four pills below my gumline and looked in the mirror. Good grief. I looked like the country boys who dipped tobacco at my South Carolina high school, my lower lip bulging.

"Hello!" I heard the front door open and my parents' voices. How long would these things take to dissolve?

Miscarriage (or, rather, "medical management of missed miscarriage") was turning out to be a lot of waiting, alone, in a bathroom. After a few minutes, I heard my mom ask where I was.

I cracked open the door and stuck out my head.

"Mom!" I whisper-yelled. I gestured for her, then closed the door to the small guest bathroom behind us. I motioned to my jaw and delivered the news completely out of order.

"I have these weird pill things in my mouth because I'm having a miscarriage, and I just wanted to tell you so you know what's going on." My voice cracked when I said the "m" word.

She hadn't known I was pregnant.

"I'm so sorry," she said. We hugged, then she left me alone to wait more. I wasn't about to go face the entire family with my lip jutting out.

After a few minutes, I thought, *whatever.* I swallowed what was left of the pills and exited the bathroom to dress for the day. The family was going to Target.

A thing we do in the South: family trips to Target. Target is a full-fledged family excursion. You can snag a Starbucks iced coffee, your groceries, cheap kid clothes, a decorative receptacle you don't need that is almost certainly wicker, and a Tabitha Brown oven mitt, all in one fell swoop.

Our entourage on this Halloween included six adults, three children, and two carts. I was managing one of the carts and policing the three children in the Lego aisle when I felt something drop out of me. This wasn't blood. I knew this feeling. A thing with mass had slid out of my body and was now being cradled, precariously, by my underwear. At least, I hoped it was.

Not wanting to risk any unnecessary steps, I texted my sister an SOS: Someone needed to a) take over kid duty immediately, and b) find the largest pads sold by Target, also some underwear, also possibly some kind of bottoms.

Ninja-style, she appeared in seconds, hurling a jumbo pack of Depends at me.

"Go," she said. "I'll bring underwear if you need it."

I did not pass Go; I did not pay for the maxi pads. I ripped them open as I waddled through the store, doing one extended Kegel as I inched my way across the vast plain that is a Super Target until I reached the blessed "Women" sign and locked myself away to survey the damage.

Over the next ten minutes, I rode out the bulk of my second miscarriage in a Target bathroom stall in North Dallas.

As I sat, waiting (more waiting), I texted Emily, since I thought she might appreciate the irony—my summer pregnancy had begun in a Walmart bathroom.

Full circle, I wrote. Ha.

Back at my sister's house, we had Halloween to get ready for. I'd bought a costume for Finn (squid/octopus) and a costume for Lucas (Mr. Potato Head) but hadn't gotten one for myself, so my sister took on the task of assembling me something workable.

"Here," she said, handing me a bright blonde wig, a pair of black pleather leggings, and a black leather jacket. "You can be Sandy from *Grease*."

We found some red lipstick, and *voila*: I transformed into one of American cinema's most iconic sexpots while, under my pleather pants, I wore a pad the size of a small diaper that I had to swap out every couple of hours.

"Your butt looks great," my sister said.

I did not feel great. But I also didn't feel the self-loathing I'd expected. It was odd. My afternoon wearing the Poshmark maternity jeans had been a peek into a different way of relating to my body, and it was lingering, the hint of kindness trailing me like Pig-Pen's dust cloud in Charlie Brown.

As I walked the streets of my sister's neighborhood at dusk, following my tiny squid with his orange jack-o'-lantern pail, reminding him to say "thank you," I wasn't thinking about how much weight I'd gained or distracted by how snug the pleather leggings were on my thighs; I didn't feel eager to "get back" to my pre-pregnancy size.

My worst fear had come true for a second time, and the one-two punch was, it seemed, the knockout required to flatten me. Last time, I'd jumped right back up, ready to keep fighting (or, at least, I tried to). This time, I'd been defeated; there was no pretending this wasn't real.

There was a quiet in surrender. The bundle had been unraveled, and inside was a white flag. I waved it in my blonde wig, trailing a squid.

15

MARY

I WALKED THROUGH THE FRONT DOOR of the yoga studio, dusty mat in hand, and approached the front desk.

"First time?" asked the woman standing behind it. I nodded. "Welcome," she said. "Follow me. I'll show you around."

The two and a half years we'd lived in Nashville had been the longest I'd gone without doing yoga since I'd first discovered it at twenty-two.

Back then, I'd accompanied a friend to a hot yoga class and gotten hooked—I loved how I sweated buckets and felt like Hercules afterward, like I could do anything.

I started going to that studio daily in between my two jobs—my day job as an admin assistant and my night gig as a bartender. (As they say, if you can make it in New York...) A workout class, that's all it was to me: ninety minutes of cathartic exercise to keep sane while I spent my days learning to quick-change from business casual to all black H&M in the five-minutes left between jobs after my forty-five-minute subway ride.

Then I decided to go to law school, which required I take the LSAT, a four-hour exam consisting of a hundred text-heavy questions. To do well, I would have to focus, and not how I'd studied my way through college, which had been sporadically, with stretches of daydreaming in between.

But I didn't know how to sustain that kind of focus. I'd never learned. I couldn't get through a single question without my mind drifting. I'd start to read the paragraph-long prompt, and, a few seconds in, realize I had no clue what I was reading. My eyes were tracking the words, but my brain had jumped to whether I was smart enough to be a lawyer or whether my ex-boyfriend still loved me.

If I wanted to do well on this test and get into law school— and I did—I had to train myself to focus.

Enter, yoga. Already, the instructors were always telling us to "focus on the breath." Already, they invited me every day to "bring attention" to the present moment. Mostly, I ignored them, following directions to execute the poses, but otherwise viewing yoga as my time to plan what I needed to pick up at the grocery on the way home.

But once I realized I wasn't going to succeed on the LSAT unless I learned to focus, I decided to give the mindfulness thing a shot.

Next class, I did what the instructor said and consciously tried to bring my awareness back to my body: Where was my leg right now? Was it steady or shaky?

I would guide my attention back to how my skin felt stretching across my lower back as I curled over my front leg, how my shoulders trembled, or how my hip pinched.

We held each pose for twenty seconds. To finish the LSAT on time, you must complete a single question in one minute and twenty seconds. Like when, as a kid, I'd ask on a road trip how much longer and my parents would say, "One *Sesame Street* and a *Mr. Rogers*," I told myself, "An LSAT question is just four yoga poses!"

It worked. I got better at taking the exam, which came and went. But yoga remained, and, in using it to prepare for the exam, I'd changed my relationship to it. Now, I couldn't just view it as exercise, couldn't just view it as a place to make shopping lists while I sweat.

When I went into a yoga studio and stood on my mat, I "dropped in," as the yoga teachers say. Outside the yoga room, I still preferred to live as if I didn't have a body. But inside it, my body got to exist. The duality was striking and reminded me of a poem I'd written about my bulimia years earlier:

My fingers taste like power
until I leave the stall.
Outside, the aftertaste makes me
want to run back in.

Yoga wasn't bulimia. But in the same way, I craved the way I felt inside that room, and only that room. For the next decade, I'd go to yoga several times a week, but when we moved to Nashville, I stopped. Over two years, I'd passed this studio three blocks from our house nearly every day but had never gone in.

I blamed the pandemic in part, but I'd also felt "too busy"— writing, starting a business teaching, parenting. Who had time for yoga?

Now, I didn't feel too busy. I felt defeated. And for whatever reason, I'd awoken that morning with an impulse to go, so there I was.

I placed my purse and shoes in a locker, then pulled open the heavy wooden door of the practice room. It was open and airy, with giant windows along the back that filled the room with morning light. A few students sat or lay quietly on mats scattered across the glossy hardwood floor. Everyone faced the mirrored wall in front.

I found a spot, unrolled my mat, sank to my knees, and looked at myself.

There I was, kneeling.

I closed my eyes, which were beginning to leak, as more people quietly entered and laid out their mats. Once my cheeks were wet enough that I needed to wipe them, I dropped my forehead to the ground and stretched my arms out in front of me, assuming child's pose to hide.

As I silently wept amidst the rustle around me, an image entered my mind, an image I didn't even know I remembered, of a sculpture I'd never actually seen in person: Michelangelo's *La Pietà*, Mary holding Jesus's corpse. A grieving mother.

For years, I had treated my body more or less the same way I did my old car: using it to cart me around, servicing it as needed when a light started flashing or the engine began rattling—when I got sick, basically—and feeling only slightly embarrassed when someone called attention to it.

"Oh, my car? I inherited it," I'd say. "At least it works!"

But, like pregnancy, miscarriage had upended this approach. If pregnancy had elevated my body from old car to beloved asset, miscarriage had basically shut it down, smoking, on the side of the road.

STOP! my body seemed to be screaming. I NEED YOU TO STOP!

My therapist, Elizabeth (Dilbert), had helped me see that I couldn't time or schedule my grief, but I'd walked away from that earth-shattering conversation still thinking that my grief would take place where everything important did (right?): in my mind. To grieve, I assumed, meant to think sad thoughts. Remember sad things. Imagine sad futures. Head, head, head.

But the pain of my losses was trembling through my limbs, not through the abstract clouds of my mind. And I mean that literally: A fetus's DNA can be detected in its mother's blood as early as six weeks gestation, and it's been found in her blood decades later. (Fascinatingly, researchers at the National University of Singapore found that, not only do the cells linger, they proliferate. Mothers of male sons have *more* male DNA in their blood over time.)

Day's death had befallen us both. My heart had ceased to pump blood into his as it rolled to a stop, and his DNA still flowed inside me. My body had housed a life, then a death, then the promise of another life, then the remnants of it, as well. (Why hadn't we named the second one, which had turned out to be only a sac? Maybe I'd sensed there was no one to name.)

Call it holy, call it haunted; my body held phantom children, and they were unsettled.

"Okay, let's begin in tabletop," the woman from the front desk said as she entered, flipping on the music. A soft pop ballad played as I rose onto all fours.

My arms shook, my heart raced, my tears puddled on my mat, grief rattling out of me like a train.

I showed up to yoga again the next day. And the next, and the one after that, always crying at least a little bit, grateful that no one ever mentioned it.

In *La Pietà*, Mary slouches under her son's corpse resting on her lap. There's absolutely no pull in her body; it is devoid of strain, of rigidity, of exertion. She's taken root.

Though I'd tried to move on since my first miscarriage, worked so hard to "bounce back," my body had other ideas. *We're not bouncing anywhere*, it seemed to insist. *This is where we belong.*

After a few weeks, I learned that the woman who'd given me my tour and taught most of my classes, Amanda, owned the studio. I paused by the front desk on my way out one afternoon to speak with her.

"I just wanted to tell you that I had a miscarriage recently," I said, my voice cracking, unable to say that I'd actually had two. Great, I was the crier in *and* out of class now. "Coming here is saving me. So thank you."

"It saved me too," she said. "It does that."

16

SCIENCE

BEING IN THE YOGA STUDIO was one thing; being outside of it was another.

I moved through the world with an itch that was growing worse and worse, the kind you can't scratch away. With Elizabeth the therapist's help, I finally named it: anger.

I was angry. But at whom or what?

In religion's absence as an adult, I had fallen into a kind of unarticulated faith in something, an order beyond my comprehension—not a moral one, but a beautiful one.

The Mandelbrot Set, if you will. The Mandelbrot Set is basically a set of fractals. A fractal is an infinitely complex mathematical shape created by very simple rules—the same process repeated over and over to create never-ending patterns.

If you google "Mandelbrot Set," you'll find a video illustrating this—an endless generation of beautiful shapes based on the same, original equation.

Lucas first showed it to me when we were dating, and I was mesmerized. It made me feel the same way I'd felt in the bushes at seven.

If a simple math rule yielded beautiful, infinite complexity, which dot was I? Which star, which hexagon, which slow-bending curve?

I saw myself as a part of this tapestry, a stitch in a magnificent, boundless web. Sometimes I thought of it as "the universe," other times just as "The Thing."

The Thing was behind the good, unexplainable moments I knew had defined my life, though I'd had no control over them. I could point to moments when I felt I'd glimpsed it—the pattern, the logic.

The Thing had brought Lucas and me together on a cold night in January in 2013, a first date I almost canceled because it was frigid and I was tired. I'd already ended my subscription on the dating site, which had led to little more than a handful of awkward dates, when I'd received his message.

Why not? I'd thought, finding nothing offensive about his profile. He was a musician who taught voice and had a nice face.

I was his first-ever date on the site.

His first, my last.

The Thing was also the magic I felt two weeks later, standing in a coffee shop, listening to a song I'd never heard before, feeling like I'd met my person.

"Come on, sit next to me. Bury my feet, bury my feet in the sand."

I returned to my apartment to pick out the chords of that song on my electric keyboard, jotting them down, along with the lyrics I remembered to the chorus on a sheet of notebook paper.

A few weeks after that, the Brooklyn marathon kicked off a few blocks from my apartment. Forever in search of extra cash, I took advantage of the influx of runners and rented out my one bedroom on Airbnb for the weekend against the building's sublease policy, crashing with Lucas in Queens.

That Sunday morning, across from him at a diner, I got a text from the woman staying in my apartment.

Did I send you Aoife's song? she wrote.

I was confused. Who?

It's on your keyboard. Did I send you her song?

That song I'd loved so much that I'd looked it up and transcribed it—it was by her daughter, Aoife O'Donovan.

Now Aoife's mother was in my apartment.

Two years later, Lucas and I would dance to it as our first dance at our wedding.

That was a glimpse of the Thing—the pattern I didn't understand but that ultimately moved toward beauty, toward love.

The Thing was the near stranger sitting next to me, grabbing my hand at the funeral of a classmate who died our first day of law school, and holding it for the next hour. The Thing was that girl becoming my best friend, and answering my phone call many years later when, alone on a street corner in Manhattan, I'd fall prey to a migraine so severe I wouldn't be able to speak or explain where I was. I'd only be able to press "call" on her name.

"I can't speak," I'd say when she picked up.

"Don't move, I'll find you," she'd say. And she would, somehow. In a city of millions of people, on a random street corner miles from our apartments, she'd find me and take me to the ER.

The Thing moved us all toward beauty, or so I'd believed until now. Because I couldn't fathom a logic to this, this pain over nothing. As the Villagers sing, "I waited for nothing, and nothing arrived."

It felt like the universe had reached out to hold my hand by giving me a pregnancy, and I'd taken its fingers, and then it had dropped me into a free fall.

I felt betrayed.

And the sense of betrayal was freshly motivating. Because I still wanted a second kid badly enough that I didn't care whether or not the universe was on board, and, if it wasn't, it was really just in my way.

The universe had changed categories. No longer a wise and prescient guide, it was now a slightly annoying co-worker who didn't quite get it, the kind who'll eat an inferior sandwich to save a buck and judge you for not making the same choice. Instead of a spiritually attuned friend, it was someone I wished would go away so I could focus on what I needed to get done: my next baby.

"Why did you keep going," a friend would ask me later, "after the second miscarriage?"

I would blink at her like I was talking to an alien life form.

Was she kidding?

Lucas had once casually mentioned that a colleague of his said that "IVF makes women crazy." I was furious at this—furious at the colleague, and furious at Lucas for telling me without the appropriate horror in his voice. (And this man's wife hadn't even done IVF! So who was he even talking about, his *neighbor*? Was her stomp to get the paper extra loud?)

"That's ridiculous. IVF hormones absolutely don't make women 'crazy,'" I'd said, bristling at the inherent misogyny in the term.

But later, as I'd watch friend after friend do another failed cycle and another failed cycle, I'd wonder if the colleague, despite his poor choice of words, had meant something other than the hormones.

"I'm just glad I could stop," a mom friend would say to me at the playground. "Some people can't."

Of course they couldn't. It was like Russian Roulette, but some people win a baby. How do you walk away from that, when a baby is what you want most? How on *earth* do you walk away?

To Lucas's colleague, to my friend who asked why, I could say: If someone offered you a seat at a high-limit craps table, and the prize was you getting your deceased parent back, would you say no? Or would you go, "Nah, I'm good, I prefer to keep my twenty grand?"

Your mom might be on the other side of that door right now. She could be back here to spend Christmas with you. How much do you want to wager, sir? How much is she worth to you?

Because that's what it felt like. I was not giving up.

My key source of hope was that statistics were in my favor. Most women didn't have three miscarriages in a row—in fact, fewer than one percent. Surely I wasn't special enough to be that unlucky.

It was time to call in reinforcements.

The little jade cardboard box was labeled *progesterone wands*.

Back in July, during my long first miscarriage, I'd purchased the digital fertility tracker—an egg-sized machine that came with a bunch of wands you peed on. The little egg paired via Bluetooth to your phone, where an app presented your hormone levels in a colorful, scientific-looking chart.

The wands tracked both estrogen and luteinizing hormone (LH) because right before ovulation, both surge. First, the estrogen climbs. Then, LH shoots up like a rocket, peaking on the day of ovulation.

Every time my LH peaked, I (a) was overcome with relief (my cycle was back!) and (b) made sure we had sex, ideally as soon as possible. An egg only lives for twelve to twenty-four hours once ovulation occurs. After that, the possibility of conception drops to near zero until the next month.

If scheduled, procreation-driven sex sounds about as hot as a lukewarm jacuzzi with broken jets, that's accurate.

"I'm ovulating," I'd say, looking meaningfully at Lucas as he tied his shoes before work and Finn threw his shoe at a spider on the wall. *Sesame Street* would be blaring, and the rumble of the garbage truck outside would remind us that it was Wednesday, and we hadn't put out the trash. "Can you come home at lunch? Please?"

"I don't know, Mary. I can try..."

After two miscarriages, Lucas was far less gung-ho than I was to get pregnant again.

"I'll probably regret it later if we don't," he'd said, "but I'd be fine if you didn't want to do this anymore."

I heard this as him caring about me, as worrying about the pain the losses had caused *me*, which made the response to it straightforward: I do want it, so get upstairs, I'm ovulating.

That he was also suffering was something I wouldn't understand until much later. If I was queen of hiding my vulnerability, Lucas was king. I'd seen him cry twice in almost a decade together. Through the miscarriages, he'd hugged me and held my hand and asked me how I was doing, but he himself had yet to shed a tear, as far as I knew.

Moreover, I'm not easy to stop once I set my mind on something. I'm a Taurus. If I'm going down, so is the boat.

Because I'd read somewhere (the Internet) that lying on your back with your legs raised in the air could improve the chances of conception for the first two minutes after intercourse, more than once I found myself on the shower floor with my back against the cold tiles while Lucas shampooed his hair.

Already, in the second week of my monthly cycle, I was peeing on a $4 fertility wand every day, searching for that LH peak so I could herd us into mandatory copulation.

I was up for any tips, tricks, or products that might accelerate the conception process, so in November, when I'd received an email from the tracker company with the subject line, *Now*

Available: NEW Confirm Wands: Confirm Your Ovulation!, of course I opened it. These hot-off-the-press wands—not to replace the old ones but to supplement them—tracked a third hormone: progesterone. If one peed on a wand every day for a week *after* ovulation, one could confirm via progesterone levels that one had ovulated.

This confused me. I thought if a woman had a period, she'd for sure ovulated. Apparently not. Google informed me that ovulation causes a woman to produce higher levels of progesterone.

High progesterone = you ovulated.

Low progesterone = you didn't.

I ordered a box of fifty.

This wasn't the first palm-size device I'd used during a pregnancy. Years earlier, twenty weeks pregnant with Finn, I'd been diagnosed with gestational diabetes and given a glucose monitor. I was to prick my finger one hour after every meal and log my blood sugar on a sheet of paper with 140 squares on it— one for every day left in the pregnancy.

We wanted my sugar to remain under 120. If it surpassed 120 a full hour after I'd eaten, I might have to go on insulin.

Lucas and I had been sent to meet with a nutritionist who stressed to me the importance of eating protein every time I consumed carbs, and of limiting my sugar intake. I'd absorbed her every word, terrified of doing something that could hurt the baby.

Every day for 140 days, I ate dutifully: eggs and oatmeal for breakfast. A salad with protein for lunch. A dinner to make the nutritionist swoon—look at that palm-size portion of protein, those fists of starches flanked by piles of green!

I'd show up to my weekly appointment at the diabetes clinic with a chart peppered with numbers in the hundred-teens: 117, 116, 119.

"Wow," my friend said when I told her. "It turned you into, like, the best anorexic ever."

She wasn't wrong. My obsession with controlling food and my inability to do so had tormented me for years. Suddenly, with someone other than myself to care for, I was *acing* gestational diabetes. At the clinic, they'd pat me on the back and tell me to keep it up.

And so when Finn's blood sugar dropped the first night in the hospital, my fear that I'd already failed as a mother was not just because I felt vaguely like I should have sensed his needs. I'd stopped tracking, and it had almost killed him before he'd been alive even a day.

Now, years later, I was back to it: obsessively tracking.

The new wands for my new device would accompany the slew of pregnancy tests I was already taking as every period approached. This amounted to three weeks out of four that I was now peeing on some kind of stick in the morning—75% of the month.

The little device took sixteen minutes to register a result, no matter which breed of wand I used, so every morning as we had breakfast, it sat next to us on the kitchen counter ticking down to a loud BEEP!, which told me it was time to check my phone app.

BEEP! It's time to have sex.

BEEP! You did, in fact, ovulate.

BEEP! Now we wait.

17

ART

IT WAS DECEMBER 14ᵀᴴ, eleven days since I'd ovulated.

I wasn't testing positive on a pregnancy test yet, but my progesterone wasn't going down—it was hovering at the "high" mark of 15 ng/ml, exactly how the Internet had described it would if I was pregnant. (If you're not pregnant, your progesterone falls after a couple of days.)

This struck me as a sneaky way to use the progesterone wands as a kind of homespun, *extra* early pregnancy test. The most sensitive at-home tests could detect pregnancy as soon as ten days after ovulation, which, in my case, met the "6 days before your missed period!" claim on the box. But this was even earlier.

Was I…a genius?

I felt like a sneaky, brilliant bastard, like I'd just gotten in on the shorting of GameStop. Had other people figured this out? A quick Google search didn't produce any results…maybe because the wands were so new.

The next day, day twelve, I was still at 15.0 ng/ml.

Day thirteen: 15.0 ng/ml.

Day fourteen: 15.0 ng/ml.

Suspicious, the plateauing. Then it hit me: Last pregnancy, when I'd gone in for labs, my progesterone had been 18 ng/ml. Was it possible that my new tracker just didn't go that high, that it was maxing out at fifteen?

I messaged customer service.

Hi Customer Service Team,

I'm writing to ask if the analyzer caps out at a progesterone level of 15 ng/ml, because I have tested at exactly 15.0 ng/ml every day for 6 days, and that seems unlikely given that, on other days, I'd had more precise measurements (5.3, 9.2, and 10.6 for example). It seems like the analyzer is reporting 15.0 when my progesterone level could actually be higher. Could you please confirm?

But, three days later, before anyone at the company had gotten back to me, I woke up to bleeding.

I wasn't surprised. The day before, my progesterone had started to drop, finally.

And then came their response:

Sorry, Mary. We had to track down someone who knew. The engineers confirmed that 15.0 is the highest the analyzer will register. Hope this clarifies.

I read the message with a tinge of self-satisfaction—I'd uncovered a feature of the tracker even its staff didn't know about! Did that make me clever, or just crazy?

Gearing up for the next cycle, since time was now measured by my menstrual calendar, I checked my next ovulation date: December 29th.

Ah. Great.

We'd be at the beach with my parents and sister's family for the holidays, crammed into a rental house with thin walls, almost certainly sharing a bathroom.

"You know what that will mean," I said to Emily.

"Muffled, timed sex a few feet from your dad in the next room?" she said.

"Bingo."

The next day, a crisp and bright December morning in Nashville, my friend Jackie and I were walking her dog when she asked, "Do you want to throw paint?"

An entrepreneur, she explained a business idea she was exploring. A customer would get to throw paint at a wall, not to make art, but as a kind of therapeutic experience. She had set up her garage as a test site and needed a guinea pig. All I had to do was show up in clothes I didn't care about ruining. She'd leave me alone in the room with a giant canvas and a bunch of paint to sling, and, afterward, I'd share my thoughts.

"Sure," I said, the most excited I'd been about anything in months. I'd recently googled *rage rooms in Nashville* out of curiosity, wanting to hammer a VCR or rip open a stuffed animal, and had been disappointed to discover that the only one had shuttered its doors during the pandemic.

"Are you sure?" she asked. "No pressure."

"I cannot even tell you how sure I am," I said.

On a Friday morning, after dropping Finn at school, I put on my oldest pajamas and two single socks that had lost their match and drove past twinkly lights and bow-weary wreaths to Jackie's.

"Come in!" she called from the garage. All four walls had been draped in sheets, so that I had to pull one aside to enter. She stood before a giant white canvas attached to the back wall. A blue tarp covered the floor. Along the right side of the garage, eight cans of fresh paint sat behind eight clean brushes. Jackie held out what looked like a cheap astronaut costume.

"I got you this painter's suit if you want to wear it," she said.

"Absolutely," I said, zipping it on and pulling up the hood. We laughed and took a "before" photo.

"I left you a brush for each color," she said. "Don't be afraid of making a mess. That's the point."

I nodded.

She told me she was going to walk her dogs, and I would be entirely alone. "Take as long as you need," she said. And then she left.

The quiet was a little much, and I wondered if I should get my headphones out of my bag to listen to music. But Jackie hadn't mentioned that option as part of the business plan, and I was the guinea pig.

I'd just start then.

I picked up the brush in front of the orange paint, dipped it, and flung. A tiny storm of orange no bigger than my foot sprung onto the wall.

I stepped back. The giant canvas was the size of a VW van, my effort a few measly specks in the bottom right quadrant.

This was going to take more effort than I thought. The Jackson Pollock paintings I'd stood before in museums over the years suddenly seemed more impressive, simply for the physicality required.

I flung the orange more, careful to target different sections of the canvas until the majority of it had a nice, even spattering of bright blobs. I stood back from my work, pleased. It looked pretty nice! And I wasn't even an artist! Go me!

Mary, said a voice in my head, *you're missing the point.*

Gah. Jackie had been very clear; the point was not to make art. The canvas would be destroyed or re-used afterward. The point was to release emotion.

Release emotion, I thought. What color matched my emotion?

Using the edge of the can, I carefully wiped the excess paint off the brush and set it down on the tarp, then picked up a new brush.

I flung. A little jolt of something popped in my chest—oof. That felt good. I liked the black paint.

I dipped again and wound back my arm, slinging the hardest I had yet. The black spray looked mean against the happy orange behind it, and I wanted more of that. I heaved and lobbed and flung, feeling like a baseball pitcher, but what was on the canvas still wasn't matching my insides.

My brain wanted to paint *something.* I couldn't just sling paint and feel something about it.

I need a goal, it said over and over.

Your goal is to express your emotions, I said back.

But I don't know what I'm feeling, it said.

I took a deep breath.

Okay, self, I decided, *you get a task. Paint this year. Paint the year you just had.*

And my brain unleashed.

I stopped being cute. I hurled paint so hard that my shoulder ached, and I did it again and again, and when the tears came, and I couldn't throw anymore, not because my arm hurt, although it did, but because splatters weren't doing it for me anymore—my year had not been splatters or evenly spaced, or what was expected of me—I lunged at the canvas and slammed the brush into it.

Fuck this year.

I lunged again, ramming my brush against the wall, beating the paint.

Fuck. This. Year.

Why did this happen to me? Why was I having to feel this way? It wasn't fair. I didn't want to be smearing black paint all over Jackie's garage. I wanted to be in my third trimester with my baby due February 10th. I was dreading February 10th, less than three months away. I would not be at a hospital giving birth. I would be home, feeling purposeless and sad, and it would suck, because I couldn't fill the hole, and I didn't get to decide when the hole filled.

It isn't fair.

This isn't fair.

It hurts.

I didn't even get to meet them! I thought as I pounded the wall, scooping out paint in goops and slathering it across the canvas until I was done, breathing hard, wiped out.

I couldn't wipe my cheeks with my hands because they were covered in paint, so I didn't.

I carefully opened the door with two fingers and called for Jackie, my tears only partly dry.

She appeared, a big smile on her face.

"How was it?" she asked.

"How long was that?" I asked, disoriented. It could have been ten minutes or an hour, I had no idea.

"About forty-five minutes," she said.

"It was good," I said, recovering my composure. "Pretty intense."

"Do you mind if I look?" She still stood on the other side of the sheet that hid the canvas.

I gestured for her to go ahead, then followed her inside the makeshift tent.

The canvas was a disaster, chaos, nothing artful about it. But unmistakably, staring back at us through the muck, were two circles, one large, one small. They touched, forming the abstract shape of a swaddled baby.

18

RISING AND FALLING

"DO YOU WANT SOME of my starter?" my friend Lexi asked.

At our feet, our two toddler boys rammed trucks into each other. Before me was a cheese board with warm, homemade bread that I couldn't stop eating. It was moist and crunchy with a tinge of sourness—I liked it even more by itself than with the cheese and had told her so.

"I don't know what a 'starter' is," I confessed. Early in the pandemic, when I'd stumbled on posts about "sourdough starters," I had scrolled past, utterly uninterested in what appeared to be a massive amount of work in order to make tangy bread. I'd gradually pieced together that it was a jar of bacteria…and then I *really* had no interest.

Lexi stood, walked over to her counter, and picked up a jar full of something spongey and beige.

"This is a starter," she said. "I've had mine for two years." She explained that she could spoon a clump of the beige mess into another jar and *voila*—it would become *my* starter. "Then you just feed it every day until you're ready to bake bread. It's no harder than owning a plant."

Right, a plant.

I'd never had a green thumb, but that hadn't stopped me from trying. Our house in Nashville, like our apartment in Queens, was speckled with orchids that hadn't bloomed in years alongside other plants that, while alive, clearly weren't thriving, and not for neglect.

One of these was a ZZ plant my sister had sent me after my first miscarriage.

Water every 2 to 3 weeks, the instruction card had read. *Allow to dry out between waterings.*

This was hard for me. When it came to plants, I was always convinced more water was needed, as if even the succulents were, like me, suffering an unquenchable thirst.

"You're over-watering," my plant-whisperer friend Jeremy had told me again and again over the years. "You have to let them dry out."

It was so hard for me to imagine over-watering a plant. They were a mirror, and we were bottomless.

So plant after plant yellowed and cowered in my care, and it was embarrassing and disappointing and made me feel like a child disguised as a grownup.

I'd even written a poem about it during the pandemic, two years before I'd ever miscarried:

I have killed my basil plant
after I killed the first one.
Drowned them in their nests,
drenching all three of us
in fatal tap water.
How easy it is to kill.
How much easier when

it's the one thing, the only thing,
between you.

When I stumbled on it after my second miscarriage, I found it eerily prescient, especially "the three of us." *Who is the three of us?* I wondered, then decided I must have meant the two basil plants.

How easy it is to kill.

In the wake of my second miscarriage, the stakes of being a plant owner suddenly felt much higher. Letting a plant die felt too symbolic, a metaphor for my inability to sustain a life that left me feeling frantic and helpless.

The fiddle leaf tree in the living room had been sagging since I'd bought it, and I recalled hearing that some fiddle leaf plants like to take showers, so I began hauling it upstairs to my bathroom for a regular wash.

"Can I...take a shower? Or is the tree not finished yet?" Lucas said more than once.

I poked at the ZZ plant's soil daily to check for moisture, sweating whether I could trust my judgment. Fortunately, it appeared to be doing fine...for now.

"Feed it..." I echoed Lexi.

"Equal parts flour and water," she said. "Here." She went to her bookshelf, pulled down a hardback with a crusty loaf on the cover, and let it fall open to a well-read page in the middle. "The recipe starts here...and goes to..." She flipped two pages, four pages, six more, and then stopped. "You want to borrow it or just take photos of the pages?"

A multi-page recipe?

Before I knew it, I was photographing pages nine to twenty-two of a bread-baking book—single-spaced. A *fourteen-page, single-spaced* recipe.

As I positioned the book in my camera frame, I thought, *Am I actually going to read this, then do it?*

A little while later, I left her house with my jar of yeast and bacteria, along with instructions to feed it at least once every twenty-four hours, ideally twice, and not to let it get "hoppy."

I'd nodded, wondering what "hoppy" meant—wasn't that how people talked about beer?

At home, I set the jar on my counter and stared at it.

The beige stuff inside looked like it was gurgling. Lexi had just "fed" it that morning.

Was it hungry now?

It had been at least ten hours, if she'd fed it that morning, so it probably was.

Don't kill it, Mary, I thought.

I measured out one-fourth cup of the beigey stuff, one-fourth cup of water, and one-fourth cup of flour. I stirred and set the jar by the stove.

Throughout the afternoon, I peeked at it. It looked a little taller, maybe?

By evening, I'd put Finn down and was pouring myself a glass of wine when I glanced over and couldn't believe my eyes—it had doubled in size. The goo was full of holes and was nearly grazing the lid resting on top of the jar.

I'd done it! I'd grown my starter!

Why I was growing a starter, and what it was supposed to do for bread, I still didn't understand. But one step at a time.

First, I had to keep it alive.

"Look!" I held the jar up to Lucas, beaming.

"Is that good?" he asked.

"Absolutely," I said, as if I had any idea. That it had worked the way it was supposed to felt miraculous.

"Should I feed it again before bed?"

Lucas shrugged. "What did Lexi say to do?"

"Feed it at least once a day, ideally twice."

"*Twice* a day?" he said. "It's more like a pet."

I was already hand-washing the measuring cup so I could feed it before bed.

Lexi had tied twine around the jar so I could measure how much it rose and fell.

The next morning, I found the goo at the same level I'd left it the night before, but from streaks along the sides of the jar, I could tell that it had risen and sunk. This made sense: If it had doubled in size in about six hours the day before, it had risen, then fallen, as Lexi had told me it would, in nine.

Holy smokes, I had a starter, and it was alive.

Making coffee in my pajamas, I kept stealing glances at it, inordinately pleased with myself.

Now, how did I make *bread*?

I opened the book photos on my phone and navigated to the first of the fourteen recipe photos, zoomed in.

Making bread with natural leaven can be divided into three basic stages...

Leaven? What was *leaven*, other than a term I vaguely remembered from the Bible?

I grabbed my glasses and headed to the couch.

Here went nothing.

"Well?" I asked, watching my brother-in-law chew a chunk of warm crust.

We were at a beach rental on the Gulf, the three of us, along with my parents and my sister's family. In the ten days since Lexi had given me her starter, I'd transformed from a person who didn't know what a starter even was to a sourdough maniac.

I could. Not. Stop. Baking. Bread.

First, I loved the rise and fall of the starter—the fact that if I fed it, it would rise, was immensely satisfying. Every day, I measured what it needed, then watched it thrive, billowing above the string of twine.

Next, there was the breadmaking, for which the fourteen-page recipe turned out to be very helpful. I'd incorporate the starter into the flour and water, then set it aside to let it rise not once, but twice.

The rising was where the magic happened. It was up to factors beyond my control but made possible by circumstances I created: the yeast itself and how active it had become, invisible to my eye; the temperature and humidity of the spot where I left the dough; the length of time I allowed the dough to rest.

Finally, there was the rise in the oven. The scoring—slicing an indent into the top of the dough to allow it to expand while baking—revealed how much life I'd captured inside the loaf. If I scored an X that barely cracked open, the loaf may be edible, but it tended to have a dense, heavy texture rather than the light and airy interior that bread dreams are made of. A bursting X, however, was heavenly.

I had baked at least twelve loaves in the ten days since getting my starter, thinking, *alright, pandemic bakers, I'm late to the party, but I get it now.*

I'd also driven to Florida—nine hours—with the starter at my feet in a soft cooler, like, indeed, a pet.

Now I was baking loaves for my extended family.

"It's amazing," my brother-in-law said.

I beamed.

"Tomorrow, I'll make a fresh loaf for dinner," I said, as if I were an 1800s farm mother who'd been doing this for decades, not a woman whose friends had made her an apron for her bachelorette party that said, "I wear this when I apply heat to food."

It was the day before New Year's Eve, the last day of a year that I'd spent mostly pregnant with nothing to show for it. It felt like a dead end, a firework that petered out before ever exploding.

But I had the bread.

The next morning, while people groggily poured cups of coffee and snuck back to their rooms for a few more minutes of quiet, I weighed cups of flour and warm water on the kitchen scale I'd brought from home, assessed the humidity of the microwave versus the stove while turned off, and speculated on the heat retentiveness of the rental's plastic and glass bowls.

That evening, the last day of 2021, the whole family trekked down to the foggy beach to watch the fireworks. It was early evening but late for children, nine o'clock, and Finn and his cousins were excited for the show.

Pop! Pop, pop!

The explosions began—we could hear them—but the sky before us remained a smoky black. Every pop was as loud as if it were mere yards away, but I couldn't make out even a faint hint of light in the dark expanse before us.

"The fog is too thick," Lucas observed as we stared into the empty sky, hoping the fog might lift, or a particularly bright firework might pierce its veil.

After a few minutes, we gave up and made our way back up the pier and down the road to our house, where my brother-in-law lit sparklers for the kids on the porch. Inside, I was cleaning up from dinner when Finn came running in, wailing, his hand outstretched. He'd been burnt by the sparkler.

"I touched fire, and it feels me sad!" he cried, crashing into my legs.

I kissed his burnt thumb and gave him ice, then watched as his burn turned from red to white, bubbling up from his tiny finger.

I touched fire, and it feels me sad.

Why did those words seem to capture so much, so well? If I'd never gotten pregnant in Mexico at all—if I'd never touched the fire—where would I be now?

And yet I couldn't, and wouldn't, have made any other choice. Imagining an alternate history made me think of Eve, whom I'd always loved—another Bible story where my interpretation had diverged from my Sunday school teacher's.

God had named a tree "The Tree of Knowledge" and expected her *not* to eat from it? She'd just wanted to know the truth, and she'd gotten it and been vilified for the rest of time.

I was terrified of another miscarriage and devastated by my year, and yet it had been the most real, the most alive, I'd ever felt, apart from giving birth to Finn. The opposite of numbed scrolling or making a chart of wellness goals. I was touching fire, and I would touch it again and again, even if it made me sad, even if it burned me.

That night, stationed around the living room on sofas and chairs, everyone but my sister and me fell asleep by 9:30 p.m. My parents eventually dragged themselves to bed. Our husbands snored across the room.

My sister joined me on the same couch, like we had when we were kids. Her head rested on my shoulder, both of us sharing a crochet throw. She held the remote, like she always did. It didn't matter that she was the younger sibling by four years. My sister had assumed the driver's seat since she was old enough to, and I welcomed it. Cars, remotes—she was our captain.

She'd even gone first as a mom. When my nephew Jackson had been born six years earlier, I'd stared at him in the hospital room, in awe. I hadn't expected becoming an aunt to be the best day of my life up to that point, but it was. I hadn't known that to witness human birth is to witness a miracle.

Looking at his tiny face, I imagined his life, played out: He would fall in love, he would hurt, he would wonder, he would feel alone and afraid, he would want a place to belong, he would experience joy.

When I left the hospital for the night, I wrote him a letter. It was didactic and earnest and too annoying to actually ever give him, and I used the word "kind" a lot and talked about how the popular kids always peak in high school.

But as my final point, I wrote this:

You have done nothing wrong. You are not inherently sinful, or guilty, or disposed to some evil temptation or traits for which you must constantly struggle and seek penance or forgiveness. You are a human being, Jackson; you are going to make decisions you regret, and you are going to hurt others whether you mean to or not, and sometimes you will mean to. You are going to disappoint your parents and yourself and you're going to be ashamed, and for all the times that you are proud and joyful and feel loved and adored, these darker moments are going to cut through it all like banana in a smoothie. But these don't make you flawed or bad. They make you a person. Forgive yourself as many times as it takes. You are a miracle.

I'd believed it from the moment he was born—that he was a miracle.

If he was a miracle who should see himself that way, was I, too? It wasn't a question I even asked.

Now, my sister flipped back and forth between New Year's shows: Miley Cyrus's in Nashville, Dick Clark's in Times Square.

There was no way we were going to make it to midnight.

"Where is it almost midnight?" my sister wondered aloud, casting for a countdown that we could follow live, on TV or online. "Oh, I know—Puerto Rico!" One of the New Year's specials on TV was in Puerto Rico.

As it approached 10 p.m. Central Time—midnight in Puerto Rico—the beautiful woman on the screen hyped up the crowd for the countdown. The two of us raised our plastic champagne flutes.

"Ten!" she began, and we joined in. "Nine! Eight! Seven! Six! Five!"

The counting stopped. The screen fizzled out, and when the picture turned, she was gone. In her place, a white man in a gray suit stood before a weather map, looking far from enthused.

"Justin Smith here with the weather report..."

The local news had interceded our countdown before it even hit four.

"Well, couldn't ask for a more fitting end to this fucking year, huh?" I said. We laughed.

We ended the year without a countdown, but at least we were laughing about it.

"Love you," I said as I went downstairs to bed, leaving her sitting in front of a jigsaw puzzle, still awake.

"Love you too," she said.

In the darkest corner of the kitchen, my starter was rising.

PART III

STILL

19

HEARTBEATS

EARLY FEBRUARY IN NASHVILLE is like stepping into a Land's End catalogue, everyone in shiny boots and thin cardigans. It's rare for breath to cloud, and the occasional snow flurry or ice storm wreaks havoc on traffic flow.

After living in New York for fifteen years, where I would have sold my soul for a few degrees by Valentine's Day, I found Nashville's mild winters quaint, barely noticeable.

Comfortable in a light sweater and just over seven weeks pregnant for the third time in nine months, I sat, content, on a couch in the lobby of my OB's office as Lucas entered, flustered. He'd meant to be there in time for the ultrasound but had accidentally gone to the wrong location. Between the multiple pregnancies, doctor's offices, and remote radiology labs, it was easy to get confused. We'd been to many.

I waved cheerfully at him.

"Heart rate is 135," I said to Lucas, joyous to be offering happy news for once. "I'm just waiting to be called back for bloodwork."

This pregnancy felt utterly different from the last. I'd not lapsed into the same frantic tracking, having taken only a handful of pregnancy tests. (I'd even managed not to buy out Target this time!)

It wasn't only that I didn't think I was special enough to fall into the one percent of women who have three miscarriages or more.

No, this difference was more elemental: I *felt* pregnant, like there was someone in there other than me. It escaped me then, but doesn't now, that the pregnancy in which there'd only been a sac and no fetus was the one during which I'd been anxious from the beginning. This time, there *was* somebody, and my body sensed it.

And the latest ultrasound had just confirmed it, along with two earlier sonograms, all of which had shown us a heartbeat in the "normal" range.

At the end of January, I'd spent a week in New York for a short teaching gig, and when a blizzard shut down the city two days into my trip, I'd spent three days stuck in my hotel room alone.

But I hadn't felt alone. I'd felt an inarticulate companionship, as not-lonely as if I'd been with Lucas or Finn. My friend Haley had once speculated that the loneliness of miscarriage was easy to explain: One went from not being alone to being alone.

"Because you had the baby with you before, so you weren't alone," she'd said.

I'd found this poetic and lovely in theory but unrelatable at the time. Now, I felt it.

Plus, my friend Greg described the roller coaster of fertility as *Groundhog Day.* You think you've steeled yourself against disappointment once you've been sidelined by it, but the amnesia is real. One hopes despite oneself.

It wasn't rational that I was so full of hope that winter. But I was.

Around us, the room was full of women at various stages of pregnancy. Finally, I wasn't quietly resenting them and hating myself for it. Finally, I got to be one of the smiling ones in the room.

My phone buzzed with a text. Photos of my ultrasound, sent from the office.

I opened the familiar, black and white, grainy images.

One was a video. I clicked "play" and watched the baby's heart flickering. The bottom of the screen read: *135 bpm.*

I sent it to my mom and sister.

Baby looks great! I wrote with a smiley face.

They sent back trails of happy emojis, and my mom asked how I felt about a baby shower in April.

The Super Bowl was coming up, and my neighbor—the woman who'd told me she was pregnant eight months earlier and I'd responded with "I'm miscarrying"—asked if I wanted to watch it with her. Eminem was performing in the halftime show, and we were both mega fans. (I didn't admit that I didn't even know who was playing in the game itself.) She was due in a few weeks.

On Super Bowl Sunday, I made a taco bar and put Finn to bed, then Lucas, my neighbor, and I lined up on our kitchen stools with the game on my laptop, which I'd set up on the counter.

During the halftime show, we were singing along to Kendrick Lamar and Mary J. Blige. Lucas was drinking wine, and my neighbor had brought over O'Doul's nonalcoholic beer for her and me, which I'd never had and found surprisingly good.

"When are you due again?" Lucas asked at one point, and we all laughed.

"Be more specific," I said. "Everyone here but you is pregnant."

Suddenly, a sharp pain shot through my abdomen, sharp enough that I snapped erect, and my hand leapt to my belly.

"Oof," I said.

"Are you okay?" my friend asked.

"Yeah, just a cramp," I said. *Laughing hard and sitting on a stool for hours while pregnant*, I thought.

Our next checkup was in two days—two weeks after our last, which had gone swimmingly.

The next day, for seemingly no reason, I decided I wanted to try again to find a memoir about miscarriage.

I poked around online until I came upon Emma Hansen's memoir *Still*, which wasn't about miscarriage but stillbirth: Hansen gave birth to her deceased son Reid at 39 weeks 6 days.

I downloaded it and read it in a sitting, sobbing my way through it, enchanted by the parts where her departed son visits her and her family in dreams.

When I recommended it to Kate within minutes of finishing, she asked, puzzled, "And why are you reading this particular book right now?"

She was right; it was an odd choice for a time when I was working hard to remain optimistic, to keep pregnancy anxiety at bay.

I told her I didn't know.

"No more feeeeeear, no more paaaaaain!"

I sang along with Mary J. Blige as I made my way through morning rush-hour traffic. As usual, Lucas was going to meet me at the appointment; he was dropping Finn off at school first.

Since the Super Bowl halftime show two days earlier, I'd been playing her on repeat.

As I dumped the cup of decaf I'd poured myself earlier, too nauseous to drink it, I briefly imagined how I'd feel if the ultrasound went badly. Standing over the sink, I laughed aloud. A cackle.

Punked. That's how I'd feel, I thought.

It was all looking beautiful, unlike the previous two pregnancies: I'd had my hCG levels assessed three times—check, check, check.

At the sonograms, the gestational age (size of the fetus) had been right on track: check, check, check.

Given all of this, my odds of miscarrying, according to the most conservative sources I could find, seemed to fall between 6 and 11 percent, possibly lower if I factored in my nausea.

As Melissa, the nurse I'd been conversing with for months, performed my intake, it was clear that she, too, was feeling optimistic.

"I'm so happy for you, girl," she said, pulling out the same print-out of the yearly calendar she'd marked up for me three months earlier—the one I'd left sitting on the counter in the patient room months earlier during miscarriage number two. I watched as, once again, she highlighted the second week of each of the next seven months, this time with a purple highlighter—March through September.

This time I'll get to make my appointments, I thought.

Melissa was very pregnant—at least twenty weeks, I thought, eyeing her large belly. I didn't feel envious. I was in the club too.

Everything was the same: We were escorted to an identical room; Lucas sat in the same chair in the corner. I shed my jeans and underwear and perched myself on the table under a paper sheet. But it all felt different, because this time, it would be okay, like we'd erased the slate and were rewriting a happier ending.

A knock on the door.

"Hi," a woman in scrubs said. "I'm a physician's assistant. Dr. Morrow is delivering a baby, so I'll be doing your ultrasound today."

Lucas, accustomed to how this worked, moved to stand on my left.

She inserted the wand, and after a few seconds, we all saw a sac, and in that sac, a blob, notably larger than it had been weeks earlier.

But we were all silent. Because the blob wasn't moving.

"Hmm," she muttered. "Let me, hmm... Let's... Where..." She made the sounds of someone who didn't trust her skills with the equipment, but every direction she turned the wand, the blob was still. No flicker, no life.

"How sure are you about your period date?" she asked.

"Sure," I said as I felt Lucas's hand on my leg.

His touch made it real.

It was happening again.

It was happening again.

It was happening *again*.

"I really thought it was going to be okay this time," I mumbled.

"I want you to get an official ultrasound across the hall," she said. "I'm not a technician and so I'm, you know, not skilled enough to trust what I'm seeing for sure, but..." She paused, then went on. "I'm pretty sure there's no heartbeat."

"Wouldn't we hear it if there was?" Lucas asked.

"Well, no," she said, launching into a long, nervous, technical explanation of how she would have to zoom in and go into M-mode and hit this button, then that button, for us to hear anything.

"I was so hopeful this time," I whispered again when she finished talking. I hadn't budged.

"This has happened before?" she asked.

"In October. And in...July," I said, taking a second to remember which month.

Later, on the drive home, I'd recall how her face pinched hearing my words, like someone was pulling a drawstring on her features, and I'd think: *Oh yeah, I guess three miscarriages in nine months really is that sad.*

The official scan across the hall confirmed it. Our baby measured 8 weeks 5 days when the heart stopped beating.

The day before.

The moment watching the Super Bowl when I'd laughed and felt the sharp pain—had that been it? Could laughing kill?

By the time we finished the second ultrasound, Dr. Morrow had finished delivering someone else's baby and was able to meet with us.

Lucas and I sat in silence, waiting. I still hadn't shed a tear but stared into space, feeling floaty and untethered.

What was real?

"This is fucking brutal," Lucas said, dropping his face in his hands.

"Yes," I said. Correct. Fucked and brutal.

The door opened and Melissa entered, her arms opening.

"Girl," she said as she wrapped them around me.

My tears came then, with her pressing her warm, pregnant belly against my own. My fetus, at 8 weeks 5 days, was no longer alive.

Dr. Morrow came in.

"I'm so sorry," she said, taking a seat. "I think this time we do a D&C. This way, we can collect a good sample and see what's going on." She explained that we'd make an appointment at the hospital for surgery to be performed under general anesthesia. Then, we'd send off the fetus to be tested, figure out what went wrong.

My gaze drifted to Lucas's face—it was stricken.

"What do you think I should do?" I asked him.

"It's up to you," he said, but his eyes were dancing, full of alarm.

"Okay," I said to Dr. Morrow.

She nodded. "I'll see if we can get you in on Friday. Once the results are back, we'll make you a pre-conception appointment with a high-risk specialist," she said.

For the first time in a year, the word *conception* left a bitter taste in my mouth.

After the previous two miscarriages, I'd been desperate to get pregnant again; if I'd been given the option to start trying again the next day, I'd have said, "Hell, yes."

But now, the idea of trying again, of even getting pregnant again, sounded almost...destructive.

Again, I left the calendar of highlighted dates on the counter.

Again, I walked out with the gray envelope. But I didn't open it this time. It would sit on my kitchen counter, unopened, for weeks.

Lucas and I hugged in the parking lot, and he asked if I was okay to be alone. I assured him I was, then climbed into the driver's seat, where I drafted a message that I started to send to my friend group text, but the idea of "reply all" condolences stopped me. I deleted it and picked one person at a time.

Hey, I don't know why I want to text you all separately about this but I'm miscarrying again. I'm sad but okay.

Copied and pasted, copied and pasted.

When I turned on my car, "No More Drama" started to play where it had left off, the words jumping out at me in a way they hadn't before:

Broken heart again
Another lesson learned...
Why'd I play the fool?

I did feel like a fool.

The other times, I'd felt angry, betrayed, crushed. This time, I felt foolish.

Back at home, I noticed the memoir *Still* resting on the armchair, the spine curved from my fast read.

Had my body known? Had that been why I'd bizarrely found my way to it and devoured it, just as my own baby's heart was stopping inside me?

20

THE END

"IT LOOKS LIKE WE CAN SCHEDULE your surgery for Friday," said the hospital clerk over the phone. "Do you have a few minutes to answer your pre-surgery questions with me?"

"Oh, I can't do Friday, actually," I said. "I have a work thing."

"Then it will probably be Wednesday of next week," she said. Crap.

Wednesday, Lucas was taking his board exam—a genetics licensure test for which he'd been studying for months. It was critical he pass it; his new job required it.

"I can't do Wednesday," I said. "I'm sorry."

"Let me see if I can get you in Monday or Tuesday," she said. "I'll call you back."

I hung up, feeling a little guilty about turning down Friday. It was true—I was teaching a class on Friday.

But also, Friday was so soon.

If, during my first miscarriage, I'd been desperate to purge myself of the baby and placenta and during my second I'd been less so, this time, I was downright reluctant.

I knew that the baby no longer had a heartbeat, but I was so aware of its presence that, more than once, I wondered if the techs (both of them) had made a mistake, or if, somehow, its heart had started back up again. I knew it was irrational. But part of me wondered if we'd show up for surgery only to learn that, miraculously, the baby was well again.

Sitting on my couch after hanging up with the surgery scheduler, I recognized that this wasn't actually possible. I thought about how I was still pregnant, just pregnant with death. When I pictured myself escorting a tiny spirit out of this world, just as I'd begun to escort it in, the fact of miscarrying felt more active, less like something happening *to* me and more a responsibility that I held, a role that hadn't ended yet. I found I wanted to perform it gently, perform it well, as I would if a child were arriving. If I were giving birth, I would do so with love. Why shouldn't I show a departing life the same tenderness?

I knew what this felt like. I'd been here before; these trees were familiar.

I counted. Over the previous eight months, I'd spent as much time ushering life out of this world as I had ushering it in. And ushering out this life, this time, I felt no need to rush.

I didn't know I was afraid of you, I'd thought months earlier, during my first miscarriage. I hadn't known what to make of it at the time. Death had felt contagious and despairing, like I might catch it, a bad cold that ends in eternal shadow.

But since then, I'd lived with it, literally. I'd held it in my belly as my own heart pumped blood into it, believing the babies to still be alive. I'd nurtured death.

Perhaps that was why it no longer felt like a stranger or an enemy. It felt like the friend who currently understood me best.

My D&C was scheduled for Tuesday, five days after our appointment.

Over the coming days, I didn't alter my behavior in the way I normally would, resuming the substances and activities pregnant women are discouraged from doing. Just as I had when I'd believed the baby to be fine, I continued to refrain from caffeine and alcohol. I slept when I was tired, going to bed by eight. I didn't resume exercise, moving only if and when I felt like it.

My knowledge of the Jewish tradition of sitting shiva—the gathering of family to sit and mourn for seven days after someone's passing—was limited to what I'd gleaned over the years from friends and popular culture. But it didn't escape me, as I moved through those slow days, that there were seven, total, this baby I spent together after its heart ceased to beat.

The night of my book launch for my first novel, my friend Kate had interviewed me in front of forty or fifty people—friends, family, and strangers. Kate and I sat on stools holding mics and copies of my novel in our laps. Finn was ten months old. He was back at the hotel, sleeping, with a babysitter.

Someone asked a question about my writing process and how it had changed since having a kid. I started to answer by saying, "When Finn died…"

I stopped. Everyone laughed uncomfortably, including me.

"Whoa," I said. "That was weird. Um, when Finn was born…"

I don't remember the rest of my answer. But in remembering a birth, my brain had instead jumped to death, as if they weren't all that different, as if they were, in some sense, the same thing.

In "Master and Man," the short story I'd read the day of my first miscarriage and that I thought about as I faced my own seemingly endless, solitary night awaiting a death, the selfish master realizes that his servant, too, is going to die. In an uncharacteristic act of compassion, he blankets the man's body with his own, and, as he dies, feels love for the first time. The servant survives as a result, awakening in the daylight under the heat of his master's corpse. Death and love are one.

I'd thought of that story often since, and with death inside me, I did once again. As I quizzed Lucas each of those seven nights, reading flashcard after flashcard aloud, I kept one hand on my belly and wished nothing away.

Instructions for a D&C, as issued by the hospital:

Wash with Dial soap (anti-bacterial) both the night before and morning of
Sleep on clean sheets
No lotions, creams, or scented anything
Remove all jewelry
No nail polish on at least one finger so oxygen level can be monitored
No eating after 11 the night before
No drinking alcohol, or taking any meds or supplements, 72 hours prior to surgery
Morning of, you may brush your teeth, but be sure to spit out all the toothpaste

I woke up at 6 a.m., climbed into the shower, and unwrapped the bar of Dial soap I'd purchased days earlier, having felt too tired to shower with it the night before—or to change my sheets.

Downstairs, I found Finn at his small table eating Cheerios and watching *Peppa Pig*, and Lucas on the couch glued to his flashcard deck. His board exam was the next day.

A D&C and a board exam—what a twofer.

I wasn't allowed any coffee, and there was time to kill, so I went to the kitchen and started to load the dishwasher.

Throughout the previous nine months, there had been so many moments where I'd outsourced my understanding of what was happening in my body to a machine: Instead of asking *what do*

I feel?, I'd google. Instead of noticing my body's sensations—whether it was panic, nausea, or achiness—I took another pregnancy test, peed on a fertility wand, checked a forum online, scheduled a blood test. Machines, machines, machines, all created to help me diagnose what was happening in my body, but still just *machines*. They weren't the body itself.

Repeatedly, these machines hadn't brought me any closer to the security I'd craved.

Sinking deeper and deeper into my quest to get pregnant, increasingly desperate for it as the losses piled up, I'd felt my own flesh and bones grow louder while working harder to find sources of assurance outside of them.

Perhaps the strangest example was my fertility tracking app, which included a calendar to track my cycle. It would highlight the days of my period based on what I reported; I manually clicked on the days I bled. Bright checkmarks appeared.

But one day, I noticed the app would sometimes change my period dates.

"It adjusts your period to what it thinks your period would have been based on hormone levels," was the response I got when I reached out to the company about this.

But that wasn't my period, I thought. It was as if the real period didn't matter—what mattered was the hypothetical period created by statistical probability. Real period dates: gone. Science-based predictive dates: real. History is written by the apps.

By the morning of my D&C, I had been dwelling in the land of machines and statistics for so long that I didn't recognize at first that what I was feeling was panic.

After loading the dishwasher, I started to make Finn's lunch and, as I peeled a clementine, realized I was shaking. The fruit trembled in my hands.

Lucas, seated across the room, looked up at me from his notecards.

"Are you anxious?" he asked.

202 | MARY ADKINS

"Yes," I said quietly, adding no more.

"At least they don't have to cut you open," he said. "It'll be okay."

He looked back down at his cards.

And standing there, I dropped into a sinkhole. Lucas and Finn were still in this world, in our bright house, living an ordinary morning, and I was somewhere else entirely.

"Are you upset I'm reviewing flashcards?" Lucas asked, picking up on something wrong.

My chest exploded as I yelled, not just at him, but at myself, too, "THIS IS A BIG DEAL!" No, I wasn't going to be sliced open. But I was about to undergo general anesthesia so a surgeon could remove my miscarried fetus and placenta, the third this year.

As he stood and came over to me, I yelled it again, starting to sob.

"THIS IS A BIG DEAL!"

He hugged me.

"I feel so alone. I don't want to do this alone," I begged. "Please be in this with me."

"I'm sorry," he said. "I know it's a big deal. I was trying to distract myself too."

I could breathe again. The idea that he was truly regarding the day—the surgery—as insignificant was unbearably isolating, but trying to distract himself? That I could identify with.

We stood there for a long time. I cried. Miraculously, Finn remained transfixed by *Peppa Pig*, engrossed in whatever shenanigans were playing out on the screen. (The power of *Peppa*, man.)

By seven o'clock, we were pulling into Finn's school. Lucas usually dropped Finn off on his way to work, but today I wanted to walk him in.

He was the first one there. His teacher was alone in the classroom as he sprinted in, yelling, "Ms. Ashli, our mailbox fell down! We hit it with our car!"

This was half-true. A drunk driver had flattened it a few nights earlier.

Ms. Ashli and I laughed at his storytelling. It was weird to laugh on the way to my D&C.

As Finn hugged me goodbye, he said, "Have fun to work!"

My heart ached; I loved him so much.

At the hospital, only three blocks from his school, we parked, headed inside, and checked in at the registration desk.

"Take the elevator to the second-floor waiting room," the clerk told us.

We selected the vinyl couch farthest from the other patients, and Lucas put his arm around me. I rested my head on his shoulder.

"Here we are," he said.

"Here we are," I said.

Of all the moments that year, all the medical buildings we'd waited in, all the hard minutes we'd endured together, sitting with Lucas in that waiting room with my head on his shoulder is the one that I go back to. I had never felt more married. We were passing through fire together.

"Mary!"

A nurse called me back and escorted me to another floor, where I changed into a gown and was hooked up to an IV and a heart monitor. I was handed a plastic bag in which to stuff my clothing, my sweater and jeans and fake Uggs that were too big and flopped off my feet. As I slid my phone into one of the boots, the nurse stopped me.

"You can hold on to your phone for now," she said.

"Okay," I said, unsure why I'd need to keep it on me but obeying.

I lay on the cot, resting my phone next to me. I was freezing, my whole body shivering. Were hospitals always so cold? The nurse covered me with a sheet.

My phone buzzed, a text from Emily.

I love you and am holding your hand, she'd written. I squeezed my phone like it was her hand, another machine in place of a human. I closed my eyes.

"I'm Dr. Drake, your anesthesiologist," a woman in scrubs said, approaching with an outstretched hand to shake mine. "I'm sorry for your loss."

"Thank you." My voice cracked. I hoped no one else said that again. So far, I'd kept it together.

I was told that I'd be administered propofol, better known as the anesthetic that killed Michael Jackson. Was this meant as a fun fact patients were supposed to enjoy? Because it struck me as pretty dark…and also interesting enough that I was, indeed, distracted as I watched her prepare a shot.

"This will only pinch a little," she said.

"Mary?" I opened my eyes.

Above me, a clock on the wall that hadn't been there before. An hour had passed.

A new nurse stood over me, smiling kindly. This room was much larger. I was surrounded by people on cots.

"I know you told me you're O-negative," she said, "but we just need to confirm that in the lab before your RhoGAM shot."

My RhoGAM shot: what I'd come to believe, thanks to Google and a lot of time to develop a conspiracy theory, was the reason I kept miscarrying.

When a mother with Rh-negative blood has a child with Rh-positive blood, she must be given this particular shot twice: during the pregnancy, and also within seventy-two hours after giving birth (or having a D&C, apparently). The shot prevents her body from making antibodies toward the Rh-positive blood type, both for her current pregnancy and any future ones. If she isn't given the shot and *does* develop antibodies, her immune system could see the baby as a foreign object and attack it.

I'd known none of this at the time, but over the previous few months, desperate for an explanation for my recurrent miscarriages, I'd become convinced that I was never given a RhoGAM shot after having Finn in 2018. My labor and delivery were largely a blur, between the high drama and hurried administration of various drugs, plus the haze and fatigue, but I didn't remember receiving one. I planned to discuss this theory with my OB the next time I saw her. Perhaps my body was attacking these babies.

"It'll only take about forty-five minutes to run your bloodwork. You just lie here and relax," she said.

"Okay," I said.

I stared up at the ceiling, white and smooth. The clock ticked. Forty-five minutes passed. Fifty. Ninety.

This is no way to live.

Lucas had said the words months earlier after our car ride from Atlanta, and they played in my head now on repeat.

This is no way to live.

It wasn't working. What was I doing to my body and spirit, to Lucas's spirit, to Finn's spirit? I didn't want to look back on these years—these precious, fleeting years of Finn's late toddlerhood—and remember them as a period of fertility struggle, of obsession over timed intercourse and pregnancy tests and medical checkups. I was at my OB's office so often these days that it had begun to feel like my second home.

Even before the previous year, there were so many moments, so many times I'd been missing from my life because my brain had jumped ahead: enduring high school by planning to leave it; skipping nights of bowling with friends in college so that I could study to get into a good law school; worrying my way through law school over finding a great job. Even with my bulimia, it was true. The present was a necessary evil, to feed myself. The future was the key to undoing the wrong, to get rid of it. The solution to my insatiable hunger was always one hour ahead.

The morning after our wedding, in the airport awaiting our flight home, Lucas and I had sat on our computers, side by side, working. We were, each independently and as a couple, striving for a future we'd agreed to pursue: financial stability, new careers. Worthy goals. World-approved goals. That he was forward-looking was something I admired about him. I knew he admired it about me, too. Our relationship was built, in part, on our shared ambition.

But now, I looked back and wondered, *why were we working? Why weren't we basking?* It was our first day married.

And yet, of course, we were already focused on the next thing. I was a future dweller. It was how I'd always lived, and I didn't question it.

Until now.

Lying on that cot, staring at the ceiling, I knew I couldn't keep living in the future, always looking ahead, always waiting for or planning the next thing.

The tracker would go in the trash. The wands. The piles of tests.

This wasn't just about trying to get pregnant. I had to learn to be present in the life I had, in this family, in this body. Not in a fantasy family of four, or a fantasy body three sizes smaller.

After nearly two hours, I received my shot, completing the procedure. I was officially discharged. The nurse wheeled me down to the front entrance, where Lucas was idling in the car.

"How're you feeling?" he asked as I fastened my seat belt.

"Okay," I said. "I don't feel loopy at all. Or even sore." I was shocked, actually, by how little impact I felt, physically.

"Good," he said, and put the car in drive. But as he pulled away from the curb, my tears started up. He pulled over to hold me.

"We can't keep doing this," I said.

"I know," he said before I'd barely gotten the words out. "No more trackers."

I nodded. No more trackers.

As we drove, I tried to let it sink in. It crushed me, because it was hard not to think that what we might be giving up wasn't just trackers. It was a person. Our person.

21

STARS

THE NEXT DAY, LUCAS PASSED his board exam. Before we could even toast, we got word that Mary, his stepmother who lived in Atlanta, was in her final days of life. Hospice had arrived at their home.

Lucas's father was disabled, and Mary had been his caretaker. After she passed, Lucas's father would move to Oklahoma to live with Lucas's brother's family. But in the meantime, his father needed someone to care for him.

Quickly, we planned for Lucas to go to Atlanta to tend to his father at their home through Mary's final days, which she would also spend at home.

I understood he needed to go, and I wanted him to go. But the thought of being alone in our house with Finn lit me up with panic. A close childhood friend of mine had been murdered in her home when we were twenty-seven in an act so random and gruesome that it literally became a *20/20* episode, one that I nauseatingly made myself sit through when it aired. Ever since, I'd struggled to spend the night alone at home.

My panic would begin with a fantasy of what could happen once Lucas was gone—someone breaking in in the middle of the night—then my heart would race and I'd freeze, unable to contemplate anything but my terror.

But I didn't want to burden Lucas, who was facing a major loss.

"We'll be fine," I lied. "I promise."

The morning he left, my fantasizing about a break-in grew relentless, so I told my mom about it. She said she would come up to stay with Finn and me, but she had a doctor's appointment she couldn't skip. She insisted I book a hotel.

"Now isn't the time to challenge yourself in this way," she said. It was true that I was only thirty-six hours out of surgery. I still sobbed at every red light, had devoted seven hours to searching for the ideal piece of carry-on luggage, and still hadn't had a bowel movement. "Book a hotel," she said, "or I'm booking one for you."

I went on Orbitz and found one out by the airport where they were cheapest, and, after I picked Finn up from school, we stocked up on groceries and headed east.

"You get to stay in a hotel tonight with mama!" I said. *Also, tomorrow night and the next, and probably a few after that*, I did not say.

"Yay!" he cheered from the backseat.

In our room, Finn jumped on the bed while I opened a bottle of wine and FaceTimed my mom. I propped the phone up on a pillow so we could chat with her.

"What are you having for dinner?" she asked.

I looked around.

Whoops.

On our grocery run, I'd thought to buy chicken nuggets and apple slices for Finn but forgotten that I was also a person who ate.

"Cheez-Its, I guess," I said, eyeing the snack bag I'd haphazardly thrown together at home.

I found *SpongeBob* on the TV, and Finn and I both fell asleep to it, Cheez-It crumbs scattered on the sheets around us.

The next morning, Lucas called early. Mary didn't have hospice care overnight, and so he'd administered her morphine every hour, taking turns with his brother, who had traveled to Georgia as well.

Lucas had gone down to care for his father, but, instead, he'd be escorting his stepmother out of this life. I didn't see this parallel until much later: There I was in Nashville, still miscarrying (even after a D&C, I'd bleed for over a week), while he tended to Mary as she took her last breaths. Both of us holding hands with death, two hundred miles apart.

Finn and I headed downstairs to open the continental breakfast bar, along with a swarm of construction workers, all orange-vested and booted up.

As we sat in the middle of them, both still in our pajamas, munching on dry Froot Loops (Finn) and swigging weak coffee (me), a man approached our table.

"Check your car yet?"

"Pardon?" I said.

"Bunch of cars busted in the night," he said. "Broken glass everywhere out there."

Oh, for the love of God. I grabbed Finn's hand and, with him still in his footie PJs covered in aliens, dragged him out to the parking lot. Sure enough, it was peppered in shards of glass.

"Careful where you step. Stay next to me," I instructed as we wove our way to the Volvo. Though the windows of the vehicles to our left and right had taken hits, our car seemed to be fine.

Mazing our way back inside, I didn't view the situation as having been spared. I saw it as a narrow escape, a threat still looming. I saw it as not being safe anywhere, home or not home.

"Do we know who did it?" I asked the hotel clerk, a bored-looking twenty-something.

She shrugged.

"This doesn't happen that often," she said. "Don't worry."

That often?

Between the break-in and our finances, I knew we'd have to find another solution. Mary's doctor had said that she could live for weeks more. We couldn't live in a hotel. But I couldn't bear the thought of returning home and staying there alone. I couldn't do it.

"Time to get dressed for school," I said to Finn, gesturing for him to press the elevator button.

"We're in a hotel because I was having panic attacks after my D&C," I said to one of my closest friends from college, also named Lucas. He lived in Austin with his husband Greg, and although we'd had a steady text conversation going for well over a decade, he and I hadn't spoken much about my miscarriages. He knew about them, of course. But apart from the basic facts, I didn't bring them up with him, because I didn't bring them up with anyone, really, except Emily and Haley. No one else spoke the language.

It was night three in the hotel, and Finn and I were in bed watching cable cartoons. College Lucas and I happened to be chatting about the non-miscarriage parts of life, as we did—what we were reading, what was good on Netflix, what cringey thing some college classmate had posted on Twitter—when my current location came up.

"Wait why?" he said. "Because you're scared alone in the house?"

I confirmed this.

"Gene!" he said, our mutual nickname for each other from I don't remember what; it's just what we've called each other for twenty years. "I'll come to Nashville! You should have told me."

I was touched and reminded that I had friends—friends who were willing to show up if I just asked for help. I resisted the urge to tell him no.

"Really?" I said.

"Yes! Let me look at flights."

That night, merely knowing he was looking into it, I fell asleep calmer than I'd felt in days.

But the next morning, just after six, I awoke to a text from the other Lucas—husband Lucas. Mary had died in the early morning hours. He'd been alone with her, having just administered what would be her final dose of morphine.

I'm going to try to get a few hours of sleep. Love you, he'd written. He'd sent the text at 4 a.m.

Earlier in the night, he'd told me that the first thing she'd said when he'd arrived, still in a suit jacket from work, had been, "You look nice."

"So do you!" he'd quipped. He hadn't expected that it would also be the last thing she'd say, but she'd closed her eyes after that.

Everyone was waking up now and texting. My sister-in-law wrote, *Do you think once Lucas showed up, Mary knew Tim would be okay and she could go?*

I imagined Lucas alone, discovering that she was gone and going to get his brother. I imagined him and Nathan, and the two little boys still inside their adult bodies, waking their father to break the news. How fast we have to grow up; how suddenly we become the ones doing the hard thing.

So I didn't think about Mary at first. I thought about Lucas, and his kid heart that had to be a grownup to the people who had been the grownups.

I got Finn ready for school, and we packed up the car to move back home.

My phone connected to the car stereo, which started to play a song I didn't know and had added to my playlist by mistake. I'd been looking for the song "Who Am I" from the musical *Les Misérables* (feel free to judge), but I'd accidentally clicked on a different song with the same title. It played, and I didn't turn it off.

I am a flower quickly fading, here today and gone tomorrow, a wave tossed in the ocean, a vapor in the wind.

Barreling down the interstate, I envisioned Mary's spirit soaring over the car as we drove under the rising sun. I thought about the babies she'd lost during the hard life she'd lived.

At some point in the previous year, my friend Meadow had asked why I wanted to have another kid so badly.

Because I didn't want it to be over, I told her. I wanted to do it again: the first giggle, the first time dancing, the mixed-up words and funny utterances.

"I be carefuled!" Finn would say, or, "My nails growed up."

Arkansas was "Bark-and-sauce."

Once, on a plane, he yelled, "Keep an eye out for giants!"

He still called skunks stunks, which made so much sense.

"But it *will* end," she'd said. Her daughter had recently turned eighteen and left for college. "Another kid won't change that. Finn will stop being small enough for you to pick him up. Then he'll stop playing with kid toys, and at some point, his childhood will be over. And that will have been it."

Listening to her tell me these things I already knew, I'd felt like I was speeding down a hill toward a cliff with no way to stop.

"So, what's the hopeful part?" I asked, swallowing the ball that had formed in my throat.

She shrugged.

"That you got to do it," she said, her voice cracking. We'd both wiped away tears.

Even if we didn't lose our children, we did.

"I don't like this song!" Finn yelled angrily from the backseat. "I want to hear a princess song!" A princess song meant any pop song that sounded like it might feature in a Disney movie. Once, when an Ariana Grande song had come on, he'd asked, "Is this Rapunzel?"

I ignored him. The song kept playing, with more lyrics that tore me apart, and I cried harder. Livid, he started to cry with me.

"Turn it off!" he yelled over and over, both of us bawling as we hurtled toward the tall buildings downtown.

"Where is Dada?" Finn asked. We sat with my mom at Whole Foods, eating an early dinner. Lucas was still in Atlanta. My mom had driven up from Louisiana to stay with us when we realized he would be needed more in Georgia, not less. There were funeral preparations to make and boxes to pack.

"He's with Papa," I said.

"And Meemaw?" Finn asked.

My mom and I looked at each other.

At the same time, we both spoke.

"She's in heaven," my mom said, as I said, "Meemaw isn't here anymore."

Again, my mom and I made eye contact. She waited for me to continue, deferring to me.

As a child, I hadn't found the notion of heaven very comforting. The way it was presented, it seemed kind of spooky: pearly gates, nowhere to sit, floating amongst people who were perpetually happy for no clear reason. When I got older, it sounded more like my version of hell, given that my favorite social gatherings were the ones where I found a misanthrope or someone irreverent to talk to.

Heaven aside, I wanted to tell Finn the truth about death, because I believed that the truth was never to be feared. But what was the truth?

In the weeks after my D&C, I seemed to develop a new place—an emotional place—that I either didn't have access to before or that I'd chosen to avoid; I could picture my past self skirting around it like a pit of quicksand, year after year.

But now, that place was where I felt most at home.

If I used to live in the future, my new dwelling was in grief—and it didn't feel temporary. It felt like I might live here forever. Because it felt like the truest place I'd ever been.

In an episode of *The Good Place*, a comedy that takes place in the afterlife, a human is trying to explain to a demon what it's like to be mortal and says, "All humans are aware of death, so we're all a little bit sad, all the time. That's just the deal."

When I'd watched that scene years earlier, it had struck me as the best definition of humanity I'd ever heard.

Now, I understood that it didn't go far enough. Death wasn't just waiting in the wings or on the sidelines. It was in our evenings and our goodbyes; it was in our cells, which died daily. It was in the melting core of the planet. It was in everything.

For over a year, Finn had been in an octopus phase (I mean, who isn't?), and one afternoon that spring, he and I had sat scrolling through octopus photos on Instagram. Most of the photos and videos were of live octopuses, but when we inevitably reached tentacles on a plate, I'd hurried to swipe past.

I wasn't fast enough. He swiped back while I braced myself—how would I explain death?—until he said, "Oh, that one is made out of food."

Like a sea creature he'd craft from construction paper or Play-Doh, this one was just "made out of food."

I was like Finn with that octopus. My entire existence, I'd been living as if life was made out of what I accomplished and not the other way around.

But life wasn't made out of accomplishments.

Life was made out of death.

Having held it in my body for much of ten months, I saw now that it surrounded me all the time. Finn's childhood was ending as it unfurled. My fertility was ending. Life was closing in. And that was *sad*.

In his book, *The Beauty of What Remains*, Rabbi Steve Leder writes that in the twenty-third Psalm, the line *Yea, though I walk through the valley of the shadow of death* is hopeful, because a shadow doesn't exist without light.

When I read that, I thought about how Finn and I would make shadow puppets on the wall, and how, to really make them pop, we needed *more* light: The greater the light, the more vivid the duck's beak.

This was how my new center felt: shadowed, because the good was so good.

If I hadn't loved Finn so much, I wouldn't have been so hungry to do it again with another child.

If I hadn't been so saddened by his childhood coming closer to its end even as it was beginning, I might not have worked so hard to distract myself from it with fertility obsession.

If I hadn't felt the glow of new life blooming in me, I wouldn't have mourned its loss.

And that was the other surprising truth—when I stopped forcing myself to adopt the world's scripts for how to think about them, I did not wish away my miscarriages.

It seemed impossible, but I didn't.

Their deaths had shown me that death could live inside me, and that I could befriend it.

But I wasn't going to try to explain all of this to a three-year-old.

"She turned into a star," I said to Finn.

"A star?" he repeated, amazed. "Whoa."

The next day, we'd be playing in the front yard when he'd point to a dead ladybug on the ground.

"Look, mama," he'd say. "This one turned into a star."

He understands, I'd think, shocked.

But of course he did—he was a child, not a rock. And death wasn't something humans had invented, like reading or calculus. It was in our bodies.

22

THE ACHE

EIGHT DAYS AFTER MY D&C, I was cooking dinner while, at my feet, Finn played with the giant tow truck we'd given him as a reward for his recent strides in potty training. The truck had sat atop the fridge for months, enticing him to go a streak of days without an accident. That afternoon, we'd made a big deal of lifting it down and unpacking it from its box, and he'd literally jumped, clapping like a cartoon.

I'd turned on "Shivers," an Ed Sheeran song Finn and I sometimes danced to in the car.

I was chopping carrots and cabbage to make fried veggie cakes and bopping my head to the song when I had the strangest sensation. It was physical, almost like I was about to cry, but not from sadness.

It took me a moment to recognize it as joy. There was nowhere I wanted to be other than in this kitchen, making dinner for my family on this warm and windy day in March.

Was this what had been on the other side of fear the whole time?

I googled "flashes of joy in grief," and while most of the hits were about *how* to rediscover joy in the midst of grief, one blog post, written by Heidi Pottinger, a doctor who'd lost both of her parents, both of her brothers, and several friends all by age thirty-one, wrote about exactly this: *Surprisingly,* she wrote, *as I was forced to navigate the waves of grief again and again, I sometimes found myself experiencing something I never could have expected—profound joy. How could this be possible?*

A few days later, we were driving to breakfast when Lucas took my hand.

"You seem so sad," he said.

I did? Sadness had become so baked into me that trying to parse it would be like picking out the flour in a loaf of bread.

"It would be weird if I weren't, wouldn't it?" I said. The moments of joy were fleeting. The sadness was not.

In truth, I wasn't sure I'd ever stop being sad.

I certainly wasn't scrambling to escape the sadness; it was a pleasant enough companion—easygoing, not too demanding, low-key.

"I think we can be happy," Lucas said as we pulled into the parking lot. He didn't have to say "without another kid."

I pondered the word *happiness*.

If I was honest, when I hadn't been escaping into the pursuit of achievement, I'd found being alive sad since I was a little girl. Driving to school in fifth grade with my dad at the wheel, listening to nineties ballads on the radio, I'd been overwhelmed by a mourning sense that this was *it*, our life. We were in this car, in this city, on this morning, driving to this school; there weren't any other cars, cities, mornings, or schools we'd get to call ours. Every moment precluded a zillion other possible moments, life closing in as it unfolded, and that left me aching. I ached for my parents, and I ached for me.

The ache was different from the hole. The hole was a void I couldn't escape. The ache was a presence I tried to escape, and sometimes could. If the hole was a "why am I here, what is my point?" the ache was a sense that regardless of the answer to that question, everything was still going to end. Life would end, whether I answered that question or not.

At the time, I thought, *well, I must need to find a way to a different life: Move to a big city, become successful enough to warrant admiration, become someone who defies odds. Then maybe I won't feel this ache.*

But living in New York City twenty years later, when I'd find myself without distraction, alone in a subway car, I'd feel the same ache. And so, I'd find a dream or goal—something to work toward—to pull me out of it.

Recently, in the midst of the third miscarriage, we'd taken Finn to his first-ever soccer practice.

As all the kids and parents rooted for him on his turn—*go, Finn, go!*—he'd dribbled the ball down the short field and kicked it into the goal, then turned around, smiling hugely, and yelled, "I did it!"

I was already nostalgic for that moment. It was his first soccer practice, but it was also his *last* first soccer practice, and within thirty minutes, it was over.

I'd noticed a mom standing nearby with a baby in a baby carrier. At some point, when I hadn't been paying attention, Finn had outgrown those.

That same weekend, to get Lucas's attention, Finn had yelled, "Dad!"

Dad?

Not even Daddy?

DAD?

Was he a damn teen?

Finn's childhood was gaining speed, and there was nothing I could do about it.

Before I was a parent, I would see parents post crying emojis on social media when their children started new grades each fall ("He's getting too big!" [sad face]), and I didn't understand.

Didn't they want their kid to grow up? Wasn't that the point?

But now I got it. It was heartbreaking not because it was progressing, but because "progress" by another name was "ending." No wonder I sought to distract myself.

Then there was the reality of my own waning fertility.

All year, the looming reality of my body aging out of its childbearing years had been in the background.

Since I was thirteen, the possibility of pregnancy had been ever present, month after month. In my twenties, it was a risk to steer clear of. In my thirties, it was a distant dream, then a hope, and then a reality. In my forties, it would cease. And who would that make me?

Of course this was going to happen, Mary, I thought. *People age. It's better than the alternative.*

But it still hurt.

I'd spent the previous ten months teetering on the rounded edges of pregnancy, holding lives as they bloomed and faded. I hadn't ushered a life into this world as a human being. But I *had* ushered a life out—and that was a gift I never knew to want.

I'd learned to live in the presence of death. But how to be alive?

PART IV

WONDER

23

CHROMOSOMES

THE HOSPITAL FORGOT to send our fetus to be tested.

After two weeks, I checked in and was told that it was still sitting in a fridge, waiting to be shipped.

We hadn't unpacked what it even meant that we were no longer trying to get pregnant. We hadn't parsed the nuances—did it mean we were done having kids? Or just taking the if-it-happens-it-happens approach? Would we resume trying at some point, had we just agreed to hit pause, or was this cessation of effort permanent?

We didn't talk about these questions. I certainly hadn't given up on having another kid. I very much still wanted one and hoped it would happen—the *how* was another matter. But at the moment, it felt like too much to discuss. Like someone asking you what your next steps are when your house just burnt down and you're standing next to a pile of ash. It was a physical reality that I needed time to recover from my D&C—six weeks or so.

And so the news about the fetus still sitting in the fridge I took with a shrug.

I wanted to know the results as a kind of closure, an understanding of what had gone wrong. I thought maybe getting an answer would feel like how scattering someone's ashes might feel: final. So what was another two weeks?

A full month after my D&C, my OB's office called.

"Can you come in tomorrow at 10:45 to discuss the results with Dr. Morrow?" the nurse asked.

"Yes," I said, although I had a meeting I'd have to move. Why couldn't she just tell me over the phone? There wasn't any news worse than what had already happened. Our baby was gone. That's about as bad as it gets.

The next morning, Lucas and I decided to drive together. I picked Lucas up at his office a few minutes before our appointment.

"Just going back to that office is triggering," I said as I pulled into traffic. "My heart is racing."

"God, me too," he said. "I feel like I've had five cups of coffee." I was glad it wasn't just me.

"Don't wait, just come straight back," the nurse had told me over the phone. And so we headed directly to one of the same rooms I'd lain in over the previous year, hooked up to ultrasound machines.

Out of habit, I sat on the table and Lucas took a chair.

Dr. Morrow entered, apologizing that the lab had taken so long to come back.

"Anyway," she said, sitting, "it was Trisomy 21."

Huh?

I glanced back and forth between Lucas and Dr. Morrow. She knew Lucas was a genetic counselor—perhaps, because of that, she figured I knew what Trisomy 21 meant. I didn't.

"Down syndrome," she said.

"Whoa," I said. "Whoa."

"I know," she said. "This can be a lot to process since babies with Down syndrome can live. You're probably having a lot of reactions right now."

Mainly, I was shocked. I knew how rare Down syndrome was. Even for a woman my age, though the risk was increased, it was still less than one percent.

My mind then went straight to an alternate reality. At twelve weeks—only three weeks after I'd miscarried—we'd have taken the same genetic test that we'd taken with Finn, the one highly recommended for pregnant women over the age of thirty-five. It would have told us if the baby had any of three chromosomal anomalies, including Trisomy 21.

If the baby had survived, we would have found out then. What would *that* Mary have felt? Perhaps because imaginary Mary's imaginary feelings were easier to contemplate than my own real ones in this moment, I found myself dwelling in that reality instead of this one. I was sitting on the patient table, but my head was traveling.

"That's so weird," I said, looking at Lucas, who, as usual inside this little room, appeared more concerned with my reaction than his own. We both were. This year had been about my struggle, my wishes, my feelings; that's how we'd treated it, as something I was primarily suffering alone. It would be months before I'd even think to ask him how this year had affected him personally.

"Wait, so is that why I miscarried?" I asked.

Dr. Morrow nodded. "Almost certainly." She explained that although Trisomy 21 pregnancies can make it to term, the vast majority don't. Most end in miscarriage.

Just before we left, Lucas said to the nurse, "Would you mind sending us the genetic report?" He wanted to see it for himself.

"Sure. I will now," she said.

By the time we'd driven back to Lucas's office and were sitting in the parked car talking, my phone dinged.

I opened the report.

To my surprise, it was an actual photo of the baby's chromosomes—twenty-three sets of squiggly little worms, some long, some short. They were numbered.

"Look," Lucas said, pointing to the slot labeled "21." There, instead of a pair of worms, there were three—the "tri" in Trisomy 21.

It seemed so small, so trivial. A tiny extra blob meant the difference between life and not life. If ever there seemed an example of humans as fractals—the simplest rule yielding complexity—this seemed it.

"It was a girl," Lucas said quietly.

"Huh?" I said, clenching for some reason, like I was bracing for a punch.

He pointed to the top of the form, which read: *fetus: a female with Trisomy 21.*

"Oh my God," I said.

Lucas smiled sadly at me. It reminded me of when the ultrasound tech had looked at me and I'd seen on her face what I wasn't allowing myself to feel. His face held longing, and not his own.

When Lucas dropped me off at home a few minutes later, I stood in the foyer alone.

I had a writing class to teach in an hour, and I needed to prepare.

But facing the fridge covered in photos—of Finn; of friends' wedding invitations and holiday cards; of Lucas, Finn, Lucas's mom, and me making goofy faces in a photo booth only a couple of days after my D&C—I sensed a presence.

Her.

What strange things the brain will do, I thought. I'd learned two key details about her—her sex, and that she would have had Down syndrome—and so now I was conjuring her.

I sat down at the counter and opened my laptop, but every time I tried to type, my eyes pulled away from the computer toward the fridge. The presence had a location in the room: in front of the fridge. There was nothing I could see with my eyes, no blur or cloud or sprinkling of light. But my eyes filled in what my body sensed: a little girl around seven, with almond-shaped eyes, one hand on the fridge, smiling hugely at me.

You're creating a vision because you're mourning, I thought.

But I did that for a living, as a novelist. I made up fictional characters as my profession: I embodied them; I cried when they suffered; I got angry on their behalf. I felt defensive of them when I read online reviews in which readers said they didn't like them. (Rebecca in *Palm Beach* is an Enneagram One, okay? She's particular!)

This felt different.

I didn't believe in ghosts. When people told stories about places being haunted, my curiosity was much more about the storyteller's psychology than about which wall the ghost knocked on or how many chairs they flipped.

As I nervously tidied the kitchen, shaken, the little girl's presence only grew in realness. She felt as real as my hands, as real as the faucet I was turning on to get a glass of water. The sensation of knowing someone has entered the room without seeing them— my body was saying, *we aren't alone.*

Nothing about her presence felt like a loss. She didn't seem there to say goodbye. It was more like she had come to visit...maybe to let me know she was okay.

Sitting at my kitchen counter, I had the extraordinary and unexpectedly spiritual experience of coming to believe she might exist somewhere.

I thought of the theory of the multiverse—that all possible universes are happening all at once. I remembered once watching a talk from Neil deGrasse Tyson on "nothing"—that's what it was on: nothing. He said that in the multiverse theory, if there are universes with higher dimensions than ours, then entering ours is as simple as stepping into another room. Had she just stepped in?

I taught my writing workshop then quickly dressed for yoga—the only place I could think to go. I walked in one minute before the doors closed.

As I moved through yoga, I felt the same rattled feeling I'd felt earlier, the feeling that something had happened that I wasn't prepared for and couldn't get my head around. It was how I imagine I might feel if we discovered life on another planet—bewildered and a little terrified but kind of excited.

At the end of class, lying on my back with my eyes closed in *savasana*, I heard the people around me leaving the studio, but I wasn't ready yet.

The music that the teacher had turned on as we lay there—soft and acoustic—had transitioned into a kind of spoken-word poetry overlaying the instrumental accompaniment. A man's deep, soft voice was so quiet that it was difficult to make out the words. I strained to listen.

"We complicate things," he said. "But joy isn't complicated. It's the simplest thing, joy."

Breathing slowly on that hardwood floor, the afternoon sunlight hitting my sweaty face, I pictured the little girl standing at the fridge, beaming at me.

That's what was on her face in my apparition, my vision, my whatever it was: *joy*.

The child suddenly seemed so much wiser than me.

What if the point wasn't fleeing the ache but experiencing simple joy *within* the ache?

What if she'd come to show me that? Or what if my brain had just invented her, and *it* was trying to show me that?

Either way, I felt thrust into an awakening, and it was going to take me a minute to process.

Well, I thought, driving home, *guess I'm someone who believes in ghosts now.*

24

GHOSTS

I WAS NERVOUS to tell Lucas. As fastened to observable reality as I often felt, which had rendered me a closeted skeptic as a child and a slightly more open one as an adult, Lucas had been out of the closet for decades. He was grand marshal of the skeptic parade.

The ghost thing was *weird*. As Finn once said after choking on carrot, in his sweet, three-year-old voice, "That was fuckin' weird" (we laughed for hours).

It was a fuckin' weird story. Of course Lucas would be dubious, just like I was dubious as it was happening, just like I *still* was. And as my partner, he had a lot of power over what I felt. I worried that with a single lift of the eyebrow, he could recast my own understanding of the experience. I didn't want that; I didn't *want* to be talked out of my visitation. It was eerie and cool, and made me think about just how big and mysterious the universe really is. It felt important to me, and it felt real.

I decided to tell my sister. I knew that no matter what, she'd be gentle with me.

The weekend of Finn's fourth birthday, we traveled to Louisiana to celebrate at my parents' house. My sister and I went for coffee, and I told her the story.

"I believe you," she said, the best thing she could possibly say.

As I began to ask around, I found that, to my surprise, more people had these kinds of stories than I thought. Many in dreams, or waking dreams.

On Mother's Day, the poet Maggie Smith posted a poem about her two pregnancy losses on Instagram that ended with the line: *If you swim, swim here.*

There seemed to be a secret world where people—mothers who'd never met or who'd lost their babies, children who'd lost parents, people who'd lost friends—had, in moments, experienced what they were certain were visits.

As I dug, I found that a surprisingly large percentage of people who've lost loved ones—not just pregnancy or infant loss—report being visited by them. The scientific articles reporting these findings generally refer to them as "hallucinations," a label that I was also tempted to adopt. But when I tried to write off my own experience as a hallucination, which, to me, implied falsehood, I found that I didn't actually buy it. I didn't buy that something that felt *more* real than my day-to-day existence was the only part that *wasn't*. Indeed, wasn't all of what we perceived as reality constructed, our eyes filling in gaps based on prediction? And why did an assessment by the cerebral cortex ("a hallucination!") warrant greater regard than the more ancient, animalistic sense of the body?

It was the opposite of my Jesus experiences growing up: wanting to believe but not being able to buy in. While a significant part of me was tempted to convince myself that these experiences were delusional manifestations of grief and therefore dismiss them, in truth, they felt as real as it gets. Dismissal of my experience felt like a patriarchal view I'd internalized, a kind of narrow-minded rejection of a profound moment rooted in my femaleness: my biological connection to a being that had passed through me.

Sharing my experience and hearing about others' gave me a kind of hope that ran deeper than rote optimism or positive thinking, and that felt truer than the conditional "if-then" statements I'd quizzed students on for years as part of the formal logic training required for the LSAT.

I had found something spiritual that I didn't need to muscle my way into. I wasn't choosing, or effort-ing, to believe it. I just did.

Perhaps more importantly, whether it was a hallucination didn't really matter. If my brain had produced an image of what my body had felt, how remarkable was *that*?

One afternoon after the ghost-child visit, I was on my daily trek around the park near our house, a three-mile loop. This wasn't, to be clear, exercise; I did this braless in a muumuu and cheap Target sandals, which blistered my feet by the end of the first week, so I swapped them out for thicker, cheap Target sandals, only to blister in a different spot. The choice was intentional: If I put on socks and sneakers, I might be tempted to jog, and this wasn't that kind of practice.

In therapist-speak, one might call it processing, or grieving, or whatever the word is for doing-the-thing-that-sounds-the-least-insufferable-in-the-wake-of-heartbreak.

With all the hills and my refusal to be in a rush, it usually took well over an hour. I recognized how slow my pace was the day a kindly gentleman wished me a good day while passing me with his walker.

I would bird-watch without knowing the names of any of them, except for the cardinals. When one cardinal stayed with me for what felt like half the loop, fluttering from branch to branch as I moved with it, I wondered, *is it her?*

This day, I had a memory. Back in 2016, on a visit to the Indianapolis Art Museum, I'd found myself in a small, dimly lit gallery that featured what appeared to be a single, large painting on its back wall.

I had wandered over and stood in front of it for a moment before a woman's voice behind me said, "It's not what it looks like." Then she left the gallery.

I moved closer to the painting, getting as close as I could possibly get without touching it. As my eyes adjusted, its edges started to blur...was it painted *on* the wall? Was it painted at all? I reached out to touch it, but my fingers kept going through the wall.

The painting wasn't a painting at all, but a hole made to look like one. An optical illusion, like the ones I'd found wondrous in sixth grade: Was it a lady's profile or a goblet? A pair of identical lines or a longer and shorter one? A duck or a rabbit?

What if all those years of filling the emptiness with food only to purge, followed by my years of filling it with work, I'd indeed been empty, but not because something "out there" was missing, some spiritual truth.

I wasn't there. I was missing. Like the painting. I was looking ahead, jumping forward, fleeing the present. Finn would ask me to read him a book, and I might say yes or no, but either way, my head was halfway across town on what I needed to pick up for dinner, or who I needed to email, or whether I'd miscarry this baby too.

My future dwelling wasn't a symptom of my emptiness; it was the reason for it.

Talk about an optical illusion.

What was real?

Later that day, I was driving Finn home from school, flipping through my playlist, starting songs and skipping forward.

"Go back!" Finn yelled from the backseat. "Go back to the ghost song!"

"What's the ghost song?" I asked, skipping back. "This one?"

"No," he said.

"This one?"

"No... Yes, this one!" Katy's Perry's "Dark Horse" started to play. "This is a ghost song," Finn said happily.

"What makes it a ghost song?" I asked.

"The ghosts are singing it," he said. "A boy ghost and a girl ghost."

Another time, he told me that his brother and sister live far away, not on Earth.

"Sometimes my brother thinks I'm his mom and I have to tell him I'm his brother," he said, laughing.

I tried to recall if Finn had talked about ghosts before, and I remembered he had. A few weeks earlier, we'd gotten an email from his teacher in the middle of the afternoon that had made us laugh:

Today at nap time we were having trouble with our listening ears. We were choosing to take our sheets off to pretend we were ghosts. Just thought you should know.

Ms. Ashli

Lucas and I had cracked up, because, well, that's funny. Both the first-person plural, and the joke.

When I'd picked Finn up that day, I'd said, "I heard you were a ghost at nap time," and he'd said, "No, I was *two* ghosts!"

Now, I pulled up her email and checked the date: the day of my last miscarriage.

Lucas and I sat in a steakhouse booth sipping gin and tonics while, next to us, Finn colored a bunny with the crayons supplied by the restaurant. It was where we went when I didn't feel like cooking and Lucas didn't feel like doing dishes, our current marital arrangement.

I needed to tell him about the ghost. I'd talked to my sister and a few close friends about it, but I still hadn't told my own husband.

Part of my future-dwelling lifestyle had always been that I simply didn't enter important conversations without a goal and a roadmap. That's how I approached them—with an agenda and determination to get my way.

While the other person was talking, I'd be drafting my reply in my mind, as the purpose of listening was to craft my response so I could ultimately persuade them to agree with my point of view (charming, no?).

Lucas had called me out on this before, more than once.

"Why are we even talking about this when you already know what you're going to do?" he'd say. "We're going to end up doing it Mary's way because that's what we always do."

"That's not true!" I'd insist, knowing it was true.

I was scared to bring up the ghost because I didn't know how it would go. I wasn't sure what I was more afraid of—that he might cause me to question my belief that it had been real (and I didn't *want* to doubt it; I cherished it), or that, if I perceived him as judgmental or dismissive, it might drive a wedge between us. But it was time. It was becoming a secret that was weird to keep from him.

I handed Finn my phone to occupy him with dinosaur videos.

"I had an experience I need to tell you about," I said to Lucas. "It happened the day we found out about her chromosomes."

I told him the whole story. He didn't smirk or lift an eyebrow skeptically. He listened.

"Why didn't you tell me before?" he asked when I finished. It had been weeks.

I explained that I was afraid he'd write it off as delusional and that his reaction would diminish the experience for me. I wanted to protect myself and my memory of it.

"I don't want you to feel like you can't tell me things," he said.

Now that we were broaching hard topics, there was something else on my mind.

"It's very hard for me to let go of the idea of having a second child," I mouthed, checking that Finn was engrossed in his cartoon. He was.

"I know," he said.

There was more. I could tell that my inability to let go of the dream of a second child was connected to my grief, though I didn't understand how, because I still didn't understand the grief itself.

As Finn would say when he was struggling to express something as a three-year-old, "I don't have the words."

I didn't have the words. Sometimes I felt so deeply sad— weeping alone at the steering wheel—that it was as if my body was able to sense everything those unspent lives would have blossomed into, all the joys and sorrows and disappointments and silliness.

And who knows? We know how being born works, mostly. You're born, and you embark on a human lifespan.

But if you are created as a life and are never born, does your destiny play out like a movie reel on high speed in the womb? Does your mother house a lifetime, or two, or three, or infinite? Because my blood now carries memories that aren't my own, and that makes no sense.

We have a word in English for when we long for someone we've known: miss. We say we miss them. But what to call longing for someone you never knew? "Miss" felt as silly as it did true.

It seemed impossible for any non-born entity to have an identity I could feel and know. Even considering it left me a bit cringey and embarrassed, like looking over one shoulder to see who might think me crazy. (But then, we, as a culture, aren't even willing to accept a live birth as the moment existence begins: After my friend's son died at two weeks old, people would sometimes talk to her as if she lost a pregnancy, not a child. As if two weeks alive doesn't count as alive at all. When someone gave her the book *Spirit Babies: How to Communicate with the Child You're Meant to Have*, she wanted to scream, *I did have him! He is my actual child!* Or, as her husband put it, "It's like we want to get out his birth certificate and social security card and say, 'Look, he exists.'")

I didn't and don't know when existence begins. But I'd realized that I didn't just want any baby now—I wanted *those* babies. It reminded me of something a scammer of a medium had once told me, even though the rest of what she'd said had been nonsense: that we arrive on this planet as fully formed souls.

Finn once said, in one of his child poet moments, that if love can be invisible, anything else can be too. He sounded so excited to have figured that out (because, of course, *he* wanted to be invisible).

"I think there's still a part of me that thinks having one will bring the other ones back," I said.

"That's understandable," Lucas said, "but you know a new baby won't make you not sad over these losses, right?"

I started to cry.

Lucas had long since described his life as a kind of before and after: before age twenty-two, when he lost his stepdad, who'd raised him, and afterward.

Now he grabbed a cocktail napkin and one of Finn's crayons.

"Before David died, I thought the world was like this." He drew a circle. "When he died, it was like realizing it was this." He drew a much bigger circle around the smaller one.

I looked at my husband across the table and saw him in a new light. He'd been in the bigger circle this whole time, while I'd been splashing around in the smaller one, thinking we were seeing the world from the same vantage point. Meanwhile, I hadn't even realized there was a bigger circle, that grief was water, that we were fish.

I supposed I'd been lucky, in some sense, that it had taken me thirty-nine years to encounter this sobering perspective, that I'd been not-so-blissfully ignorant for so long. It was only a matter of time before it came for me.

Grief seemed to be a great leveler, a fundamental flattening of the hierarchies that divide us. Billionaire? It'll get you. Impoverished? It'll get you. No matter where you live or who you are, it's coming for us all.

25

ODDS

I WANT TO TELL YOU that, from here, I let go. That I learned to love my body and my family as is. The writer in me suspects this makes a better narrative, that if I could shove this next part into that shape, it would read better.

But that's not what happened.

Lucas had come along on my daily walk, and it seemed like as good a time as any to broach what I'd been thinking about: a last strategy. A Hail Mary. A final attempt at creating the family I wanted.

"I know it won't end my grief to have another baby," I said. "But can we just look into IVF?"

IVF made sense to me now that we knew at least one of my miscarriages had been chromosome-related, and possibly all three. As a woman approaches forty, her chances of ovulating a chromosomally abnormal egg increase. Because a fertility clinic could genetically test the embryos, we could screen for the viable ones. I saw it as a detour around miscarriage. An expensive one, sure. But how much was my child worth? What would I pay for my dream?

I'm not being hyperbolic when I say that the answer was: anything. I would have paid anything.

I made my case to Lucas. He sighed.

"When does life get to be easy, Mary?" he asked.

We walked in silence for a bit. I saw where he was coming from. He'd spent years slogging his way into a new career, and the week that career officially started, we'd gotten pregnant again, then miscarried the first month of his new job. My D&C had fallen the day before his board exam.

Another kid felt worth the hardship to me, but I agreed that's what it was: hard. Or as Finn might say, "fuckin' hard."

"The brunt of it will be on me," I said, code for, *since it's my body, shouldn't my vote count more?*

"Okay, we can look into IVF if you want," he said in the same voice he might use to offer to drive twenty minutes across town and pick up a pair of sunglasses I'd left behind—slightly annoyed but willing to take one for the team. "But not multiple rounds. We're not getting on that wagon."

"One round," I said, agreeing. "No more."

Nothing could bring back the others, but maybe I didn't have to give up on a second kid, not yet.

A few weeks later, we sat across from a fertility doctor in a white coat and a nurse next to her. Before us was a spread of glossy brochures; I'd absently flipped through them in the lobby, registering very little.

Next to me, Lucas radiated unease. He did not want to be here. It felt like someone could let him go and he'd shoot across the room, he was holding in so much agitated energy.

"Do we know the reasons for the first two miscarriages?" the doctor, a pretty woman who didn't look older than thirty, asked. I shook my head.

"But at least one was a chromosomal issue, the Trisomy 21. Okay," she continued, talking mostly to herself. "And given that you've had a successful pregnancy before..." She paused. "Yeah, I think going right to IVF makes more sense than trying IUI first." She looked up at us. "Do you know how it works?"

I turned to Lucas. He was leaning back in his chair with his hands folded, his face in the expression that our friends and I sometimes call his "serial killer face."

We exchanged a whole conversation in a single look.

Me: Participate, please?

Him: I am.

"No," we both said at the same time.

She flipped over one of the information sheets to its blank side and uncapped a pen.

"First, we see how many follicles you have. This will help us estimate how many eggs you might get on an egg retrieval. Let's say you have...thirteen."

She drew an oval with thirteen dots inside, then wrote "13" above it.

"We'll give you medicine to start growing these follicles. You'll take it from ten days to two weeks, based on how many eggs are growing and how quickly. We want to get as many eggs to twenty millimeters as possible before we go in. All the follicles won't grow, so let's say we get...ten."

She drew an arrow coming out of the oval that I now inferred represented my ovary. She wrote "10" above it.

"Of these, not all of them will be mature. But let's say most are, like eight. That would be good." She wrote "8."

"On average, half of those will fertilize. So that's...four." She drew another arrow and a "4."

"Now we wait to see if they grow over five days. What we want is a blastocyst—an embryo with enough cells that we can test it." She took her time drawing what looked like a pomegranate. Lucas, the nurse, and I watched silently as she meticulously completed each tiny circular cell inside the blastocyst. I wondered how essential the detailed illustration was going to be for making her point. "The attrition rate at this stage is about fifty percent. So now we're down to two."

Arrow. A "2."

"So if we have two embryos that are going to be sent off for genetic testing, let's see. At your age, only one in three on average will be euploid, meaning genetically normal. So that brings us to..."

We all stared at the page, which was now full of arrows leading from thirteen down to a blank: 13 → 10 → 8 → 4 → 2 → ___.

"Zero," I said when she didn't continue. "One in three when we only have two is zero." I chuckled, thinking she'd made a mistake in choosing numbers that landed us at zero, but she didn't flinch.

Oh. That was intentional, I realized.

She was staring at me.

"This is why, at your age, the number of eggs we're able to retrieve is critical. Because of the attrition as you move through the stages."

"How common is it to get a lot of eggs"—I pointed to the first stage, the egg retrieval—"at my age?"

She half-smiled sympathetically.

"Not very," she said. Then, more brightly, "But we can take a look. See how many follicles you have. That'll give us an idea. I just want to be honest with you before we move forward."

I couldn't look at Lucas.

"I mean, it's still more efficient than natural human reproduction?" she said with a question mark at the end, like someone sifting through the charred remains of the burnt-down house and going, "Hey, look, this lamp made it?"

"Are these numbers affected by the fact that I've had a successful pregnancy before?" I asked. Surely there had to be some way I could weasel my way out of these stats, find a reason to count myself the exception, not the rule.

"No," she said. "The only factor is age. Age is it."

While Lucas chimed in with questions about the particulars of the genetic testing, I sat quietly and processed what she'd just told us.

When we'd finally decided to potty train Finn, it was later than his peers—he was already three. Most of his friends were in underwear, at least during the day. (The previous year, we'd been more concerned about speech than diapers, and tackling two big developmental challenges had felt overwhelming.) A few months after his third birthday, I'd bought a potty-training guide, and when I cracked it open, the first sentence read, "Far more important than *how* you start is *when*." Start no later than two, it instructed.

Ah, great, I'd thought. Failing before we'd even begun.

This was like that, but a million times worse. *Zero?*

"Okay, thank you," I said as we gathered up our brochures to leave.

Until this moment, I had still—out of sheer will, denial, or entitlement—believed that, eventually, I would have another baby.

Didn't women (celebrities) have babies into their forties all the time? Or was I making that up? I'd assumed that IVF was the go-to, pretty-much-always-works solution when you reached an age where things stopped functioning on their own. It was like calling the fridge repairman once you gave it a go yourself; it wound up costing more than DIY, but, in the end, your fridge got repaired. Or you got a new one. No one was leaving you with a broken fridge.

But no. According to the doctor, even IVF couldn't make my body have a baby at forty. In fact, it seemed pretty damn bad at making forty-year-old bodies have babies, especially for the price tag.

On our way out, as a final stop, we met with the finance officer, who estimated that an IVF cycle would cost us $13,000, and that didn't include the embryo transfer (into my uterus) if we actually wound up with one. This was, apparently, *good* news.

"Your insurance covers part of it because you've had recurrent losses."

"Oh, so is it less?"

"No, this is the price after the insurance contribution." Ah. Yay?

A $13,000 bet for which the odds of winning had been spelled out as: zero.

As we walked to the car, the years leading up to this moment suddenly felt dumb. What had I been *doing* throughout my thirties when my eggs were still chilling viably down there in my ovaries? Living, is what. Writing books. Getting married. Going to happy hour with my friends. Running the New York Marathon and feeling immensely proud of myself. Moments I didn't regret, moments I cherished, but what irked me was that I'd been doing it all while believing that I had time to burn.

All year, I'd been facing the harsh reality that reproduction wasn't a test I could ace or a goal I could work hard to reach. Nonetheless, I'd assumed that things would eventually pan out. I hadn't realized that my fertility didn't play by my agenda or hopes, that, in utterly non-feminist fashion, it continued to do what it had been doing for thousands of years: phase out.

In the maternity ward of the hospital after Finn was born, the nurses had joked to all the moms as we were discharged with our newborns, "See you in two years!"

Who was supposed to tell me? The nurses? My sex ed teacher? My gynecologist? Was it a failure of women's healthcare? It suddenly seemed like a glaring omission that our rapidly diminishing egg reserves aren't mentioned at our annual checkups.

I thought about how, over the previous year that I'd been miscarrying, I'd watched, one by one, my girlfriends struggle alongside me. All at once, we were trying to have babies, and all at once, we were failing.

There were the few lucky ones, mostly the ones who had frozen their eggs in their late twenties or early thirties (Who told them? How did they know?). And even they weren't guaranteed anything, not even close.

At one point not long after this appointment, as I was venting to a friend about this, she said, "But it's not necessarily true. Have you read *The Atlantic* article?" She sent it to me. It argued that the idea that women age out of fertility is misogynistic and outdated, rooted in old science. Women over forty, the author argued, don't struggle to get pregnant if you look at more recent research.

But the problem wasn't getting pregnant. The problem was staying that way.

I closed the article, angry at how it was misleading us, my peers and I, the girl babies of the eighties pushed to chase our dreams. Here we were: We'd earned the executive roles and PhDs and law degrees. But approaching forty, that's not what we were talking about behind closed doors.

In the months after my year of miscarriages, I'd watch a stunning number of my friends struggle to conceive. We'd pile up pregnancy losses, dry egg retrievals, and unsuccessful transfers, throwing our money and prayers and wishes against biology in desperation to build the families we thought we had time to build because no one told us we didn't. If anything, they told us *we did*.

Earlier in the year, I'd ordered fancy fertility vitamins that promised to help me get pregnant. Each little packet of daily pills was branded with the phrase: *Science is on your side.*

But that wasn't true. Science was not on our side. No vitamin could change that, and nobody had told me that, and I was, to put it simply, pissed.

From Finn's books, I'd learned the collective nouns for all kinds of animals. Rhinos were a crash, zebras a zeal, eagles a convocation.

What might we, the women enduring these disappointments, these devastations, be called?

A cemetery?

A wake?

A generation?

26

SUGAR

IN SPITE OF THE TERRIBLE ODDS laid out by the doctor, I still wanted to try IVF. Lucas did not.

The one thing we agreed on was that we weren't going to continue to try to conceive naturally. Neither of us wanted to face another miscarriage, and the odds at my age, higher now that I'd had three, were too high for our comfort. Lucas continued to respond with the enthusiasm of someone gearing up for a colonoscopy.

"When do we just say, hey, we have a great kid, let's live our lives?"

But I wanted to continue imagining what I'd always imagined: two Christmas stockings. Two adults bringing their girlfriends or boyfriends home for Thanksgiving. Two backpacks every fall, two school supply lists. Two, dammit.

"It's my body," I finally said, laying it out bluntly.

"Yes," he said, "and it's also my life."

But we had started the ball rolling with the clinic, and we had agreed to one round, so he shrugged it off as I continued scheduling the required preliminary procedures—a mammogram, blood draws, and an extra fancy ultrasound that involved squirting water into my uterus. Lucas's sperm would also need to be tested, a procedure that was booking eight weeks out. (Bitterly, I wondered if they said "eight weeks" because they thought it sounded shorter than "two months.")

I told myself that he didn't really know what he wanted, that he'd come around and thank me in twenty years when we were playing bridge on a cruise liner while our kids were off at college.

In the meantime, my dream deferred was turning me into an increasingly sour person. I was the stink of rotten meat in Langston Hughes' poem, my thoughts growing more vinegary by the day.

I would spot a pregnant woman in the produce section of the grocery store and topple headfirst into envy. Why did she get to be pregnant? Why did *she* get what *I* wanted?

I would fight the impulse to stare at her belly, which she'd be stroking lovingly, and curse the universe for its unjustness.

I muted acquaintances who posted pregnancy news, then felt guilty about it. I had ungenerous, petty thoughts when they announced at six weeks, or even sooner—the photo of the at-home test itself captioned, "Coming in October, Little So-and-So."

Yeah, we'll see! I'd think. *You might be surprised.*

I didn't actually wish ill fate on anyone. I wasn't that malevolent. But I was as salty as the Dead Sea, so dense that I was pruny from floating in it.

And I hated it. I hated that it was petty and that it was predictable. More than one close friend called to tell me she was pregnant and opened with an apology, as if becoming pregnant were a personal offense to me. One cried.

"I feel so bad telling you this," she said. "I feel so guilty." It broke my heart that she didn't think I would be happy for her. I was so happy for her that *I* started crying—she'd also struggled to have kids, and this was a beautiful and joyous outcome for her family.

This friend had left a gift in my mailbox on the anniversary of my first miscarriage, which had just passed. She'd known that I'd bought SweeTarts, Cheez-Its, and gummy bears at CVS while I waited for my medicine that day because she'd seen a photo I'd taken of them in my lap, back when I was trying to make light of the whole situation ("miscarriage snacks" I'd texted to friends). On the first anniversary, which was far more painful than I'd even expected, I went to check the mail and found a note from her, plus all three: SweeTarts, Cheez-Its, and gummy bears.

Now that she was pregnant, I begged her not to feel guilty for sharing her joy. I wanted to be a part of it, not excluded. I was as elated for her as she was devastated for me. It was all true.

But when it came to strangers, who were easier to objectify since I had no personal connection to them, the green monster would regularly rear its head.

Like one afternoon at the park when two little girls couldn't find their mom. Finn and I helped them look for at least fifteen minutes before a woman casually strolled up carrying a baby. The two girls were around Finn's age, terrified, crying.

"Mama!" they screamed, running to her.

"What's up?" she said, as if she hadn't been missing.

As Finn and I had walked away, I thought bitterly, *how did she get to have three kids and I don't even get two?*

Like I said: not proud.

Underneath the saltiness, I was, of course, hurting. Sometimes the hurt would break through the bitterness and stop me in my tracks. Like another afternoon at the park, when a mom stood at the top of a slide holding a very small toddler, too small to walk yet. She wanted to go down the slide, which wasn't big enough for the mom to go down with the child on her lap.

The only adults on the ground were Lucas and me.

"Want me to catch her?" I offered.

"If you don't mind," the woman said. She placed the baby at the top of the slide and let go. Her tiny body was so light in my arms, and as I waited for her mom to climb off the play gym, my heart raced. Handing her over to her mother, I had the strange compulsion to overshare with this stranger.

I was pregnant until a little while ago, but I miscarried, I had to hold myself back from saying.

I remembered months earlier, after my first miscarriage, when I'd responded to my friend telling me she was pregnant by assaulting her with my own news.

It seemed to come from a place of wanting to be seen, wanting to be acknowledged. A woman with a pregnant belly or an infant in tow is visible. A woman who's mourning that she has neither is not.

Several days later, I was driving to pick up some groceries before an afternoon of teaching, and as I turned left at the end of my street, I saw the dog—a small, fluffy, white terrier. It raced toward my car, and I slowed, searching for the human hurrying to catch up with it.

But there was no one in sight. Rolling down my window to stick my head out, I spotted, on a hill two streets over, a group of young guys in baseball caps smoking on their balcony, watching.

They've got an eye on him, I thought, and rounded the corner, pulling onto the main street of our neighborhood that leads to the busy, four-lane thoroughfare a dozen or so yards ahead.

But as I turned on my blinker and approached the busy intersection no animal should ever venture to, I checked my rearview mirror once more, and there he was, following me, still yapping away in the middle of the street.

I parked and got out.

The dog barked at me angrily.

"It's okay," I cooed, reaching out my hand, palm up.

I coaxed him closer until I could slip a hand under his neck to check his collar—*Sugar*, it read, with a phone number that I spoke aloud to memorize.

Keeping an eye on Sugar, I hurried back to my car, grabbed my cell, and called the number. No answer.

I sent a text: *Hi, I'm outside on 35th Avenue with your dog Sugar!*

A few minutes passed before the door of a house on the block flew open, and a woman with wet hair came running out.

"Sugar! Oh no! Thank you!" Sugar ran to her, as she explained that he must have gotten out while she was in the shower.

I climbed into my car and continued to the grocery store, and, as I drove, I began to weep. I mean a full-blown ugly cry.

Why on earth was I crying?

Partly horror at myself. The dog had been in danger, and my impulse had been to turn away. I hadn't wanted to deal with it. I had a to-do list to knock out, so I was telling myself the dog would be fine, even though it clearly was very close to *not being fine*, to being hit by a car going fifty or faster.

THE DOG WAS WORTH SAVING! my brain yelled as I cried.

I KNOW! I yelled back.

BUT YOU ALMOST DIDN'T STOP!

BUT I DID, DIDN'T I?

I cried all the way to the store and back, confused about why I was so sad.

"What's wrong?" Lucas asked, seeing my swollen face. Collapsing onto a chair on the porch, I burst into tears.

"There was this d-d-dog..." I told him the story. He listened, the whole time looking like he was waiting for a punchline that never came. When the story ended with Sugar's owner coming outside, it was the ultimate anti-climactic ending; nothing bad had happened.

"And *why* is this making you so sad?" he asked, confused.

"*I don't know!*" I sobbed.

I thought about it for days. Why had it made me so sad? Because I almost turned away? Did I feel like a terrible person? Was this guilt?

I'd suffered my share of guilt, but it didn't typically make me bawl.

A few days later, I saw Sugar being walked by his owner, and when I waved, I could tell that she didn't seem to recognize me.

One strange thing about a pregnancy ending without a baby is that you're pregnant, then you're not. You go back to being you, and no one sees you as pregnant, and no one sees you as a parent because there's no baby, and so it almost feels like nothing ever happened.

It's easy to question your own history, your own scars. Was that even real? Was that a dream?

Was the reason I'd been so triggered by Sugar that, while getting him home had definitely been the most important act of my day that day—possibly the *only* thing that mattered in my whole day—no one else knew about it? The owner didn't even know my name or remember my face. It had been an invisible act, a shuttling of the animal from one circumstance to another. I was the woman catching the baby at the bottom of the slide, wanting to scream, *I almost had a baby, too!* I was the nameless carrier.

If a tree falls in the forest and no one is there, it makes a sound no one hears. But what if only one person hears it? How long before she starts to question what she heard? How long before she wonders if she imagined it?

For a year of my life, every memory is filtered through my state of being at the time: pregnant, trying to get pregnant, or miscarrying. But it's a filter that exists for no one else, not even Lucas.

"Remember when you impulse-ordered a treadmill and immediately canceled it?" My sister sometimes pokes fun at me, and I laugh while thinking, *yes, I was forty-eight hours into a miscarriage.*

"Remember how much fun we had dancing at my wedding?" a friend asks. *Yes, I miscarried through my dress and onto the dining chair and was just glad I was in a dark dress and the room was dim.*

Checking out at the Target where I miscarried, I pass the bathrooms and remember how I bled on Halloween, how I'll always be in that stall bleeding on Halloween, how my ghost will never leave it.

27

THE MISSING PIECE

IN THE END, WE TRIED two rounds of IVF. The first yielded no viable embryos.

As we waited for the results of the second, it increasingly felt like I was squeezing a shriveled lemon. The energy of our fertility struggle had begun to feel desperate, anemic. Like the whistle had been blown, and the game was over, but I was still running around the field with an imaginary ball.

One morning, I woke up angry at the doctor. She should have told us that, at my age, we would very likely need three rounds or more of IVF to get a viable embryo. Driving home from daycare drop off, I fumed. Why hadn't she made clear that, now that I was forty, our decision should be whether to plan for *several* cycles, that a single round would just result in a big financial hit for nothing, money squandered in a night gambling?

"What difference would it have made?" Lucas said when I vented back at home.

"Knowledge is power," I said vaguely. But he was right. I would have a done a million rounds if we'd had the money. He'd begrudgingly agreed to a second only after several strained conversations.

But then I thought of the circles the doctor had drawn, the zero at the end of her equation. *Didn't she tell you, Mary? Wasn't that what she was saying?*

I'd been the one to look at her paltry numbers and think, *I'll be different. I'll be the one to skew the curve.* Because I had to be.

We found out the second had produced no viable embryos via message in the clinic's portal. I read it aloud while standing at the kitchen counter, close to the spot where I'd yelled "This is a big deal!" months earlier on the morning of my D&C. Lucas stood a few feet away, snacking on chips and salsa we'd set out. We hadn't expected this news right now.

"So we're really done," I said, the realization finally sinking in. "That was it."

I'd recently been texting with another friend going through IVF hoping to have her second child. Her attempts had also failed so far, and we were talking about how hard it was to imagine letting go of the dream.

Like being told I'm moving to Mars, I'd typed. What's the air like there? Would the adaptations I'd accrued here on earth allow me to survive there? How about thrive?

I started to cry. This time, Lucas didn't come to comfort me. He sat on the railing of a tall stool Finn used to help me cook. It looked uncomfortable and unstable.

"I'm sad, too," he said. "I didn't think this would happen. I wanted it, too."

I wasn't surprised. He'd never not wanted a second kid. He adored being a dad. He just wanted to be done with the struggle.

So this was it.

Impossible not to think of the closing lines of the T.S. Eliot poem I fell in love with in high school, "The Hollow Men":

This is the way the world ends

Not with a bang but a whimper.

I texted my friend the news: *I guess I'll be learning to live on Mars.*

After sympathizing, she acknowledged that she might be joining me there. *Take notes,* she wrote.

The only thing I could think to do was to talk myself out of wanting what I wanted.

I reminded myself how fortunate I was to have Finn, how insanely, insanely lucky. My recognition of how miraculous Finn was had indeed ballooned over the previous year. But instead of subsuming my desire for another, it put a fine point on it. I'd eaten at this restaurant before and didn't just think that the chicken cordon bleu was my favorite, I *knew* it was.

Still, I felt guilty for being so devastated when some people could have zero children, and I did my best not to seek comfort from friends in this category. But friends with multiple children were dismissive, saying things like, "At least you have one beautiful one." *True,* I'd think, and my gratitude for that kid was so big it could turn into a moon and start orbiting the earth. But also, I'd think, *easy for you to say.*

I started digging up Reddit threads on why only children are preferable to multiple children, googling celebrities who had only had one child, and making a list of the "pros" of being a one-child family:

One college tuition

Less risk of having a serial killer

Some of my favorite people are only children (Claire, Harrison, Christine!!!)

Families with two or more kids on airplanes and at restaurants seem miserable; families with one kid seem fine

The list was stupid. I didn't care if dinners at restaurants were hard or travel was prohibitively expensive or if I had a little delinquent. We'd cook at home. We'd go to Italy as empty nesters. I'd bail him out.

One morning, I awoke from a dream I'd forgotten much of but of which I remembered one moment: screaming, at the top of my lungs, "THIS IS NOT THE LIFE I WANTED!"

Climbing out of bed, I felt hung over with desire.

"I found a new one!" Finn marched out of his closet, where we stored books he hadn't yet aged into, holding *The Missing Piece* by Shel Silverstein. He handed it to me. "Let's read this one," he said.

The book's shiny black and white jacket cover took me back to my own childhood, loving Shel Silverstein's silly poems and drawings. Still, as Finn snuggled in next to me, I cracked it open with little enthusiasm.

I was pretty sure I remembered how this one ended: He finds his missing piece, and, *voilà*, he's happy.

Just what I need, I thought, *a story about someone who gets exactly what they want.*

I began to read.

Part of my memory was correct. The circle with a pizza-slice chunk missing rolls along but not very fast because of the divot.

He goes in search of his missing piece and tries on a lot of ill-fitting pieces. He then finds a piece that fits—now, he's a perfect circle, and he can roll really fast. He rolls so fast, in fact, that he bypasses things he used to enjoy, like flowers and butterflies.

And this is where the story takes a turn from what I remembered: He gives up his missing piece. He decides that he liked life better *before*. Wait...what? *How?*

28

SHADES

"FAKE IT TILL YOU MAKE IT" had worked for me as a new lawyer pretending to understand what *res ipsa loquitur* was, and again as a new writer pretending that I knew what an "inciting incident" was. Therefore, it seemed like a reasonable approach when it came to letting go of a dream, too. I would act like the person I wanted to be before I knew how to become her. I would start with *the stuff*.

The stuff: a category of belongings known intimately by any parent-to-be who has expected something that never came.

It's the cradles and rockers and onesies, the blankets and lovies and board books, the maternity wear and breast pumps and nursing bras.

Wherever it lives, a closet on a high shelf or dusty basement corner, hidden behind cardboard in the unused at-home office or behind the brooms in the pantry, we hear it sizzling whenever we go near. And the sizzle asks: *What are you going to do with me?*

Mine lived in a dedicated corner of my closet, underneath where my winter coats hung. There was the glass mosaic elephant I'd bought on our way out of Mexico on the off chance I was, indeed, pregnant. The knit blanket covered in hot air balloons that I'd bought in the days after my Oklahoma Walmart bathroom positive. The newborn outfits I couldn't resist during Zara's clearance sale at the mall. The children's book prints from the Salt Lake City airport.

Occasionally, I'd venture back there and take out the things, examine them like wares at a flea market, let myself feel. Sometimes I thought again of the iconic, six-word story the boy I'd briefly dated had brought up on our date: *For sale: baby shoes, never worn.*

It's iconic because it's brief and devastating. The mark of a great sentence, no? Like many writers, I'd admired it since I first heard it decades earlier, but its protagonist, the seller of the shoes, had always been a fiction in my mind, some poor soul that someone who wasn't Hemingway had invented. Certainly not me.

Until now. I held the booties I'd ordered from an Instagram ad, the ones I'd imagined one of my babies in, then another, then another, and it struck me: I *was* a story made legendary by how concisely it heart-shatters.

That particular outfit—the coming-home-from-the-hospital set of a knit sweater, onesie, beanie, and booties—occupied the greatest territory of my mind.

One afternoon, I thought of the outfit with a fresh intention. My friend Lexi (sourdough starter dealer) had just given birth to a baby girl, Mabel. It felt like it was time. I hadn't wanted to put the outfit in a generic donation bin. It was too special for that. I'd wanted to give it to a particular person, to envision the parent and child using it.

I hadn't met Mabel yet—she was hours old—but I could imagine the knits belonging to her.

Besides, I knew that keeping the stuff around "just in case" wasn't helping me move on.

On a springy, Sunday afternoon, still clinging to a secret dream that I'd wind up gray-haired and burping a cooing newborn while bragging, "we'd given up all hope, and *then*...", I wandered into the dark cavern at the back of my closet, opened the drawer I didn't like to open, and removed the knit ensemble.

I folded it and placed it in a plain gift bag, fluffed tissue, and tied a ribbon. I found a notecard and wrote to Mabel, welcoming her to the world.

I wouldn't tell Lexi about the gift's history, of course; I wanted her to enjoy it—that was the point. I didn't want her to feel uncomfortable or, worse, guilty.

"I'm going to drop this off at Lexi's," I announced, appearing downstairs with the gift bag.

"What is it?" Lucas asked.

"It's the coming-home outfit I bought last spring," I said.

He raised his eyebrows.

"Is today the day for that, you think?" he said carefully.

"I mean, it has to happen at some point," I said, my voice breaking. A sob escaped. "I'm sure."

I drove over to Lexi's, plotting where to leave the gift bag so I'd be the least likely to alert them to my presence. If she or her husband opened the door, I was sure I'd burst into tears, a giveaway that this was no normal baby gift drop-off and a less-than-ideal reaction to someone's new baby.

Bottom step? No, super weird and awkward. Top step, but I'd go fast. I'd leave my sunglasses on just in case they spotted me and came out to say hello, God forbid holding the baby, although surely, they wouldn't do that. She was too new; she belonged indoors and not in the presence of germ-carrying friends. Maybe

I should text and say I had a cold? Ack, it was getting too complicated. I was almost at their house.

I pulled into their driveway and turned off the engine, feeling like MacGyver facing down a ticking bomb. The clock had started; I was on the property. Taking deep breaths, I grabbed the bag and opened the driver's side door but didn't shut it—that would be too loud. With the car door hanging open, I snuck up their five thousand front steps and slid the bag onto the landing. I scrambled back down and into my car, holding my breath until I cruised safely to a stop at the end of their street.

Where I burst into tears. Just as walking away from the calendar of appointments had felt like walking away from my baby, giving away the outfit had felt like giving away my baby. I might as well have put the baby in a basket and sent him down a river.

Not ready to go home, I took a left instead of a right into Twelve South, a cool part of Nashville popular among people who use cooler words than "cool."

I called Emily.

"I just gave away my hospital coming-home outfit," I said. I didn't have to specify for which baby. Obviously, it was for them all—or not; it didn't matter.

"Oh my God," she said. "You are a braver woman than I." She'd shared with me that "the stuff" for her was in a box in the basement labeled DO NOT OPEN. "And that's where it will live forever," she said.

"I'm about to do something reckless," I said, eyeing a sunglasses store that was clearly going to be out of my price range; it existed inside a shipping container painted bright white. It had a door made to look like a window and an A-frame chalkboard offering free champagne inside.

"Uh, what?" she asked nervously.

"I'm about to spend way too much money on sunglasses." Wearing perfectly good shades, I pulled onto a side street to park.

Less than ten minutes later, I was back in my car, purchase in hand. I called Emily back.

"How much?" she answered.

"Four hundred," I said.

"*Dollars?*" she choked.

I explained that it was the kind of place that doesn't have prices marked (of course), so I hadn't actually known how much they were going to be until the clerk had rung them up, at which point it felt too late to back out. (Remember the tattoo I have because I didn't want to annoy a stranger?)

"Listen," she said, ever the true friend, "I support this. Because now, today isn't the day you gave away your coming-home outfit. It's the day you bought $400 sunglasses."

And even though I exchanged them for a cheaper pair three days later, handing them over to a man in one-strap overalls and purple eye shadow, she was half-right.

It became the day I bought $200 sunglasses.

Next came the bigger items—the stroller. The crib. The bassinet that rocked the baby to sleep. Things we'd chosen to haul with us in a cross-country move because we'd rather pay to move it than buy it all again for baby number two.

Donating these larger items made the most sense to me. But after a cursory search online turned up no suitable donation centers in the area, the logistics of getting them to a recipient felt overwhelming, and so for months, they sat, radioactive, in various pockets of our house: Finn's closet, the water heater closet, the garage.

And then one morning, over a visit with my family, Lucas returned from a run, removed his headphones, and said, "I think we should move to Dallas. Like, soon."

It was serendipitous that I'd been having the same thought.

We'd discussed the possibility before, but as a more distant one. Finn was close to his cousins, who lived there. Dallas was a short drive from the city in Oklahoma where Lucas's dad had just moved into an assisted living facility.

Now that Finn wasn't going to have a sibling, it made the idea more appealing. Finn could grow up with his cousins.

"Me too," I said.

Lucas and I aren't ones to sit on decisions for very long. We aren't wafflers or second-guessers or "let's sleep on it" people.

Once, at a West Elm, a saleswoman had handed us a rainbow of swatches of chair fabrics and said, "So you'll take those home and see what works best with what you have?"

We'd looked at each other and cracked up.

"We're not that kind of people," Lucas had said. We'd eyeballed the color and ordered our chairs on the spot.

We had one conversation about moving to Dallas and, within the hour, had texted our friend who was a realtor there.

Back in Nashville, the decision to move was the kick in the butt I needed. Even though moving was still an abstraction—we wouldn't for months, until Finn finished his school year—I wanted my new home to be a fresh start, a place where I didn't have remnants of fertility struggle lurking behind literal doors. I wanted my closets to contain my future, not my past.

I found Junkdrop, a local company that would come take your "junk" and sort through it to separate the re-usable from the trash, donating the former. Sold by the reviews from the recipients, I booked a pickup for two days later, and we began the process of ferreting baby equipment from the recesses of our house to the middle of the living room, where it amassed in a pile that grew taller by the hour.

Over and over, we remembered something we'd forgotten about.

"Oh yeah, that other stroller in the garage," Lucas said. "And the highchair—where is it?"

"And what about all the toddler toys?" It turned out there were full boxes of things Finn had only recently outgrown: the rattles, the rocking horse. The size 2T pajamas might as well go, too.

By Thursday, when the Junkdrop truck appeared in front of our house, our living room looked like a ramshackle buybuy BABY.

Two friendly guys in bright blue and green t-shirts made trip after trip, their arms full, and as the pile of "the stuff" dwindled from a mountain to a smatter to nothing, I didn't feel the same heartbreak I'd felt pulling away from Lexi's. I felt lighter, how pulling back drapes brightens a room.

In our final exchange before their departure, I swiped my credit card in their tiny machine, thinking it ironic that I was paying to give away useful stuff.

And yet, unlike the sunglasses I'd promptly regretted, this felt like money I'd spend again and again. Sure, in another life, in another era, I might have summoned the necessary strength to haul my own crib to a women's shelter. But as my mom might say, this was not the time to challenge myself.

Sometimes you just need to pay people to take things away.

And then there were the things that, oddly, I didn't want gone. Like my D&C socks. At my D&C, they'd given me a gown to wear that I'd changed out of before leaving, but also a pair of red tube socks with white grippers on the soles that I was told I could keep.

There was nothing high-quality about these socks. They weren't thick or warm. They had no shape and bunched at the ankle. They were hospital-issue, flimsy, papery, and I imagined most people tossed them or left them behind.

But for me, they were a keepsake, a memento of a pregnancy of which I didn't have any mementos. Unlike the unworn baby clothes and maternity wear, the socks *had* been used. They'd played a role. They'd witnessed.

And so I kept them, putting them on when I was in the mood, feeling a whisper of a connection to the past, and thinking how, only a year earlier, I really didn't understand grief at all.

29

DAWN

"I THINK YOU NEED to mark it in some way," my friend Meadow said of my letting-go quest. It was early spring. The most intrepid flowers were budding, daring an entrance even though another freeze would probably come. "Make it an active decision on your part."

Releasing the desire for a second kid, she thought, could be empowering, especially in contrast to the alternative: passively sliding into the same future but one I felt like I hadn't actively chosen or even really accepted.

I'd never been one for ceremonies. Once, in law school, I'd broken up with a boyfriend who'd insisted, as part of our split, that I take back an antique watch I'd given him. Suddenly the owner of a valuable men's watch that I couldn't imagine giving to any future partner, I didn't know what to do with it. Selling it felt too mercenary, crass; this was someone I'd cared about.

My friend Andrew, a romantic who wore an ascot every day of his life, had said, "We have to do something symbolic. Let's go to the ocean, and you'll throw it in."

We lived only a few miles from a harbor.

I'd gasped.

"No!" I'd said, horrified by the idea. It was a nice watch. Andrew had shrugged, and I'd stuffed the watch away in some box, where it unceremoniously disappeared in a subsequent move.

Now, I was intrigued, if still skeptical, that it would work. Would making some kind of concrete gesture actually help me let go?

Lucas and I had a morbid joke that never got old. Since we both want to be cremated, I'd once asked him where he wants his ashes scattered.

"I don't care," he'd said. "Dump me in the yard."

I'd responded that I absolutely would not and so he might as well choose a place that meant something to him.

"Throw my ashes all over Finn," he'd said.

That's it, that's the joke we cannot handle. We lose our minds; we laugh so hard.

My chosen spot to spend eternity was far more basic: an ocean, any ocean. I mean, okay, if I was being picky, the Côte d'Azur was my top choice, but I'd settle for a Hilton Head or a Fort Lauderdale, maybe something on the Gulf. If I wound up splashing into a PBR can on Myrtle Beach, I'd have some feedback for Lucas, should we meet again in the next life, but I trusted he knew me well enough to know this.

As I considered where I might stage my ceremonial release of my second-kid dream, my immediate thought was a beach. Problem was, we didn't live at a beach.

I'll just be open to the opportunity should it arise, I thought. *Or, you know, just never do it.*

And then, one Sunday morning not long after, over a bowl of oatmeal at my kitchen counter, I found myself reading *The New York Times.*

I would not call myself a reader of *The New York Times.* I get most of my news from Lucas, who reads me headlines while I do more important things like make food for the family.

But in a bout of nostalgia one evening, missing New York City and the endless free time of my twenties (brunches that bled into afternoons! Nights so late the subway cars were empty!), I'd re-subscribed to the Sunday paper—the hard copy. I pictured myself reading it cover to cover on Sunday mornings over a cup of coffee and a plate of steaming eggs. (What I'd forgotten was that, even in my unburdened twenties, every time I subscribed to the paper, they'd piled up, unread, on the coffee table until I finally gave in and smudged my hands black hauling them to the recycling bin.)

The Sunday paper had arrived, and I, determined to be a real adult, unbound it and immediately pulled out the section with the content I wanted to make sure not to miss: Style.

As I skimmed the section headlines, that week's Modern Love column caught my attention. *He wanted children,* read the teaser in bold print. *I didn't. What happened next was completely unexpected.*

Huh. Like us, just the opposite.

The writer, Rachel Heng, wrote about how she resisted having a baby, then gave in, then got pregnant, and even started to get excited. But the pregnancy was ectopic, a life-threatening condition that invariably ends the pregnancy.

Facing whether or not to give pregnancy another go, she wrote, *What to do when the person you love most wants something you can give him?*

I could have asked the exact same question, just the other way around: Lucas wanted us to stop, to be satisfied with our family size as it was. I could give him that...but I didn't want to.

I kept reading.

Love changes what we think we want, expands the scope of our desires, she wrote.

I closed the paper.

Whoa.

Love expands the scope of our desires.

The image that her phrasing planted in my mind was identical to the concentric circles Lucas had drawn at the restaurant, the ones representing grief.

But this time, the smaller circle was my wish for a baby. The bigger circle around it held my wishes for the whole family, not just myself.

I'd been approaching fertility as if I were my own team, a team of one. All the while, my teammates had been by my side, supporting my efforts even as I'd been too preoccupied to notice them. They were sore, grass-stained, and ready to go home.

Rachel Heng had just put it plainly for me: I could take them home.

"Do you want to fly the plane?" the flight attendant asked Finn. He nodded shyly, and she gestured for him to enter the cockpit, where the pilot was already climbing out of his seat so Finn could sit in it.

He timidly entered, as if this were his first time. But no.

My son had been in more Southwest cockpits than anyone I knew—at least four already, and considering that *he* was four, it was an astounding number. His ability to weasel his way into the pilot's seat of a commercial aircraft with a flirtatious look at a flight attendant was, frankly, frightening.

He grabbed the control stick and expertly swiveled to smile at me so I could take a photo. This was our routine.

"Thank you so much!" I said. "Say thank you!"

He thanked them and emerged triumphant while, ahead of us, Lucas was shoving our suitcases into the overhead bin.

"How many times is that?" Lucas asked as we took our seats.

"I think that makes five," I said.

We were headed to Miami for the week. It had been a year since my D&C. Finn was out of school for spring break, and we'd booked a hotel on the beach for five days.

When we decided to go to the beach, it didn't escape me that the beach was where I'd contemplated releasing my dream of a second child, making an active decision to let go. I was still dubious that a gesture like that could even work—or maybe I just didn't want it to.

I decided to play it by ear. I wouldn't force anything, but I'd be open to it, should the moment arise.

As the plane lifted, Finn, in the window seat, turned to us and yelled loudly enough for everyone in the nearby rows to hear, "My penis is getting higher!"

I looked at Lucas.

"Why do you want another kid again?" he asked. *Do*, I noticed he'd said. Not *did*.

I rose silently before dawn on our first morning and quietly slipped into a bra and flip flops. I was wide awake, and Lucas and I would need coffee. Good coffee.

I knew there was a coffee shop a half-mile south of us, and I pictured myself moseying down a blue-lit beach to fetch us steaming lattés, arriving with them just as Lucas was waking up.

But outside, the beach was still inky, untouched by the exterior illumination of the oceanfront hotels. Never mind. I'd have to take the streets.

In the glow of orange streetlamps, I trekked the half-mile on asphalt, feeling only mildly unsafe when stretches of eerie isolation passed between cars and early-morning joggers.

By the time I reached the coffee shop, I could see my own hand without the aid of a streetlamp, and so I exited with my and Lucas's orders, found a public access path, and made my way to the sand for my return walk.

After walking for several minutes, I noticed people arriving, a number of them armed with fancy cameras. The sun was about to rise.

Nice, I thought. *I'll get to see it.*

I walked a little farther, then found a metal beam that had no business being on a beach and sat to face the horizon. The beach was speckled with onlookers doing the same. We watched; we waited.

Was this it? My moment? It was sooner than I anticipated— our first day—but maybe this was for the best. I could enjoy the rest of our trip.

The sun peeked over the horizon, a glorious sliver.

Alright, Mary, I thought. *Here goes nothing.*

Buzz.

My phone rattled in my pocket. Lucas calling.

"What's up?" I answered.

"Are you okay?" he asked. It had been almost an hour.

"I went to get coffees and stopped to watch the sunrise," I said. "It's coming up now."

"Fine," he grumbled and hung up, annoyed to have to wait for his coffee.

I set my phone on the metal beam, annoyed right back. Didn't he know I was having a dream-releasing ceremony and didn't have the emotional bandwidth for a grumpy interruption?

Whatever. I'd do it quickly. The coffees were getting cold.

The sliver of gold was swelling. I gazed into it and tried to imagine handing my dream of a second child over to it. It was awkward, and even though I was alone, I felt a little embarrassed, the same way I had when I was asked to pray aloud as a teenager, distracted by whether I was doing it right.

Since I was old enough to understand that I would grow up, I'd envisioned myself with two children. Mother of two.

I took a deep breath. Exhaled. Pictured the fantasy. Pictured it rising.

Here you go, I thought. *Be gentle with this one. It's a good one.*

Like with every balloon I ever released or lost as a child, I turned away long before it had disappeared, long before I was ready. As the sun slithered its full bounty into our half of the sky, my longing still warm on my back, I walked back to my family.

"Are you going to have any more kids?" another kid's nanny asked.

Finn had found some kids to play with in the hotel pool, and I was sitting on the pool edge chatting with her. She was twenty-seven and in her last semester of college.

It was the last day of our trip, four days since the morning I'd sat on the beach at sunrise, and though this was a question I was used to, I'd not been asked it on this vacation yet.

Normally, it would sting, along with its variants: "Is he your only one?" "Are you all planning to give him a sibling?" and "Do you think you're finished?"

But I found myself surprisingly not triggered as I said, matter-of-factly, "No. I'm old." She and I both chuckled.

"How old are you?" she asked.

"Forty," I said.

She gasped.

"Wow, you look great," she said, confirming that, in her eyes, I was, indeed, quite old. (But I looked great!)

As I slid into the pool to play with Finn, I checked in. Was I okay?

278 | MARY ADKINS

I was. Her question hadn't sparked rage, or even sadness. I'd said that we weren't having more kids, and I didn't feel resentful or annoyed. What was this sorcery? Had my giving up the dream on the beach *actually worked*?

Emily had once said something about stopping IVF that stuck with me. She said that imagining ending IVF because it wasn't working was terrible, because you could only picture your future self being as miserable as you currently were, but even worse, without the hope of a kid. But calling off an IVF journey wasn't actually like that. Because you also got to *stop doing IVF*. You were free.

I'd held the same fear about relinquishing my quest for another kid. I'd been certain that if I gave it up, I'd feel just as despondent, but also like I'd forfeited a dream. I'd be sad *and* pitiable!

But here I was, wading around a family pool surrounded by parents with their multiple kids, and I felt neither. Maybe I'd made it to an after party of my own.

I climbed out and reached for a towel folded up on our pool chair. A stack of Polaroids scattered onto the ground.

The day before, I'd bought Finn a Polaroid camera in the hotel gift shop, along with a sixteen-photo roll of film. He was supposed to take no more than three photos a day, but clearly, he'd maxed out the roll while I wasn't looking. I gathered up the photos, overexposed and indecipherable shots of the pool area, in which I could make out only a palm tree or two.

But one was a close-up of the little girl Finn had been playing with all week, her cherub face and wet curls.

The girl had spent all day, every day with her younger sister and nanny while her father sat in the pool area with his laptop propped open, taking calls on Bluetooth and rarely looking up from his screen.

Lucas appeared.

"Want a margarita?" he asked. I showed him the photo. He smiled. "Nice shot, Finn!" he said.

"Will you give it to her dad?" I asked, handing it to Lucas. "I think he'll want it." He looked uncertain but took it anyway, turning to where the father sat, head buried in his computer.

He would want it, I thought again as I watched Lucas hand it to him. He would be glad to have it.

30

OUTER SPACE

IT SEEMED STRANGE to get a pap smear when I'd had over a dozen ultrasounds of my uterus over the previous eighteen months, but I was a rule-follower, so when the reminder to book my annual visit arrived in my inbox, I did.

The nurse escorted me back and told me to remove my shoes and step onto the scale. I slid off my sandals and stepped onto the old-school, metal platform, but this time, unlike ever before, I kept my gaze lifted.

"I prefer to not know my weight," I said as matter-of-factly as I could.

"No problem," she said as she jotted the number on my chart.

That was it? That had been easier than I expected.

I'd begun to refer to my year of miscarriages as "my year in the first trimester." The bizarre, surreal phrasing seemed to accurately capture the extraordinary year from which I still felt whiplashed. But I just as easily could call it the year my body got louder, the year my body sat me down for a come-to-Jesus talk and told me things were going to change around here, that if I didn't straighten up, it was leaving.

And I, like a husband who'd been served eight thousand meals without knowing how to turn on the oven, whose clothes had appeared pressed and folded in his drawers like magic for years while he uttered not so much as a thank you, said, "Huh? I thought everything was fine!"

But no, it wasn't fine.

Postpartum is a term we typically reserve for women who have given birth to live babies, but the term is meant to capture the mother's state of being—her physical body—in the wake of pregnancy. It actually has nothing to do with the baby. Whether a pregnancy results in a living human is irrelevant—it's the *pregnancy* that results in an aftermath, not the product of it.

I don't know when it hit me that I was postpartum, but when it did, it was a light bulb turning on.

After having Finn, I'd understood that some time would need to pass before I felt like myself again—it was six weeks before I was allowed to exercise or have sex, for example. In reality, my transition back to regular life took far longer. It was months before I felt comfortable lifting heavy things or going on runs, months before my personality resumed its corners.

But I didn't expect a postpartum period after miscarriage. I naively assumed, without giving it any conscious thought, that the fact that my belly never pushed past my waistband meant that transitioning back to regular life was purely a mental game. All the while, the sensations and perceptions I was experiencing weren't foreign—they were familiar, echoes of my earlier postpartum days: a tender and raw haziness, like a soft, thick fog around my thoughts, and a body that didn't want to be shoved into Spandex or onto a treadmill.

By my pap smear, I was aware that I'd gone through a postpartum period following my miscarriages, because it wasn't until eight months after my third one that something had finally shifted. I'd stopped crying almost every time I found myself alone in the car. I'd started wanting to get my heart rate up, wanting to sweat. My jokes no longer existed solely to ward off pain. Sometimes, they were just jokes.

So that afternoon, I was showing up to the appointment in a body that until very recently had been postpartum, and I wasn't interested in stepping on any scales.

A friend who also had a history of disordered eating had given me the idea of asking not to be told my weight.

"Wait, how?" I'd asked, intrigued.

"I just say I don't want to know, so don't tell me," she'd said. I'd been floored. The audacity! The genius!

Because if there ever was a device that had exclusively diminished the quality of my life, it was the scale. Who would have thought that such rudimentary technology, a $40 stack of plastic, could wreak such havoc on human happiness? (And why is the at-home scale the only battery-powered device in existence whose battery *never runs out*? The patriarchy, that's why. Mine lasted *over a damn decade*.)

I'd never met a scale that made my day better. I could be feeling just fine, then come upon a scale.

I'll just see, I'd think. *I'll just check.* Wasn't it good to know one's weight? Wasn't it supposed to be a helpful piece of information?

But "just checking" invariably turned into an ordeal that splashed through my day like a wet dog. No matter what the number, I would promptly begin planning some kind of lifestyle overhaul: more workouts, less booze, zero dairy…a restrictive scheme that would stress me out until I finally gave it up.

It had taken me to age forty, but I didn't want to do that anymore. Postpartum or not, why would I continue to torment myself?

I'm off scales, I texted my friend from the patient room, where I now awaited the doctor. *I just did the thing at the doctor!*

Bravo! she wrote back.

For years, I'd believed I was tolerating my body when, if anything, it had tolerated me. It was the smart one. It created life, then ended it when it wasn't viable. It held on to weight when it was still circulating pregnancy hormones and transitioning out of pregnancy, because perhaps it sensed that rest was needed. It could produce a headache to stop me in my tracks when I pushed myself too hard. It sensed danger; it sensed safety; it sensed human presence.

And yet body shaming is so entrenched in our culture, it's no wonder we struggle to recognize our bodies' power.

I'd begun to immerse myself in writing by Sonya Renee Taylor and Virginia Sole-Smith, writers who placed my lifetime of body struggle in a cultural context. I saw that I was part of systemic oppression, that I was playing a role in that oppression by entertaining the beauty standards of thin and white. These books busted open my self-deception and left me reeling with horror at my new understanding. But these were intellectual shifts happening in the confines of my mind. Translating them into action, into an everyday relationship with my body, was way trickier.

Which was why, as I sat waiting for the doctor, having successfully refused to learn my weight, I felt more than a little proud.

There was a knock at the door.

"Hello," a woman I'd never met said as she entered. She introduced herself as a nurse practitioner.

"You've had a rough year, huh?" she said, looking down at a tablet on which I imagined it reading, *this girl just had three miscarriages*.

"Yeah," I said.

"Do you have a good support system?" she asked.

I nodded.

"Anything you want to talk about today?" she asked.

"Just that I'm ready to get back on birth control," I said, the words sounding odd to my ears. I was really doing this. After well over a year of feeling nothing more deeply than the unrelenting desire for a baby, I was going back on birth control.

Then it was time for the pap smear.

I lay back and placed my feet in the stirrups like I had many times before. And something weird happened.

I'd been going to the gynecologist since I was sixteen. I didn't ever remember feeling anxious about it. Sure, it was invasive, but it was a doctor performing a standard procedure for my own well-being. It felt no different than a cleaning at the dentist.

But suddenly, for the first time, my chest contracted, and my breath caught. She was chatting, but I wasn't really listening. I focused on breathing my way through the exam.

It was over quickly, and as I exited the chilly office, I noticed that my fingers had gone white, and my hands were tremoring.

I had a lifetime of training in ignoring these kinds of signals from my body. To binge is to intentionally override one's instinct to stop eating, and I'd mastered that by fifteen. Assuming the duties of adulthood, even after I'd stopped binging, had largely constituted the same practice of overriding. "Adulting" meant logging hours worked, covering bills and renter's insurance and estimated taxes. Entertaining the needs of a messy, growling, finicky, demanding human body didn't fit into a philosophy regimented to maximize success and earn a good income.

Many years earlier, my old therapist had asked what I did for fun. "Read," I'd answered.

"Why don't you take a break in your workday sometimes to read then?" she'd said. "Read a novel for an hour."

Ridiculous, I'd thought. I had shit to do and more shit to do. Breaks in work—writing, teaching, or preparing to teach—were for getting the other shit done: buying groceries, making doctor's appointments, finding the right shoes for someone's rehearsal dinner or booking a flight for their wedding. Breaks weren't actually breaks from being productive, they were a switch over to a different breed of productivity.

Old Mary would have ignored that my insides were screaming as I left the doctor's office following my pap smear. I would have returned home and resumed my day in front of the computer, even if my heart was racing faster than the keys under my fingers.

But I didn't want to be her anymore. And I didn't want to model that kind of living for Finn.

As I walked to my car and it occurred to me what was going on—my body was reliving the last time it had been laid out on a table in this building, feet in stirrups—I asked it: *What do you need?*

Which was how I found myself driving to the grocery store bakery to pick up a chocolate chip cookie, then to the greenway near our house that I'd walked dozens of times in my postpartum fog.

In my sundress and gladiator sandals, I drifted along the path, eating my cookie, still clammy and unsteady.

By mile three, it had started to drizzle. I took shelter under a tree, the empty wax pastry paper balled up in my hand.

I probably wasn't ever going to be pregnant again. There wouldn't be a separate soul in me to justify caring for myself, a different person constituting a reason to treat my body well. But maybe the one already in here was enough.

I'd come out of the previous year and a half understanding my body as so much more than a vessel for my brain. It could spark a life and sunset one. Why would I want to shrink such a powerful thing?

From here, I'd go on to avoid scales; I'd find it best for my mental health to avoid numbers. To be a good parent as a pregnant woman with gestational diabetes back when Finn was in my belly,

I'd had to track numbers daily. To be a good parent to myself now, I had to put them away.

And in their absence, something brighter would come.

The rain grew heavier and I waited.

A few weeks later, I stood in front of a wall of glowing planets at Nashville's Adventure Science Center.

"What do we do on this one, mama?" Finn asked, darting around in that aimless way children do, like they have so much excess energy they'd rather run in circles than stand still. The short partition before me contained a panel of computer-generated numbers that changed rapidly whenever Finn ran past. What did they represent?

Unable to figure it out, I located the exhibit panel. I had to squint to read the small font in the dim light of "outer space."

Find out how much you would weigh anywhere in the solar system!

Finn had lost interest and sprinted across the room to where Lucas was checking out a different exhibit.

I stood alone on the carpet square. Before me, laid out in bright phosphorescence, was my weight—not just on Earth, but on *all nine planets* (because of course, they'd included goddamn Pluto).

EARTH: X POUNDS
MARS: Y POUNDS
VENUS: Z POUNDS

And so on.

An act of divine comedy. If there was a God, her joke was on me.

31

ELSEWHERE

THE PART OF THE EMAIL that jumped out to me was the line, *Saturday afternoon: hike.*

Sure, okay. It was Karen's bachelorette party; I was down for whatever she wanted to do. It's just that, traditionally, hikes for me had been like movies that started after eight p.m., or bars with loud TVs, or pretty much any professional sports game—if I was there, someone else had chosen the agenda.

I'm the kind of person who has been given a magnet that reads: INDOORSY. As my glamorous trans friend B had once put it, "There are two kinds of people who obviously don't hike: the kind who look like you, and the kind who look like me." B wears stilettos and bandage dresses and has two-inch nails; I wear cotton bag dresses with suede mules that I spot-clean after walking around the mall. You get the idea.

Despite the magnet, I did enjoy being outside. My issue with hiking was that, for most of my life, hikes didn't seem to have much of a purpose, and my rubric for physical activity wasn't so different from my rubric for writing a novel: Did it move the narrative forward? If so, I was on board. If not, I cut the scene.

I didn't get the point of hikes. The point was…the hike itself? You just, like, stomp on dry leaves and bat away branches, and that's how you spent your time for no reason?

But grief opened me to doing more things just because. Just because they felt good. Just because I wanted to try them. Hiking fell squarely into the "just because" category. Maybe I'd like it. Who knew? I never thought I'd be a person who had three miscarriages, either, but here I was.

"Maybe I'm going to be a hiking person now," I said to B. She slow blinked at me.

Packing for the trip the day before I left, I asked Emily, who would also be there, what one wore to hike.

"Do I need boots?" I asked.

"No, just sneakers."

"And a running top?"

"A hoodie," Emily said. "It might be chilly."

Good thing I asked. We were gathering in Arizona, which, in my mind, was never chilly, but apparently mountain peaks were special. I searched my closet for the closest thing I had to a hoodie and found what seemed to work best. The morning of our hike, I put it on with leggings and sneakers and breezed into the kitchen of our Airbnb.

"Oh my God," Emily said. She froze with her coffee mid-sip. "What are you wearing?"

It took me a second to realize she was talking to me.

"What?" I said. "This?" I pointed to my top.

"Everyone, look at Mary!" Emily shouted. "Come here!" People who were already in the kitchen turned. People who were not in the kitchen came into the kitchen, including Karen, the bachelorette, who screamed.

"What?!" I yelled like someone had spotted a bee on my back.

"What *is* that?" Karen asked.

"It's a capelet," I said, using the term from the website where I'd ordered it.

"Did you *make* that?" someone asked with complete sincerity.

"*A capelet!*" Emily was yelling over and over. "*What is a capelet?*"

"Of course I didn't make it! It's a sweatshirt!"

"That's not a sweatshirt. It looks like you made it."

"It's *nice!*" I insisted.

"Why are you wearing something nice on a hike?" someone asked.

"Why are you wearing a *cape*?" Emily asked between cackles.

"It's a cape*let*," I said, already heading back to my room, humiliated. "Forget it! I'm going to change!"

"Yes, for the love of God, go change!" Karen yelled. "You're going to get hooked on a branch!"

(This is probably where I should mention that my favorite movie in childhood was *Troop Beverly Hills*, in which Shelley Long remakes her wilderness girl uniform into a hiking cape.)

Two hours later, we plodded up a dusty mountain trail. I wore the only alternative I had, a bright green NASHVILLE sweatshirt I'd impulse-purchased at the airport when I'd grown nervous I hadn't packed warm enough clothing.

As I found my footing on boulder after boulder, it occurred to me that a year earlier, I'd been with these friends and white-knuckling a sled to keep from sliding too fast down a mountain. Here I was now, climbing one in the dry sunlight. Then, I'd been pregnant. Now, I wasn't.

At the top of the tallest peak, we stood arm in arm and screamed. Our voices sounded both tiny and huge. Happiness was coming back in moments, the way happiness does.

I felt it again a few months later, in Austin: my friend Rufi and I on the sidewalk as I clutched my stomach and begged her to stop telling the story she was in the middle of telling because I was

292 | MARY ADKINS

peeing a little (or a lot). Since having Finn, I've still never recovered my pelvic floor.

We'd come to Texas to co-lead a writing retreat. We'd bought matching red cowboy boots and taken tequila shots with the flirty saleswoman who sold them to us. Then, we'd gone to see the bats—a nightly phenomenon for which Austin is known. At dusk each evening, you can observe the millions of bats that live under the Congress Avenue Bridge fly out *en masse.*

We stood on the bridge for two hours, then two and a half, waiting. The sun set, our boots chilling in shopping bags at our aching feet, the sparkle from the tequila having long evaporated. Finally, after it was too dark to make out individual creatures, they emerged in a quiet whir, a puff of steam rising. The crowd had dwindled to a dozen or so determined souls on the bridge, and our collective disappointment was evident. There was nothing to photograph, only a grayish cloud obscuring the stars.

It occurred to me that, had we not primed ourselves for a certain vista—the image of a pink sky speckled black that accompanied every What to Do in Austin article—we would have found it insanely cool.

"Like if we'd just stumbled on this, it would blow our minds," I said. So many bats, they made steam that hid the moon!

It was the expectation that gave rise to the disappointment. The reality was, in fact, far from disappointing; it was magical.

Not long after, Lucas and I traveled to New York for a wedding, leaving Finn back home with my parents. With plenty of time to kill, we set off on a walk through the city, eventually finding ourselves at an intersection that held much history for us: the college where he'd gone back to school after we'd married and which he'd attended through Finn's birth, and the hospital where Finn had been born. They were on the same block.

In the final week of my pregnancy with Finn, when I'd been monitored daily at the hospital, Lucas would head there straight from class with his bookbag, student and dad-to-be. One of these days, as I approached him in my wool coat tied around my massive stomach, he'd laughed and lifted his phone to snap a photo.

"It's the leading from the middle," he said. "Your belly rounds the corner before you do."

I recalled the morning of Finn's birth, cruising this very block in the darkness at 4 a.m. in a yellow cab, having told the driver that he was taking us to have a baby.

"Congratulations!" he'd said, then told us that it was very good luck to have a baby on this day for another reason.

"What?" I'd asked, excited to share a special moment with this stranger.

"Today, my friend is going to overthrow the Egyptian government!" he exclaimed.

The next morning, marveling at Finn—he was real!—we'd recalled our driver.

"Do you think his friend succeeded?" I asked.

"No," Lucas said. He confessed that in the middle of the night, he'd googled coups in Egypt. I had as well.

Then both of us fumbling over the newborn car seat in the back of the taxi to take Finn home from the hospital on his third day of life, so terrified that we enlisted the help of the driver to strap him in. It had been a large SUV with captain seats, and instead of taking the front, Lucas had crammed himself in the back between Finn and me, crouching on the floor of the SUV as if, in the case of an accident, he might save us from that position.

Walking along this block where so much had happened, Lucas took my hand. We didn't speak. Manhattan on an early Sunday afternoon in October felt strangely quiet.

"We hustled so hard here," he said. "I associate this place with hustle."

I did, too.

The year had softened my edges, tamped down my hustling nature. Productivity as a lifestyle had lost its appeal. I saw that it had never actually worked to help me avoid the ache of being alive. I'd just managed to distract myself with it.

The ache I felt as a child was back. Or rather, it had never really gone—I just didn't feel like I needed to flee it anymore.

I cried when happy things happened. I cried when sad memories surfaced. I cried when *nothing* happened—one afternoon, just imagining being in the airport leaving Nashville brought me to tears, even though I was excited to move, and even though it was months away.

It caught Lucas by surprise every time.

"You okay?" he'd ask, unnerved.

I'd nod through tears. I was. I was as okay as any human who sees her life as perpetually ending as it unfolds.

When people said, "I'm sorry for your loss," I wanted to say back, *And I'm sorry for yours, because it's coming. And it's going to be like waking up to find out that you live on a different planet, and you'll be in the company of every human who has ever lived long enough to get here.*

We made our way back to the hotel and took a bistro table on the sidewalk to order cocktails. Our chairs faced out, ideal for people watching.

I don't remember which of us started the game, but at some point, we began improvising commentary on the fashion choices of passersby. Lucas's remarks made me giggle.

"I don't like that furry purse with the gemstone pants—it clashes."

"This guy killed a man for that jacket fringe."

We sat for hours, two drinks, three, performing our *Mystery Science Theater 3000* of New York City for only ourselves.

I didn't regret my miscarriages. I wished the babies had lived, of course. But even having not survived, they'd given me more than they'd taken.

Like the idea that one could be loved for their essence without having to earn it. For someone who'd spent her entire life trying to earn her place on earth, the discovery that love needn't be earned to exist was radical, mind-bending. The mere suggestion that I might not have to work to earn love was a surprise, blessed relief, like being misted by one of those misters at an amusement park or fancy playground.

Plus, I had secrets now: secret ghost visits, secret memories, secret suspicions.

If the present was inherently sad, death forever closing in, possibilities converging into a single path to extinguish all others, my memory of the moment in my kitchen in the presence of the child was a solace, because it meant that maybe life *wasn't* always ending…not everywhere.

Somewhere, the little dog had died.

Somewhere, my daughter was smiling. Maybe in a tiny cape.

EPILOGUE

FOR ADMINISTRATIVE REASONS, back in 2015, Lucas and I had two weddings: the one we think of as our actual wedding, to which family and friends came and we danced till midnight, and the official one a few months later that I sometimes forget about. On a rainy morning in early March, we arrived at a Queens courthouse with our friend Curtis as witness. In our minds, this one was merely a technicality. I wore a polka dot dress I'd owned for years. He wore a blazer.

The mood in line to wed was warm and festive. There were women in gowns and men in ties and lots of bouquets.

Then the clerk whose job it was to call out names showed up. Wet and grouchy, she perched herself on a stool before the door that led to the chapel where we'd all wed (a converted office space with rust-colored carpet), and declared, at full volume, "Fuck the MTA!"

The room went silent as she continued to gripe about New York City transit.

"Please, ma'am," a man gently interrupted, "there are children here."

"Hey! Hey!" She snapped and literally pointed at him. "You know what I say to that? I say this: Fuck the MTA, and fuck *you!*"

Upon which, Lucas, Curtis, and I got the giggles. What on earth was happening? Our giggles didn't stop after the angry attendant called our names, and an only slightly less hostile officiant married us while scolding Curtis for how he was holding his phone to take photos ("Flip it, sir! Sir! Flip!") and Lucas for how he was holding my ring ("Leave it in the box!"). We held back laughter as she brusquely pronounced us husband and wife and, in the same breath, mumbled, "Exit through the back door. Go left into your future, not into your past."

Go left into your future, not into your past. On one hand, I didn't get it. Who was leaving their wedding ceremony and returning to their past? But it also struck me as kind of lovely, a way of saying, no matter what's come before, don't let it hold you back. Go make something beautiful now.

After my year of miscarriages and failed IVF, the future ceased to be a place I could cultivate excited feelings about. Even when it came to Finn and his future, my hopes were more of a tender desire for good things than excitement.

I stopped fantasizing. Completely. The thing I'd spent thousands of hours of my former life doing—it was like I didn't know how to do it anymore.

I wondered if the end of fantasy was merely a rite of passage: I'd finally suffered enough that I'd discovered the other side of living, where excitement about the future dies. *That would make sense*, I thought.

Fantasy, perhaps, was childish, even embarrassing—coy pregnancy announcements with baby shoes and ultrasound photos. It was the woman whose face I couldn't see but whom I could hear behind a partition at my OB's, having blood drawn, as she told the nurse, "I'm only six weeks so I have time, but, like, I can't decide whether to speak German or English at home!" Fantasy was like some kind of estranged friend who'd betrayed me: I was bitter and trying not to talk too badly about her behind her back.

It didn't occur to me that this could be postpartum-related.

When my therapist said, "It sounds like depression," I brushed her off and we didn't talk about it again.

And then, two and a half years after my third miscarriage, I showed up to therapy with big news: I was excited about something. I couldn't believe it.

It was an idea for a new novel. I got out of bed in the mornings eager to work on it. I fantasized about people reading it and liking it.

"I thought this was over," I said, almost tearful. "I thought I just didn't get excited anymore."

If I have a soapbox now, it's that the postpartum tail of pregnancy loss is long and winding, just like the postpartum period after childbirth. It can exceed weeks; it can exceed months. It can last for *years*, and women need to be informed about this, because it helps us understand that we haven't just *become sad people.*

As fantasy crept back in, I found that I liked it.

Sure, the future-dwelling part of me had assumed too large a role in my life. But it turned out that I actually didn't want that part to die.

The day we moved to Texas, Finn and I arrived first, having flown (with, of course, a visit to the Southwest cockpit). Lucas drove, and the moving truck would arrive the following day.

When I first stepped foot into our new house as a resident, it was empty.

And filthy.

The floors were covered in a layer of grime, so my sister and I quickly gathered up all the cleaning supplies from her house, along with a couple of new Swiffer mops from Home Depot, and put the three children to work.

Lucas had told me that the home's previous owners had a sound system rigged throughout the house that was all set to play music, so I finally downloaded the app he'd been nagging me to get and connected to the Wi-Fi.

"Tipsy" by J-Kwon boomed through the house.

My sister and I began to dance.

Somewhere in the house, the children were mopping, and we christened the empty living room with a dance party that lasted the entire four minutes of the song.

This, I thought as we danced. *This is what I want my future to look like.* Dancing in a house that is empty but still full.

ACKNOWLEDGEMENTS

I STARTED WRITING THIS the day before my D&C after my third miscarriage. Doing so solidified my view that "writing from a wound," as some say not to do, can be incredibly healing. I will never tell someone there is a time when they shouldn't write.

I want to thank the friends who carried me through this time in my life. Stirba, who was always right there, even though you were hundreds of miles away. Lexi, who listened and checked in even when I was quiet. Florence, who brought me snacks and left them in my mailbox. Jackie, who handed me paint and told me to throw it. Heléne, who announced that we were going to Miami and actually booked it—probably the best thing a friend has ever done for me, and I will never forget it (POSITIVE!). Haley, who calls in the middle of the night and isn't afraid of silence. Joanna, who helped me remember that there is life outside of fertility, specifically book events to attend and salads to pair with fries. Lucas Schaefer, who is still Gene and always will be. Greg, who has become as special to me as Gene. Kathleen, who has held my nipples and my hands and my feelings, all with care. Meadow, who cried alongside me and helped me find the truth in the rubble—

there aren't words, except that I will always be grateful. Rufi, I met you at a time when I wasn't sure if I wanted to get rid my gecko tattoo, and you convinced me to put a hat on him instead. That pretty much sums up our friendship, to me: Your way of seeing the world just makes it better.

Then there is my family—Katie Beth, the best sister I could ask for. My mom and dad, who root for me, no matter what. My mother-in-law Angie and sister-in-law Kristin, who were so thoughtful and gentle when I was fragile. Lucas, I can't even write a sentence about you without tearing up. I feel like we went into a kiln and came out solid and glossy. And Finn, who, at six, already likes to wonder aloud what his future kid will be like: If you're lucky, buddy, he'll be as funny as you.

A number of friends and colleagues read versions of or excerpts from this manuscript or advised me on its publishing journey. A huge, heartfelt thank you to Claire Anderson-Wheeler, Emily Griffin, Greg Marshall, Lindy Alexander, Gayle Brown, Leigh Stewart, Kate Tellers, and Stephen Ruddy. Thank you especially to Joanna Bradley and Emma Dries for your insightful and generous edits.

I will always be grateful to my nurses and OB in Nashville for their supreme compassion. The teachers at Fahrenheit Yoga and Bend and Zen in Nashville were all bright stars for me during this time, as were the *Bachelor* crew, the New York Queens, and my brilliant colleagues at The Book Incubator, who make running a business fun every day.

Finally, speaking of stars, thank you to Alle Mudrick, whose orbit intersected with mine because it was written in them. You're a comet, you're magic dust, you're a person I want leading the way. Let's light this place up.

RESOURCE LIST

If you are looking for support during pregnancy loss, infant loss, or another kind of loss, some books I recommend checking out are:

Blue Hour Homecoming by Alle Mudrick (infant loss and miscarriage)

I Had a Miscarriage by Jessica Zucker (miscarriage)

Still by Emma Hansen (stillbirth)

Grief is for People by Sloane Crosley (loss of a close friend)

All the Beauty in the World: The Metropolitan Museum of Art and Me by Patrick Bringley (loss of a brother)

Grief is Love: Living with Loss by Marisa Renee Lee

My therapist also vouches for The Compassionate Friends, a monthly meeting group (online or in person) that has five hundred chapters around the US for family members who have lost children, regardless of age or cause.